Runaway Romances

Robert R. Shandley

Runaway
Romances

Hollywood's Postwar Tour of Europe

TEMPLE UNIVERSITY PRESS
Philadelphia

TEMPLE UNIVERSITY PRESS
1601 North Broad Street
Philadelphia PA 19122
www.temple.edu/tempress

♾ The paper used in this publication meets the requirements of the American National Standard for Information Sciences—Permanence of Paper for Printed Library Materials, ANSI Z39.48-1992

Frontispiece: The triumph of fashion over feminism: Audrey Hepburn in *Funny Face.* (Publicity still, *Funny Face,* Paramount Pictures, 1957, courtesy of Photofest.)

Library of Congress Cataloging-in-Publication Data

Shandley, Robert R.
   Runaway romances : Hollywood's postwar tour of Europe / Robert R. Shandley.
      p. cm.
   Includes bibliographical references and index.
   ISBN 978-1-59213-945-3 (cloth : alk. paper)
   1. Motion picture industry—United States—History.   2. Motion picture industry—Production and direction—United States—History.   3. Motion pictures, American—Europe—History.   4. Love in motion pictures.
5. Travel in motion pictures.   I. Title.
   PN1993.5.U6S475 2009
   384'.80973—dc22
   2008043757

2 4 6 8 9 7 5 3 1

For my daughter,
Mary Margaret Shandley

Contents

Preface

Going to Europe to discover something unavailable at home describes a good part of my young adulthood. Along that journey of self-discovery I came to understand that Europe and America shared a complicated relationship informed by both Realpolitik and fairy tales. As a student of the German film industry, which had languished under the yoke of competition with Hollywood since World War II, I generally worked with the false assumption that Hollywood enjoyed absolute power in the European market. Of course, a closer look at postwar European–American cinematic relations reveals that such was hardly the case. Upon closer scrutiny it became clear to me that in order to understand the rise of art cinema in Italy, France, and Germany from the late 1950s through the 1970s, one had to consider, among other things, from where the infrastructure to support this resurgence might have come. That line of questioning led me to research Hollywood runaway production in the postwar era. Once I started looking at runaway production in general, which was most known for bringing about cycles of war films and biblical epics, I found a group of films set in contemporary Europe in which Hollywood seemed to be trying to sort out how Americans felt about their Old World allies. The films contained both the fairy tales and the political negotiations that underlie the transatlantic relationship.

This book benefited from the assistance, criticism, and ideas of many people and institutions. My colleague and friend, Anne Morey, accompanied me to archives, gently educated me in film historical matters, patiently listened to many parts of this work at conferences, and offered invaluable criticism of the manuscript. Members of the Film Studies Working Group at Texas A&M lent their critical acumen to parts of the manuscript. Peter Lev has been unbelievably generous in sharing both research material and advice. Barbara Hall of the Margaret Herrick Library may well be the most helpful librarian I have ever met. Janet Staiger has offered tremendous advice and information on the project. Rey Chow, David McWhirter, Larson Powell, John Marshall, Pamela Klassen, and Terry Hoagwood provided very helpful readings of chapters. I would like to thank Lisa Saltzman and the Center for Visual Studies at Bryn Mawr College, Brent Peterson and Lawrence University, and Jean-Marc Leveratto at the Paul Verlaine Université-Metz for allowing me to present part of my work there. I had tremendous institutional support from James Rosenheim and the Melbern G. Glasscock Center for Humanities Research, the Comparative Literature and Cultures Program, the College of Liberal Arts, and the Department of European and Classical Languages and Cultures of Texas A&M University. The friendships of Ingrid Abeln, Roland Schmidt, Constance Hauf, Prudence Rose, Bojan and Rositza Popov, Arnold Vedlitz, Marian Eide, and Victoria Rosner made this a better book. Nell Lindquist did heroic work in preparing the manuscript for which I am eternally grateful. Ede Hilton-Lowe, Nina Morris, and Patricia Garza keep my workplace sane. I am happy to have maintained my relationship with my editor, Micah Kleit. I hope we meet in person someday. Joe Golsan continues to be a devoted friend and valued mentor while deflecting my criticism and insubordination with a consistent backhand.

I have presented parts of this book at the Society for Cinema and Media Studies annual conferences in London (2005) and Chicago (2007). A very early part of Chapter Four was presented at the Ninth Quadrennial International Conference on Comparative Literature in 2004 in Taipei, Taiwan, and appeared in the *Tamkang Review*. A much revised version of Chapter Two was presented in 2005 at a conference on 'Cinematic Rome' organized by Richard Wrigley at the University of Nottingham and was printed in a volume of the same name (Troubadour Press, 2008). Both sections are reprinted with permission. I also benefited from presenting material on *Roman Holiday* and its reception at a conference organized by Ulrike Weckel at the European University Institute in Florence, Italy, in 2007 and one organized by Janet Staiger at the University of Texas–Austin in 2005. I would like to thank the organizers and participants of those conferences for their input.

I started this project while my mother, Mary Shandley, was still alive. Her recollection of her experiences during World War II and its aftermath has always driven my interest in the subject. My mother-in-law, Margie Radzik, shared her memories of her reception of the films in question. These private connections to history made this a more personal project.

The times I have enjoyed working on this project the most were those spent in the company of my wife, collaborator, and favorite philosopher, Linda Radzik. It is difficult to separate out her work on the book except to note that, insofar as the following pages constitute an argument rather than a jumbled pile of thoughts, it was her doing. If it fails in its rhetorical attempts, she is not to blame.

And finally, I would like to dedicate this book to the one person who has made it most difficult to write, our daughter, Mary. I have spent most of her life so far working on this project. Without her, the book might have taken half as long to write, but life would not have been one-tenth as good.

May 30, 2008
College Station, Texas

Introduction

Part of the regular fare in American cinema in the 1950s and early 1960s were stories of Americans in Europe. The American, usually young, naïve, and female, arrives in Europe filled with vague but romantic ambitions. She soaks up the beauty and culture of the Old World, tours the grand monuments, and mixes with the colorful locals. Inevitably, she falls in love. She must make a choice between her old life and the romantic allures of the Old World.

The associations between Europe and romance long predate this cycle of films, and stories of American sexual awakening and self-discovery in Europe occasionally still reappear.[1] However, in the period between the end of World War II and the building of the Berlin Wall, at the point in history where American isolationism had ended for good and the United States took a dominant role in the postwar world order, America imagined itself young and in love in Europe.

This moment at which America was forging a new role for itself in the international scene coincided with a set of industrial challenges in Hollywood that made American filmmakers also ready to try their luck abroad. As a result, America's filmic fantasies of Europe were, for the first time, shot (and often processed and finished) on location as part of a trend that came to be known as "runaway filmmaking." New, larger format screens were filled with the storied landscapes of the Old World. The romances doubled as travelogue films. In this way, audiences accompanied the characters and filmmakers on their European tour.

In this book, I will examine Hollywood's European travelogue romances, 1947–1964. Read as an industrial phenomenon, this group of films shows how Hollywood weathered one of the most difficult periods in its history. As a cultural phenomenon, the films provide an insight into America's evolving sense of its place in the wider world of the postwar era.

The book proceeds from the methodological assertion that films both derive their meaning from and contribute to their contextual surrounding. Although the formal construction of the filmic text can reveal how the films produce meaning, a formalist reading provides scant suggestion about how films circulate in an ideological field, a field in which they are obvious contributors. On the other hand, as we will see, a formal component such as the wide-screen process can have tremendous ideological implications as well. Thus, while film form will be an integral part of the discussion, the book remains firmly rooted in understanding films as participating in the cultural conversation of the moment.

In the next few pages, I would like to begin to orient the travelogue romances, which formed a staple during the first decade and a half of Hollywood's runaway filmmaking practices, in their historical context. I will then defend the claim that this set of films constitutes a genre. After that, we will take a brief view of the industrial history that led the studios to Europe, before undertaking readings of individual films and production histories.

Hollywood and the American Century

On February 7, 1941, just ten months before the United States formally entered World War II, Henry Luce, founder of *Time* magazine and noted American conservative, proclaimed the twentieth century to be the "American Century." This claim was predicated on the assumption that sooner or later Americans would enter the war and that once they did, they would necessarily be victorious. Moreover, Luce suggested that the victory would then allow the United States to assume its rightful place as world leader in order to "exert upon the world the full impact of our influence, for such purposes as we see fit and by such means as we see fit."[2] Luce's frightening call to colonialist arms signaled that at least a faction of American conservatism had broken ranks and that the American industrial class now saw not only entry into the war, but a broader commitment to internationalism as in its best interests.

Whether Luce's "American Century" editorial or the attack on Pearl Harbor marks the turning point, the fact is that the United States' entry into World War II connoted a shift in American self-understanding, one that reached from the political elite class to the common foot soldier to the average moviegoer. America and Americans understood themselves as important players on the global stage. This change in identity was neither immediate nor did it go entirely uncontested. But, the conditions under which the Americans entered the war stipulated that, once it was over, it would be difficult for America to return to its traditional isolationism.

Since 1941, America has settled into its role, in its varying guises, as a global hegemon. While World War II itself provided many opportunities to display the United States' immeasurable human and natural resources, the postwar period allowed for a wider range of activities through which the United States could establish dominance. This new role meant the dedication of greater resources to national priorities and therefore an expansion of the role of the federal government. It meant that the United States would maintain a large standing army that would be deployed in bases throughout Europe and the Pacific Rim.

As companies sought to take advantage of the position America had achieved through the war, commerce became more internationalized, thus causing federal officials to establish policies to encourage expansion of international operations, especially into Allied countries whose support was deemed important to U.S. strategic interests. These interests led the Truman administration to devise means to prevent Western Europe from falling into the expanding Soviet empire. The European Recovery Act, generally known as the Marshall Plan, not only lifted the economies of Western Europe at a time when the region had little access to other capital investment, it also laid the foundations of stable trade relations between the United States and its European allies. By the end of the 1940s, America had irrevocably entered the business of nation building, creating entangling foreign alliances, and securing its influence throughout the globe.

The war and the following occupations meant that a large group of veterans had been or continued to be stationed abroad. While before the war a trip to Europe was an experience mostly limited to the American elite, the broad shift in American foreign policy brought a much more socioeconomically diverse group of (mostly male) citizens into greater contact with places outside of the American continent than ever before. In the following decades, millions of soldiers and their families would be stationed in Europe and Asia, living abroad for years at a time and bringing their stories home. Because of the demographic diversity of those serving in the armed forces, foreign deployment exponentially expanded the group of Americans with either immediate or indirect experience in a foreign culture.[3]

In addition to the Marshall Plan, other government initiatives encouraged postwar American international influence. Intended as an American answer to the Rhodes Scholarship, The Fulbright Act of 1946 created opportunities for students and scholars from around the world to study in the United States, and it sent generations of young American scholars abroad. Designation as a "Fulbright Scholar" became a prestige marker for having studied abroad. The Fulbright program spawned a host of study abroad programs in college and universities as well, such that a trip or even semester abroad became a common part of the college experience.

Thus, World War II and its aftermath created a new American ideological perspective that encouraged a high degree of self-assurance. It inserted America into the global narrative more forcefully than before. Moreover, it pushed the formerly hegemonic "Old World" into a perceived position of subservience. This shift in attitude toward the rest of the world did not confine itself to policy makers and cultural elites. The following chapters reveal how Hollywood negotiated the new and complicated relationship between the "New" and the "Old" World in the postwar era. The Americans are portrayed as liberators, conquerors, tourists, capitalists, and colonialists. The Europeans appear as war criminals, victims, children, sexual amusements, or merely attractive but blank slates onto which Americans could project a range of fantasies. These fantasies, however, remain tempered by a continuing perception of Europeans as the arbiters of sophistication, erudition, beauty, and social legitimacy, and therefore as those whose romantic attentions are well worth winning. The films under discussion in this book share a common project of investigating the newly reconfigured relationship between Americans and Europeans, one in which the American characters would, to paraphrase Luce, come to exert upon the world the full impact of their influence, for such purposes as they saw fit.

Genres, Films, and History

As America began imagining itself into the new geopolitical postwar constellation, Hollywood naturally entered the conversation. For specific financial and industrial reasons, which will be examined at length in Chapter One, studios began creating a significant number of films that were both set in Europe and filmed on location. At first, certain established genres emerged as most suitable for "runaway" production. *Quo Vadis* (Mervyn Le Roy, 1951) marked a return of the biblical epic to the Hollywood production list, a genre that would include *The Ten Commandments* (Cecil B. DeMille, 1956), which was filmed in Egypt and Israel. Producers developed a long series of narratives that employed both biblical and classical Greek stories as vehicles for displaying ancient European architecture and scantily clad young actors, such as *Ben-Hur* (William Wyler, 1959) and *Spartacus* (Stanley Kubrick, 1960), both of which were filmed at the Cinecittá studios outside of Rome, which became a sort of home away from home for Hollywood throughout the 1950s.

In the 1960s, Europe returned to the cinema as a theater of war. A cycle of World War II films premiered decades after the conflict that restructured the world. The grandest and most famous was *The Longest Day*, an omnibus account of the D-Day invasion filmed on location with multiple directors, produced by Darryl F. Zanuck, and released in 1962. Later features, such as *The Dirty Dozen* (Robert Aldrich, 1967), *Catch 22* (Mike Nichols, 1970), and the filmic treatments of World War II battles in both the European and Pacific theaters, served to interpret World War II in the face of postwar geopolitical dynamics.

The combination of a much broader and more intensive American contact with the rest of the world and Hollywood studios' experiments with globalization provide ample films of all genres made all over the world. However, Europe remained both the largest market for the export of Hollywood products and the host to the most runaway productions. The following chapters limit their exploration to America's relationship with Europe as it is depicted in those films made by Hollywood producers in Europe. Because we are concentrating on that contemporary relationship, I have chosen to talk about only those films that are also set in postwar Europe. While the biblical epics, war films, colonial adventure films set in Africa and Asia, and the "spaghetti" Westerns filmed in Italy and Yugoslavia would yield interesting readings, the attempt here is to work through both cinematic and noncinematic questions regarding the integration of American and Western European interests in the postwar years. As such, those films that animate such issues will provide the most fruitful place to start.

The Hollywood films set in contemporary Europe in the 1950s are almost invariably stories of Americans finding love in Europe. Whether the story is a comedy or a drama, whether the love interest is another American or a European, the romance is always in part a love affair with Europe itself, presented grandly on the big screen. The uniformity of the portrayal of the contemporary relationship is remarkable. Hollywood in this period portrays America's past with Europe in terms of war and its present in terms of romance. As the Cold War heats up in the 1960s, spy films will add another dimension to Hollywood's romantic framing of the American–European relationship.

The various narrative conventions to which Hollywood films generally resort when weaving romantic tales function, in the films under consideration here, to reveal much about how Americans perceived the changing relationship with their European allies. But the travelogue romances, as we will see, provide interesting variations upon and reconstructions of the generic conventions of the romance. For example, even in films that would generally be read as having happy endings, the romantic pair frequently does not end up together. In fact, with few exceptions, lasting romantic unions are formed only if the lovers are both American or if, as in the case of love stories involving American GIs, it is clear that the union will be transported back to the States. Holidays in Europe, it is understood, must come to an end, and Americans must eventually return home. The filmic stories of American romances in Europe share enough common traits and were perceived by reviewers at the time as having been related such that we can consider them a genre. Picking up on the language of contemporary reviews, which often noted how well the films captured the location scenery, I will refer to these films as "travelogue romances."

Much serious theoretical work has gone into the question of what a genre is and how we might recognize one when we see one. In his systematic recounting of the large critical literature on genres, in the broader, more literary sense, Steve Neale notes that some theories of genre "stress the primacy of expectations, others the primacy of texts, still others the primacy of categories, corpuses, the norms they encompass, the traditions they embody and the formulae that mark them."[4] Neale attempts to account for genre by considering all of these factors. Thomas Schatz thinks of a genre as an efficient feedback loop. "The filmmaker's inventive impulse is tempered by his or her practical recognition of certain conventions and audience expectations; the audience demands creativity or variation but only within the context of a familiar narrative experience."[5] Schatz later makes a claim for the social function of film genres when he argues that

> we may consider a genre film not only as some filmmaker's artistic expression, but further as the cooperation between artists and audience in celebrating their collective values and ideals. . . . If we are to explain the *why* of Hollywood genres, we must look to their shared social function and to their formal conventions.[6]

Thus, for Neale, Schatz, and many others working on of the topic, film genres and genre films are efficient parts of the culture industry in which producers, distributors, and consumers share a common notion about what films are and how these standardized film industry products should speak to us.

Rick Altman finds this public conformity a bit too constricting. He argues that most genre studies suffer from the common logical error known as a confirmation bias.[7] These studies usually include in a genre category only those films that ineluctably conform to the definition they have set up. That is to say, the genre is defined in a certain way because the scholars have only chosen to include those films in it that conform exactly to the definition they have set up. Any potential counterexamples are excluded from the start. This is only the most damning of many serious flaws Altman finds in the ways that scholars set up their studies of genres.

While Altman's critique of almost every system of understanding film genres is both valid and useful, we might find that the stakes in this theoretical question are a bit lower than his work would suggest. Jeanine Basinger, who has authored a number of fascinating books about stars, stardom, and film genres, makes a rather flippant suggestion as to how one might determine whether or not something is a genre.

> Almost anyone you ask to define a genre such as the Western will come up with a list—the saloon girl with heart of gold, the school teacher, the good guy in the white hat, the bad guy in the black hat, the Indians who try to buy rifles, the sheepherders who try to fence off the cattlemen's grazing land, and the inevitable final shootout. A simple test for any genre is whether or not you can, in fact, generate such a list. If you can, it's a genre. If you can't, it probably isn't.[9]

It might appear at first flush as if Basinger is offering an intuitive rather than an intellectual response to genre theory. But this test provides a useful set of constrictions as well as openings for how we might construct an understanding of a genre. First of all, it avoids the pitfall of presuming that everyone understands a particular film genre or genre filmmaking as a whole in the same way. My list of the characteristics of the Western would differ significantly from those suggested by Basinger. Moreover, it also leaves open the notion that such a list might change over time. That is to say, a Western may look slightly different to different people and different groups, and it may well serve a different function at different times as well.

In discussing film genre, it is useful to remind ourselves that genre categories are not natural kinds but interpretative and explanatory tools applied to an immensely complex set of phenomena. If we wanted the label "genre" or "Western" to do heavy explanatory lifting—say, to mark out precisely what a particular film is, how it is made, and how it is received—then we would likely need an Aristotelian model whereby we determine necessary and sufficient conditions for membership in a genre. As David Bordwell notes, "One could . . . argue that the concept of genre is so historically mutable that no set of necessary and sufficient conditions can mark off genres from other sorts of groupings in ways that all experts or ordinary film-goers would find acceptable."[9] However, if we follow Aristotle's own advice by not asking more precision from a discussion than its subject matter allows,[10] then we can proceed with a much more loosely constructed paradigm model of genres.[11] In a paradigm model, genre categories are defined by paradigmatic sets of characteristics, and particular films fall under those categories based on the number and strength of the similarities they share with those paradigms. Generic paradigms may shift. They take on certain meanings at certain times, but may change or lose their significance. Filmmakers, distributors, and consumers may be conscious of the patterns in which the films partake, or those patterns may only be recognizable to later audiences. A particular film may resemble more than one paradigm and so may fall into more than one genre. The point of talking about genres, when genres are as loosely formed as this paradigm model suggests, is not to provide a shorthand for industrial explanations or aesthetic interpretations but to focus our attention on a phenomenon that calls out for explanation and interpretation.

Ultimately, in the case of the travelogue romance, it is not important whether we attach the label of genre to the set of films in question. What is important is to notice that Hollywood was, for a particular period of time, inclined to tell a certain kind of story in a certain kind of way. This is not the only sort of film it made, and similar films can be found both before and after this period. But the fact that it is possible to identify a particular narrative and aesthetic form recurring over and over again in a relatively short span of time—especially a form that lends itself so easily to allegorical readings connecting it to the politics of the day—calls for our attention.

So, in the spirit of Basinger's discussions of film genre, and in hopes of opening up rather than limiting a line of inquiry, I would like to characterize the travelogue romance by offering a list of characteristics shared by a large number of films made by Hollywood studios from 1947–1964. I hope that in reading the list, the reader will feel a sense of familiarity. If so, that is some evidence that the pattern I am identifying constitutes a genre. Later chapters will show how the characteristics that form this list provided filmmakers with a reliable model of production and the opportunity to explore a stable set of ideological positions. Those explanations and interpretations will serve as a defense for treating this list of characteristics as defining a genre.

The Credit Sequence

A nondiegetic travelogue alerts the viewer that the film is set in contemporary times in Europe. Frequently the opening titles state that the film was shot, whether in its entirety or in part, on location in the particular city where the story is set.

The Arrival Scene

The main character, usually an American, frequently female, is seen arriving in the European city. (One does not see the character leaving the United States, only her arrival in Europe.)

The Travelogue

The film uses her arrival to offer another travelogue sequence, this time more diegetically bound, as the character makes her way to her lodging or receives an initial tour of the area. The travelogue footage highlights the sorts of monuments and landscapes one would see in a travel guide. There is little attention paid to geographical plausibility in the sequence. Travelogue sequences may recur throughout the film.

The Rationale

The film will need to offer a reason for the American's presence in Europe. She may be in Europe on some sort of business, on a long or a short stay, but tourism and shopping almost always form part of the object. A wish for self-discovery, reinvention, or renewal is usually explicitly mentioned.

Local Rituals

The American partakes in some sort of local ritual, whether touristic or more "authentic," that allows her to mix with the local people or the local setting and highlights the difference from home.

Class Mobility

The American moves freely and sometimes obliviously among the old and fixed European class boundaries, mixing with ancient aristocratic families and street urchins with equal ease.

The Locals

Regardless of socioeconomic class the local population is deferent to the American. The locals are often portrayed as children, regardless of their age. Those who present romantic possibilities for the American speak perfect English (which is usually explained somehow). Those who speak no English or poor English are not potential lovers, but are instead a source of the film's humor.

The Romantic Relationship

A romantic relationship is quickly established between characters from the Old and New Worlds. The Old World resident may be a European or an American exile, but he (or she) will be strongly associated with Europe and represented as highly sexualized or highly sophisticated. A sexual relationship is strongly implied. Frequently, a love triangle is formed between the main character, the European/Europeanized American and an American love interest (who may remain offscreen).

The Declaration of Difference

The American character realizes, and often says or has said to her, that what is happening now could not have happened at home, that the people she has met are not like those in the States, or that the folks back home would no longer recognize her. This moment may be celebratory or alienating or both in turn.

The Decision

The American is forced to choose to continue the romantic relationship or not, or to choose between lovers. The decision is almost always framed as at least in part a decision between returning home and staying in Europe, or between American values and European values. The main character chooses the path associated with America.

The Transformation

The American has been transformed by the events, almost invariably becoming stronger, wiser, and more independent, whether or not the relationship continues.

The Departure

The film almost always ends with a departure scene or a scene in which departure is decided upon. The tour of the Old World will come to an end, and the American will return home.

Again, this list functions paradigmatically rather than categorically. We should understand the elements as a mean. No film has all of these features, and most films deviate from the descriptions somewhat. But, in keeping with Basinger's test for genre, in the case of the travelogue romance, it is rather easy to generate a list of characteristic features.

Overview

In the following chapters, I will trace the development of the travelogue romance by examining sets of films that speak to many of the ideological and

industrial questions of the day. Each of the following chapters shall be organized around an issue with which certain productions and films were confronted. We shall often separate productions from films because in most cases
the studio or the producers were trying to respond to trends or sets of challenges that differ from the ideological content of the films' narratives. At times
the production concerns and those of the story itself appear to converge. At
other times, the connections are much more tenuous. Thus, it is important to
be attentive to production history and narrative content as well as the cultural,
economic, and political forces that influence both.

Chapter One will introduce the industrial conditions of postwar Hollywood. It will show how a long list of factors combined to undermine the
strength of the studios immediately after World War II. By the early 1950s,
the classical Hollywood modes of production, distribution, and exhibition
were each undergoing rapid transformation. Among the changes in production
practices was the advent of what came to be known as the "runaway production," that is, the removal of much of the shooting of a film to a location other
than southern California. We will see how and why European cities became
increasingly attractive to film producers. This move to Europe, in turn, led to
the development of a wider variety of stories set in the Old World.

Chapter Two is dedicated to a discussion of the film that most success-
fully piqued Hollywood's and the general public's interest in the new romantic
possibilities of the Old World, namely William Wyler's *Roman Holiday*. While
not the first runaway film with a contemporary setting, *Roman Holiday* provided a production and narrative model off of which many other films would
build. In the production history of the film we find evidence that Paramount
was quite self-consciously experimenting with both runaway production and
the combination of the travelogue with the romance in order to deal with the
industrial crises of the day. An interpretation of the narrative content of the
film itself provides both our first look at a travelogue romance and an allegorical presentation of Hollywood's act of running away.

In Chapter Three, we will examine the construction of Europe as a
narrative locale for sexual awakening, discovery, and reinvention. We will
examine how and why so many European runaway productions employ the
trope of the European holiday as sexual adventure. Through a discussion
of four films, *September Affair* (William Dieterle, 1950), *Indiscretion of an
American Wife* (Vittorio DeSica, 1954), *Summertime* (David Lean, 1955),
and *Interlude* (Douglas Sirk, 1957), I will discuss why Europe functions so
frequently as the woods in a Grimm's fairy tale, that is, the place one must
traverse in order to enter sexuality. Moreover, in each of the films discussed
in this chapter, the relationship is hampered by the fact that one of the
characters is married. This plot device ensures that the relationship will

remain temporary, and the American will return to her or his productive life stateside.

One of the Hollywood studios' most dramatic attempts to draw audiences back into the theaters in the early 1950s came from the introduction of various wide-screen processes designed to enhance cinematic experience. Chapter Four discusses the marketing strategy of using new technologies to exploit the increased interest in foreign travel and in fashion. The chapter uses three films, *Three Coins in the Fountain* (Jean Negulesco, 1954), *To Catch a Thief* (Alfred Hitchcock, 1955), and *Funny Face* (Stanley Donen, 1957), to reveal a set of production strategies designed to combat plummeting movie attendance. This chapter will show how the convergence of wide-screen technology and runaway production affected the growing series of films about the transatlantic relationship. It will also argue that the production choices carried with them ideological remnants that influence how we are to read the films' narratives.

Chapter Five will trace the evolution of the German–American romance as depicted in the travelogue romances from the end of the Second World War to the building of the Berlin Wall in 1961. The discussion begins and ends with films directed by Billy Wilder in Berlin. *A Foreign Affair* (1948) depicts the newly conquered Berlin as a den of iniquity in which American morality must prevail over the remnants of National Socialist ideology. While tours of duty can hardly be equated with the other kinds of tours portrayed in travelogue romances, many of the structural and thematic elements parallel the rest of the genre. Gradually economic occupation overtakes military occupation as the metaphor for German–American relations. When Wilder returns to Berlin in 1961 for *One, Two, Three*, Cold War tensions have superseded World War II resentments. Berlin, now a much more charming den of iniquity, is the last bastion of Western freedom against the tyranny of Soviet rule. The occupation troops have been replaced by the soldiers of capitalism, in the form of Coca-Cola executives. Between Wilder's two Berlin films we find a set of films, including *I Was a Male War Bride* (Howard Hawks, 1949), *The Big Lift* (George Seaton, 1950), *Fräulein* (Henry Koster, 1958), and *GI Blues* (Norman Taurog, 1960), in which the discourse of distrust and occupation gradually gives way to a narrative of empathy and integration. The travelogue romance negotiates the ideological transformation in American popular sentiment toward Germany as a symptom of moral decay to an example of successful rehabilitation.

Chapter Six discusses the decline of the travelogue romance. The chapter offers evidence that filmmakers and moviegoers alike began to tire of the basic conceits of the travelogue romance by the early 1960s. Films such as *Town Without Pity* (Gottfried Reinhardt, 1961), *The Roman Spring of Mrs.*

Stone (José Quintero, 1961), and *Two Weeks in Another Town* (Vincente Minnelli, 1962) suggest both a darker underside to the kinds of stories that make up the travelogue romance and a receding fascination with Old World splendors. Moreover, the films depict the American–European encounter as something other than appealing. Meanwhile *Paris, When it Sizzles* (Richard Quine, 1964) aggressively lampoons what had become Hollywood's trite uses of Europe. While the travelogue romance film did not disappear, by the mid-1960s other cultural movements were afoot that would overrun the stories of American sexual awakening in the Old World. The social upheaval at home in the 1960s as well as the shift of international attention to Southeast Asia made the self-discovery involved in a trip to Europe seem slightly less relevant than it had a decade earlier. America had to return from its European holiday and get its own house in order.

Hollywood's Move Abroad

In 1951 Hollywood studios shot three films abroad.[1] The next year the number tripled[2] and included one production, William Wyler's hit *Roman Holiday*, in which almost all production and postproduction work would be completed in Europe. By 1956 fifty five productions were shot abroad, while ever fewer were being taken up in southern California. A *New York Times* article from April 7, 1958, entitled "Movies' Decline Held Permanent" suggests that industry observers did not see the demise of Hollywood studio productions as temporary.[3] In 1961 a southern California newspaper noted that more films were currently being shot in Rome than in Hollywood.[4]

Hollywood's various union leaders in the early 1950s quickly branded as "runaways" those productions in which the principal actors were filmed on location outside of southern California. Whether or not this moniker, which implies an illicit flight from home, was justified, it became the commonly used term for Hollywood films shot abroad.[5] Hollywood studios shot in locations as diverse as Rome, Hong Kong, and Kenya, but, for reasons to be explored here, Europe exerted by far the strongest pull on the Hollywood imagination. Runaway films of the 1950s to the early 1960s ranged in genre from biblical epics to circus films, from combat films to Westerns to musicals. But, of those films with contemporary European settings, the films made are almost invariably what I will call "travelogue romances." They are films that take an American character as well as the American spectator on a tour of Europe in search of love. These films proved to be both particularly popular with the studios and uniquely informative about Hollywood's relationship with Europe. The European travelogue romance emerged as a format for discussing the new and changing contemporary relationship between the Old and the New Worlds.

This chapter will introduce the notion of the runaway film. We will examine its causes, which lay in the larger social and cultural context of postwar America as well as in the economic disparities between the United States and Europe in the aftermath of World War II. More specifically, we will examine the film industry in America and the serious challenges it faced after 1946. The United States underwent massive demographic and social change in the postwar period, which affected the ways people worked, lived, traveled, and entertained themselves. Moreover, the place that the United States occupied in the world shifted, thereby altering American self-perception. This chapter will provide a primer on these various upheavals, using them to situate runaway filmmaking in general and the travelogue romance in particular in the conditions of their production. First though, we will begin by offering a brief sketch of Hollywood's relationship to Europe before 1945.

Hollywood's Relationship with Europe before 1945

The histories of American and European cinema have always been closely intertwined, and American cinema was not always the dominant force. Before the rise of the studios in southern California and the streamlining of production techniques, movie exhibitors often struggled to find films to present in their nickelodeons and, increasingly, in the larger variety halls in which films were shown. With the slow decline of Thomas Edison's Motion Pictures Patents Company in the first decade of the twentieth century, exhibitors had a more liberated choice of distributors from which they could rent films. One of the largest was Pathè-Frères, a French company that bought the rights to the Lumière brothers' patents and that occupied a dominant position for a brief time in early American cinema, showing films with primarily European content. By 1910, when the Pathè brothers lost their hold on the exhibition market, Richard Abel argues "that the American cinema could be refashioned as a national cinema and become truly American."[6] From that point on, the American cinema would consolidate its energies mostly around narratives that would tell the American story, no matter when and where the film is set.

The decline of the Pathè brothers in America did not, of course, spell the end of the American film industry's contact with its European counterparts. The outbreak of the First World War radically reduced film production on the continent at a time when American production was moving west to

California and consolidating itself and its art. After the war, a newly consolidated German film industry, mostly in the guise of its most hegemonic studio, Ufa, enjoyed a string of successes in the American market with films such as *The Cabinet of Dr. Caligari* (Robert Wiene, 1920), F. W. Murnau's *Nosferatu* (1922) and *The Last Laugh* (1924). But with the success of, among others, Murnau, Josef von Sternberg, and Ernst Lubitsch came another trend in the cinematic relations between Europe and the United States. Hollywood, as the newly formed studios of southern California became collectively known, created a brain drain for movie industry talent from all over the world. Directors, such as Murnau and Lubitsch, began immigrating to the United States in search of the greater resources and audiences that the post-World War I American film industry could provide.

The Hollywood studios established dominance in the European market almost as quickly as they did in the United States. Their distribution efforts came with both a backlash on the part of the Europeans and a public relations effort on the part of the studios. As Thomas Guback reports, "the great wave of American film exportation that started after World War I produced retaliatory import quotas, distributor quotas, and screen quotas."[7] Hollywood then enlisted the help of the U.S. State Department in order to defend its dominance in the European market. In fact, the trade organization to which the majors belonged, the Motion Picture Producers and Distributors of America (MPPDA), predecessor to the Motion Picture Producers Association (MPPA), set up its own "foreign department" to negotiate with governments and to inform studios of foreign censorship requirements. In short, Hollywood was already an international force in the prewar period. The studios had sales forces throughout the globe and, by the 1930s, were deriving a large percentage of their income from foreign rentals.[8]

American studios did not restrict their European efforts to merely distributing Hollywood films. A number of studios, including Paramount and Fox, set up production units in Europe in the 1920s, with varying degrees of success.[9] But these efforts were aimed primarily at producing films in and for the European market. Especially with the advent of sound, any Hollywood film meant for the American market that contained scenes set in Europe was generally either shot by a second unit and incorporated into rear projection or was wholly constructed on a Hollywood back lot.

The rise of the Nazis to power in 1933 added to the connection between Europe and Hollywood. Many of the German film industry's most talented directors, actors, writers, and producers, including figures such as Fritz Lang, Peter Lorre, Billy Wilder, Kurt Siodmak, and Otto Preminger, filled the ranks of filmmakers who fled National Socialist Germany. Moreover, it increased the tendency of Hollywood to serve as a value-added producer, taking the raw talent from Europe and returning a valuable product to be sold. The arrow rarely if ever worked in the other direction.

Even through the war years, Hollywood continued to maintain a hold on the imaginations of Europeans. Although the beginning of World War II in 1939 inhibited access to new Hollywood releases in much of Europe, it only created a pent-up demand. Furthermore, as Eric Rentschler has argued, even Nazi leaders remained fascinated fans of American films, for which they arranged private screenings.[10] Once the war was over, a flood of Hollywood films poured into the European market in an attempt to sate the demand for feature films in general and Hollywood products in particular. But, as profitable as this phenomenon was, Hollywood was to face a slew of problems both at home and abroad in the years immediately after the war, problems that would change the relationship between the studios and Europe. In 1946 any ticket sales abroad provided surplus profits, long after a film had recouped its costs and become profitable at home. But the economics of production, distribution, and exhibition, as well as those of currency exchange and market protectionism, would alter radically the origin and flow of cinema products.

Postwar Industrial Pressures at Home

Although the economy of the United States experienced a long and steep expansion in the decade and a half after World War II, not every segment of the economy enjoyed this boom equally. During roughly the same boom period of the U.S. economy (1946–1960), the American film industry underwent a series of crises, realignments, and retrenchments. Attendance at the movies dropped from 80,000,000 to 45,000,000 annually. While the drop in movie attendance has been attributed traditionally to the equal rise in television set ownership during the period, a variety of factors combined to dethrone the cinema as America's primary entertainment site.

To be certain, the availability of visual entertainment in the home provided a level of competition for attention and resources that the motion picture industry had never previously experienced with other home entertainment systems, such as radio. In the same period in which movie attendance was dropping, television ownership skyrocketed. While there were only 8,000 television sets in circulation in 1946, less than 1 percent of American households, by 1960, 90 percent of America homes had them.[11] Had television been the only force with which the film industry had to contend it is imaginable that they might have more quickly perceived the advantages of cooperation with the television studios. Instead, such cooperation took the better part of a decade to develop. In fact, the industry was faced with a number of major obstacles at once, all of which threatened the continued existence of the studios.

In May of 1948 the Supreme Court handed down what has come to be known as the Paramount decision, which required major and minor studios to break up their vertically integrated systems of production, distribution, and exhibition. Some of the studios continued in vain to fight the decision. Yet, in the end, the subsequent consent decrees forced all of the studios to divest themselves of their exhibition business. Despite the evidence that this allowed Hollywood studios to rid themselves of expensive urban properties just at a time when those properties were beginning to lose value, thereby preventing the studios from further capital loss, in 1949 the studios certainly did not view their breakup as a positive development.[12] For them it meant that there was to be no guaranteed venue for the films they made. Thus, millions of dollars could be invested in a film that might never find a distributor or a screen.

Movie houses, which were no longer owned by the studios, were also no longer forced into exclusive relationships with them. Theater owners, panicked about collapsing ticket sales, were now at liberty to pick and choose among the film offerings of all of the studios, without having to buy into package deals or block bookings. The studios had to sell each movie on its merits. This, for the most part, spelled the end of B-movies, double features, and the like, which had previously been used to turn a visit to the cinema into a whole evening's entertainment but, when faced with the competition of another studio's top-shelf films, looked like comparatively inferior products. Thus, the studios had to create new formulas in order to attract theater owners. One of the studio responses to this shift in programming was to attempt to change the nature of the entertainment offered in the cinema. Studios began to revisit the scale of the productions, turning more frequently to epic films that were generally produced at a screening length that would fill a whole evening program with a single, higher-quality product. In order to produce these films, Hollywood studios would, for the first time in over a generation, radically transform their highly specialized modes of production.

The breakup of the studio theater chains and the freedom of programming were not the only factors influencing the programming practices of the movie theaters in the early fifties. The act of going to the cinema itself underwent a change. The role of stand-alone movie theaters in consumer culture was shifting. The suburbs being built by William Levitt and other developers were altering the basic organization of domestic life in America. Other forms of entertainment and activity, such as participation sports like golf, tennis, and bowling, began to occupy Americans' increasing amounts of free time. As the population spread out, as automobile culture expanded, the cinema gradually ceased to be a place to which one could walk. Going to a movie became more of a deliberate choice rather than a pedestrian impulse. Moreover, it also changed the way in which many filmgoers viewed individual films.[13]

As Hollywood studios watched their audiences leave for the suburbs, they were in no position to follow them. The studios were prevented by the consent decrees that followed from the Paramount decision from investing in new theaters themselves. And, given the drastic drop in ticket sales, building new movie palaces in the suburbs seemed like a bad investment to other entrepreneurs. This convergence of factors left a virtual void in the cinematic culture of the new suburbs, a void that rapidly would be filled. As John Belton points out,

> The quickest and cheapest solution to the problem of theater construc-
> tion in the suburbs was the drive-in. . . . The tremendous increase in
> the number of drive-ins in the postwar era, from 554 in 1947 to 4,700
> in 1958, reflects an attempt by one group of exhibitors in the industry
> to catch up with this new, highly mobile suburban audience.[14]

In the late forties, the opening of drive-ins outpaced the closures of indoor cinemas.[15] Despite the fact that the drive-ins were obviously the easiest response to the changing development patterns in America, the studios did not endorse the move to outdoor cinemas. They still adhered to the notion of the movie palace as the ideal setting in which their products should be viewed. Therefore, they limited the quantity and quality of films released to the drive-ins. Nevertheless, the development of drive-ins indicates a larger trend among those in the American film industry to find new ways to reach the newly prosperous American. As Thomas Schatz puts it, "with its clientele of young marrieds getting out of the house for a few hours with the kids in the family car the drive-in heralded the rise of the suburbs and the passing of the downtown area as the center of social and cultural activity for most Americans."[16] Despite its initial resistance, Hollywood studios eventually had to appeal to a different audience in a different place.

The general necessity in the industry to address the growing middle class shifted the traditional ground on which the American cinema was built. Small neighborhood theaters and larger urban theaters were often home to a socioeconomic mixture of moviegoers. Yet, even before the move to the suburbs, the class makeup of the audience seems to have begun to change. Once the studios began keeping track of their audiences, they noticed that they were growing ever younger and more educated. By the 1950s, the studios had long since devoted their energies primarily to programming for the middle class. This strategy responded both to the fact of an expanding middle class and the perception of an increasing desire of average Americans to associate themselves with the middle class, whether or not they had achieved that status.

The sharp drop in attendance led, by the end of the 1940s, to severe layoffs on the part of the studios, most of which had reached peak employment levels in 1946. Precisely at the moment where their revenues were declining, the studios faced cost increases that came from a number of sources. Unions, who had cooperated in the war effort, now demanded increased compensation for their members. The cost of Hollywood's highest-paid stars was also increasing, as tax laws encouraged them to market their services more openly. The status of stars changed even further in the early 1950s, with the proliferation of independent production companies and the rise of the powerful talent agencies.

In 1947, the House Committee on Un-American Activities (HUAC) took up an investigation of the influence of the Communist Party in Hollywood. That year it led to charges against those who would eventually become known as the "Hollywood Ten" for contempt of Congress for failing to answer the Committee's questions.[17] The studio's trade organization, the Motion Picture Association of America, which had originally signaled a resistance to cooperation with the Committee, reversed itself in November 1947, when it issued the Waldorf statement, in which it promised the Committee its full cooperation. While the hearings in the fall of 1947 marked the last time Hollywood would be summoned by the Committee until 1951 (again just before the next U.S. presidential elections), it marked the official beginning of blacklisting, which remained in place in Hollywood until the 1960s.

Postwar Industrial Pressures Abroad

At the end of World War II, the conditions for Hollywood's global dominance of the movie market appeared perfect. Germany, Italy, and the territories they occupied during the war were opened to Hollywood again. The ambiguous legal situation in the wake of the war left many countries without the protection they had built up for their own film industries in the 1920s and 1930s. Moreover, Hollywood studios, which had been effectively shut out of the European markets since the 1930s, had hundreds of movies not yet seen by European audiences, which they were prepared to dump on the market. The industry had also picked up influence through its cooperation with the Allied war effort and was prepared to use that influence to again take over the European cinema landscape. The formation of the Motion Picture Export Association (MPEA) in 1945 created a legal cartel with which the studios could combine efforts to compete abroad. Utilizing provisions of the

Webb-Pomerene Export Trade Act of 1918, the MPEA was "to act as the sole export sales agent for its members, to set prices and terms of trade for films, and to make arrangements for their distribution abroad."[18] It was effectively a cartel that functioned as the foreign ministry of the Motion Picture Association of America.

By the end of 1946, "the studios reported that their overseas income of $125 million was virtually identical to their overall net profits—a situation that many in the industry considered ideal."[19] If the domestic market could cover expenses, the growing international market could insure a healthy 50 percent profit margin. However, this rosy prospect soon became clouded by the economic and political realities of the postwar European context.

While the MPEA may have been able to dominate most of the screens in Western Europe in the immediate aftermath of the war, the 1948 Paramount decision and the subsequent consent decrees led to the organization's demise. Furthermore, extracting the profits from film rentals turned out to be increasingly complicated for the studios: $90 million of the foreign earnings from 1946 came from England, yet a large portion of that money was frozen and remained in England. The United Kingdom simply could not afford that large of a draw on their balance of payments to the United States. As the economic situation in postwar Britain worsened, so did the remittances from the United Kingdom. By 1949, England only accounted for $17 million in revenues for the Hollywood studios, the amount agreed upon in a settlement between Hollywood and the British government.[20]

The problems elsewhere in Europe were different. In the sectors of Germany controlled by the Allied powers, for instance, there was no functional currency until June 1948. A barter economy persisted in which the most valuable commodities were U.S. made cigarettes. While Germans were delighted to have access to Hollywood products again, they hardly had any way to pay for them that would appear on Hollywood ledgers.[21] Other Western European countries had functional currencies, but, until the institution of the Marshall Plan beginning in 1948, which added much needed capital to the Western European markets, these currencies were anything but stable. Thus extracting profit from the rental of films to postwar Europe was a problem for the studios from the very end of the war onward.

Once Western European countries instituted various currency reforms in 1948, the expectation was that it would improve Hollywood's ability to realize a profit from the huge number of films in circulation throughout the continent. Yet one of the biggest threats to the stability of Western European economies in the late forties was the balance of payments vis-á-vis the United States. The United States occupied such a large percentage of the world economy in the immediate postwar period that European currencies held very little value in comparison. The weakness of those currencies forced European nations to take measures to protect what few dollar reserves they held to be used for essential commodities. The most relevant of these measures for the studios was the freezing of earnings generated by American companies so that such earnings had to be reinvested in the national economies rather than be removed in the form of dollars.[22]

The limits placed on profit repatriation caused the MPEA during its brief but important existence to negotiate deals with most Western European governments regarding the amount of money to remain in frozen accounts annually. While they were able to arrange some repatriation, the studios were nevertheless left with large sums of weak currency to dispose of in a myriad of fashions. As Guback reports,

> The first attempts to acquire monies in blocked accounts abroad entailed such ingenious schemes as buying wood pulp, whiskey, furniture, and other commodities and selling them elsewhere for dollars. Producers also invested in ship construction and in a variety of other non-cinema fields, all with the assistance of the MPEA diplomatic corps.[23]

But soon the studios discovered a formula that would put them at the forefront of a certain practice in American industry, namely outsourcing production to foreign countries.

Hollywood Runs Away

While the MPEA was still experimenting with bartering to liquidate their frozen currencies, the studios began experimenting with making films abroad. The *francs*, pounds, *lira*, and *Deutschmarks* earned from film receipts were directly reinvested in products that would bring in dollars at home. Metro's *The Search,* directed by Fred Zinneman, Paramount's *A Foreign Affair,* and RKO's *Berlin Express*, all released in 1948, mark some of the earliest Hollywood ventures into what would, a few years later, be dubbed "runaway productions." The move abroad was also a strategy that would answer many of the challenges that Hollywood faced on the domestic front. Foreign film crews could provide much of the labor at lower costs. The higher-paid artists received tax advantages and avoided the gaze of the HUAC by working abroad. More important, the studios would discover that filming in foreign locations, especially in Europe, offered the opportunity to tell the kinds of stories and present the kinds of spectacles that could help them lure American audiences back to the theaters.

For the studios, the runaway production presented the first full-scale departure from the secure and comfortable working conditions of southern California. In the course of the 1950s, Hollywood changed its attitude entirely about location productions. Producers, directors, actors, and executives who had earlier placed a premium on the control that was possible in the studio setting became increasingly comfortable and savvy about working abroad. Under pressure to compete for American theater space in the wake of the Paramount decision, studios began making fewer films with higher production values. Cosmopolitanism in the form of authentic location shots became an important part of the studios' attempts to separate themselves from television and revive their fortunes.

Long-standing relationships, market connections, and a common language made England an attractive location for the studios. With weather and light conditions similar to those of southern California, Rome and the revived Cinecittà studios in Lazlo became an even more important home for the Hollywood runaways. In fact, on a trip to the United States in 1949, Roberto Rossellini, then a darling in the American art house circuit for films such as *Open City* and *Paisan*, complained that Hollywood's discovery of Rome had driven up the price of labor, studio rentals, and film stock such that it was becoming difficult for local directors to finance films.[24] Rossellini is presumably referring to *Quo Vadis* (Mervyn LeRoy, 1951), which was the first Hollywood film to engage Cinecittà, as well as various international coproductions, such as his own *Stromboli* (1949), which was coproduced by RKO.

Notably, as the trend toward runaway production blossomed, the studios and production companies looked most often to those directors born in Europe to return to the Old World to make pictures. Thus, European expatriates such as William Wyler, Billy Wilder, Jean Negulesco, Douglas Sirk, Alfred Hitchcock, and Otto Preminger all took part in Hollywood's journey to Europe. This could be seen as an attempt to choose directors who had some experience with the continent and who might, therefore, thrive under those conditions. It was also a way of marketing the films in Europe, namely as European films made by Europeans. In either case, this list, which contains many of the most prominent directors of the day, also shows what a priority runaway production had become to a number of the studios.

All of the majors undertook efforts to film abroad, with some much more engaged in the process than others. It is perhaps not an accident that the two studios that had been involved in European production in the 1920s, namely Paramount and Fox, would be the ones to make the most notable efforts abroad in the 1950s. Nevertheless, Metro was the first studio to exploit the Cinecittà facilities in Rome with the *Quo Vadis* production.

While Hollywood studios began to plan productions abroad almost immediately after the war, such activity blossomed by the early 1950s, such that it began to cause added strife to the already contentious relationship between the studios and the film industry trade unions stateside. By the beginning of 1953, the term "runaway production" had become a point of contention. As Peter Lev puts it, "the term took on a pejorative force . . . suggesting that the Hollywood studios were acting irresponsibly when they did not protect the California-based labor force."[25] W. R. Wilkerson, founding editor of *Hollywood Reporter,* on January 15, 1953, dedicated his weekly "Tradeviews" column to the rising controversy of foreign productions. In it we see both to what degree outsourcing had become a hotly contested topic in Hollywood and what sort of force "runaway production" carried as a label. Wilkerson begins his piece:

> THAT TAG, "runaway productions," slapped on the foreign produc-tion efforts of our Hollywood producers by the IATSE [International Alliance of Theatrical and Stage Employees] is a bad smear on a most necessary effort. Dick Walsh, Roy Brewer and other top brass in the IA know why our companies design products in foreign fields and the necessity of making those pictures. Consequently, it's unfair to slug the effort with 'runaway productions.'

The labor–management relations that Roy Brewer had done so much to nor-malize were clearly threatening to come unraveled around this issue. Brewer had gained favor for himself with the studios by helping break up more radical spin-off labor organizations as well as by serving alongside Wilkerson as an avid red-baiter during the early HUAC hearings. Yet, as the exchange indi-cates, the two could not agree on why it was that Hollywood was moving its productions abroad. Wilkerson continues:

> There are two main reasons why we make pictures abroad: (1) to get the use of our frozen earnings, and (2) to establish better relations with countries and governments that are now paying off the better than 65 percent of the entire earnings on our pictures, world-wide.
>
> Walsh and Brewer know we have to cater to our foreign customers and have to toss some money into their motion picture pots, in return for the big heap we are taking out. These IA men know that, when we make an occasional picture abroad, it gives employment and helps build production in the countries where we spread our production effort. Too, these men know, without the foreign haul, few if any of

their organization would be working, because few if any studios would be in operation. So why the smear of "runaway productions."

Every big industry in this country manufactures in various foreign fields. Through this type of operations better foreign sales are created, making better working conditions here in the U.S. AND greater employment. Have you ever heard one of the unions in any of the other industries yell "runaway production" at their foreign effort?

Mr. Walsh, Mr. Brewer and their whole IA can be assured that our picture-making is not running away to foreign shores and they can be certain that some of it has to be done and will be done and through it IA gets better protection.[26]

Wilkerson's confidence that foreign production was undertaken only when necessary and that "picture-making is not running away" was not shared by everyone, least of all by the IATSE, whose membership was suffering high unemployment. Moreover, Wilkerson's support for building up the production facilities in places such as London, Rome, or Munich was not going to appease union bosses who were opposed to just that. IATSE representative Roy Brewer responded in the pages of Wilkerson's journal. In February 1953, Brewer writes a letter to the *Hollywood Reporter* laying out his union's position on foreign productions. He carefully eschews the "runaway" label, while disputing the full set of rationales for undertaking such productions.[27] He and Wilkerson also disagree on the level to which production profit was based on foreign sales.

The letter is introduced in an article and then quoted in its entirety. Brewer begins by claiming Wilkerson's editorial expresses a misunderstanding of the IATSE position.

First let me say that at no time have we, president Walsh, myself or the IATSE, officially ever objected to production abroad which was necessary in the pursuit of the best interests of the industry as a whole. We have always recognized that our industry is a world wide industry, which derives a substantial portion of its revenue from the foreign markets. (There are no statistics available at this time, however, to bear out your charge that it is anything like 65 percent.)[28]

Indeed, the percentage of overall receipts accounted for by foreign sales by the early 1950s was again on the rise, after having suffered from the general economic downturn in Europe in the late 1940s. But Brewer is certainly right to doubt that foreign sales amounted to such a high percentage of the receipts. If so, it would mean a complete inversion of the market since 1949, when foreign sales reached only 35 percent.[29] Brewer fails to note here that there was little evidence at the time to suggest that films made outside the United States fared better in the international market than those made domestically.

Brewer concedes that certain circumstances dictate a film being shot abroad. He continues:

> We recognize that story content of foreign locale may at time require shooting abroad. However, only in rare instances does it require that the entire picture be made abroad. In most instances authentic locale can be had in American made pictures by shooting on location and the utilization of background plates, which our technicians have developed to a high degree of perfection. Such a picture as 'The Snows of Kilimanjaro' is a perfect example of this type of production. It was set almost in its entirety in a series of foreign locations, but the bulk of its production was done in Hollywood.

Here Brewer seems to be responding to the recently completed experiment by Paramount with its production of *Roman Holiday*. As we will see in Chapter Two, the entire production was completed abroad using Italian facilities and labor, as well as location shots in which the characters interact with the foreign locales.

> Such a picture as 'The River,' however, would have been, in my judgment, seriously injured were it deprived of the natural setting of life in modern India. We recognize these problems and we do not intend that our judgment should at any time displace the judgment of the producer as to when the creative qualities of a picture will be enhanced by photography in its natural setting.
>
> What we are trying to do is to minimize the pressures which are being established by those who have a special interest in having pictures produced abroad.
>
> The pressures are from many sources, the first of which is frozen foreign financing. Individuals and groups who hope to profit at the expense of our Hollywood industry are making enticing offers to independent producers in the way of financing by which they hope to build up a foreign competitor by utilizing the ability of our creative artists and craftsmen. This we think is basically injurious to our industry and we feel we should be united in our opposition to it.

While Brewer may have been right in his claim that frozen financing was injurious to the American film industry, he fails to appreciate how much was at stake for the countries in question. The governments that set up these currency arrangements were far more concerned with their countries' balance of payment situations and their ability to sustain their economies as a whole than whether or not a wealthy American industry suffered as a consequence.

An important argument in his favor that Brewer seems to miss here is the fact that, because of the favorable conditions abroad, an increasing number of scripts were being developed that required a foreign setting. As the next chapter argues, the quality and quantity of these projects would become firmly entrenched by mid-decade. Thus, by the time any such picture was announced, the studios had the built-in argument that it could only be produced abroad.

Having failed to counter both the aesthetic and economic arguments for lensing abroad, Brewer reveals his credentials as a red-baiter.

> There is the ever recurring problem of the communist influence of which you should certainly be aware. Persons who have been called before the committee and who have refused to testify have gone abroad and are working behind the scenes to build up a production center where their pro-communist view will not interfere with their employment as it has done here. These people are being joined by persons, who, while never having been communists, but who were active in front activities, now find themselves uncomfortable in the anti-communist atmosphere that prevails here. Certainly you cannot disagree that every possible effort should be made to resist this type of pressure.

Again, Brewer was likely referring to the *Roman Holiday* production. As we will discuss in Chapter Two, the studio hired, either directly or indirectly, a number of people who had been blacklisted, as well as others, including William Wyler himself, who were "active in front activities." This is also true of a number of the other foreign productions of the period, including John Huston's numerous films from the early 1950s. Huston, who like Wyler had made known his sympathies with the Hollywood left, settled in Ireland and made numerous runaway films before returning to southern California in the latter part of the decade.

Wyler, Huston, and many other Hollywood dignitaries were indeed vulnerable to Brewer's last critique.

> And last, but certainly not least, is the more recent problem of those persons who have gone abroad to take advantage of the eighteen months tax exemption. We are not unmindful of the problem of the

individual in the high income brackets, whose position requires him to maintain a standard of living which the tax collector makes it so hard to maintain. Nor do we expect them not to take whatever advantages they can in reducing their tax load. But there is certainly no justification in the minds of the people of our industry, whose income is meager by comparison, for being deprived of employment and thus reduced to a lesser standard of living so that the big earners can avoid payment of taxes. From an industry standpoint no one can justify such a situation and as an industry we should rise up in indignation and demand that it be stopped.[30]

Brewer is mindful of his own position as a moderate union leader, one who had maintained a healthy rapport with the studio bosses. This allows him to close his letter with diplomatic language that reveals his willingness to cooperate.

Perhaps there are other lesser pressures which I have not mentioned, but these are the principal ones. We are trying to deal realistically with the entire problem of foreign production. We fully recognize that we cannot take any position which will hurt the industry without hurting ourselves. But we also contend that what we do to help ourselves in the proper way will also help the industry. We believe that basically we are all on the same side of this fight and we sincerely hope we can tackle it—constructively together.[31]

While certainly not intended as such, Brewer's letter is an accession that the unions had very few weapons with which to fight studio outsourcing. The fight would go on for another decade, although the union could do little to control the outcome. IATSE, an American Federation of Labor affiliate, did manage to keep television production from moving abroad as well. At the same time that Brewer was responding to Wilkerson, he was also fighting to keep a television series from moving abroad. *Variety Daily* ran a headline on February 11, 1953, "Labor Whips 'Runaway' Vidpix."[32] The article suggests that Brewer was able to dissuade the series' sponsor, a local brewery, from backing a project that was to be shot abroad. This would be one of few victories in the outsourcing wars that Brewer would be able to report. Despite Wilkerson's reassurances to the contrary, there was in fact a widespread fear that Hollywood was running away from home.

IATSE was not the only union worried about Hollywood globalization. In June 1953, the Screen Actors Guild (SAG) asked for a congressional investigation of the increase in filmmaking abroad by American producers.[33] SAG discounted the possibility that the increase could be attributed alone to the tax clause that allowed high-income earners to escape income taxes by living abroad for eighteen months. In general, SAG was looking to have the federal government place pressure on foreign governments to lift the freezing of film company earnings. But, by 1953, the studios had geared up completely to film abroad and saw advantages that would continue well beyond the point at which currency could flow freely.

The development of travelogue romance scripts allowed studios to announce productions that would necessarily have to be filmed abroad. Once they had developed certain story packages and sets of narrative and visual expectations, runaway productions would take on lives of their own that the unions would be unable to combat. Presumably, the unions, as well as others in the southern California region, saw this danger early and sought to articulate an opposition on other grounds in an attempt to ward off the inevitable.

Los Angeles Times columnist Edwin Schallert entered into the fray, writing a column that is little more than a plea for producers to stay home. Schallert prophesies "contemporary stories will probably have very little appeal in foreign pictures, even when they are made with American stars, unless the stories are unusually rich in drama or comedy."[34] In his survey of current or announced productions abroad he continually contradicts himself. The article starts out in praise of *Roman Holiday* and *Little Boy Lost* (George Seaton, 1953), both of which were recently made foreign productions of the sort he claims will be unsuccessful. His argument is that those who were a part of the exodus of Hollywood professionals in the early fifties heading to Europe for a tax break would find themselves at a disadvantage when they eventually returned to southern California. Among other things, these professionals would not be able to keep abreast of the technical developments in Hollywood. However, he also decries the then recent technical advances, such as CinemaScope and 3D, as gimmicks, claiming that all that the industry needs is good old-fashioned storytelling. This too, he claims, can only be done in Hollywood: "It is a question whether even the British will be able to contrive such subjects as to appeal to this country." This supposed handicap apparently, in Schallert's opinion, stems from the notion that producers working in Europe would see their talents shrivel when not exposed to the sunshine of southern California. However poorly stated their arguments, the supporting media around Los Angeles also feared that the film industry was running away for good.

In the 1950s, southern California faced a set of circumstances that has recurred throughout different industrial regions of the United States ever since. Not unlike the textile mills of the South, auto manufacturing in the upper Midwest, or lumber mill jobs in the Pacific Northwest, the well-paying jobs in the movie industry that anchored the economy of southern California were outsourced to countries with lower wages and related production facilities. Studio employment was on a steady decline for at least a decade.

Studio management and producers were also under rather severe financial and political pressure. While their arguments were often predictable and occasionally disingenuous, they were made with force equal to that of the union representatives. In 1954, producer Walter Wanger countered the criticism of the AFL's Hollywood Film Council, which was lobbying to curb runaway production. Wanger argued that "if everyone stays home, and pictures are dull, it won't help the Council. . . . If the backgrounds are different and interesting, on the other hand, and films do business, labor—like everyone else—is bound to profit."[35] The film industry was in decline and, according to Wanger, the only way to reverse its fortunes was for Hollywood to leave the studios and back lots of southern California and use as its background the larger world in which Americans had grown more comfortable.

Eric Johnston, head of the Motion Pictures Production Association, defended overseas production in a meeting of the Motion Picture Industry Council, a group of management and labor officials formed in 1948 to protect the interests of the industry. Johnston claimed that three-quarters of Hollywood films did not cover their costs in the domestic market. Therefore, producers simply needed the foreign market in order to have films make money.[36] Johnston was reacting to pressures on Hollywood to seek trade protection from foreign made films due to the currency protections abroad. Claiming that Hollywood still enjoyed tremendous market opportunity abroad that he was loathe to undermine, Johnston noted that in 1953 the motion picture industry "brought back $165,000,000 from abroad, and American pix still occupy almost 70% of the total screen playing time of the world."[37] Thus did Hollywood producers provide a model for capturing world markets and remaining profitable by outsourcing labor.

Despite union protestation Hollywood did run away. For over a decade runaway productions would be an important part of Hollywood studios' search for a new business model. Producers began by developing stories, hiring directors and stars, and then moving entire productions abroad. In the course of the 1950s producers started taking advantage of new incentives established by European governments. The practice of the government subsidized international coproduction, in which projects received certain significant subsidies from European governments, boomed in the 1960s. As Guback notes, "through the 1960s, American films financed abroad rose from an estimated 35 to 60 percent of the total output of U.S. producers."[38] Guback points out that in Italy, "in the decade up to 1967, American companies spent a yearly average of about $35 million to acquire and to finance Italian features, and to make their own films in Italy."[39] Thus, many of the fears of those in southern California proved to be well justified.

In the early sixties, the trade papers were claiming that the wave of American-interest filmmaking abroad had abated. Yet, the statistics show that runaway production, although changing in nature, was still a major part of the mix. The director and producer Otto Preminger noted in 1963 that "it's still about 33% cheaper to make a picture abroad."[40] Preminger dismisses all of the talk of rising costs in Europe eventually making it more economical to work in the States again as a "Hollywood Dream." It is important to note that while Preminger and other producers reveal themselves clearly to be motivated by the cost-savings of foreign production, they always follow up their economic argument with an aesthetic one. Preminger reiterates an opinion that was shared by many producers at the time. "I only like, at least at the moment, to shoot pictures where a story takes place."[41] Audiences, it seems, had grown used to the look of location work and were no longer accepting of the rear projection techniques of an earlier age. "Today's audience," Preminger asserts, "is more demanding. To get authenticity you must shoot all over the world."[42] Enough evidence does exist to suggest that filmgoers responded well to and therefore likely began to demand the look of location shooting.

Given this entwinement of causalities, the studios' strategies for survival involved a tremendous shift in production from southern California to Europe and the rest of the world. At the same time, the studios themselves shifted their emphasis away from actual filmmaking. Instead, they became a combination of financing companies, studio leasers, aesthetic consultants, and distributors. In the most extreme case, at the beginning of 1963, Twentieth Century Fox suspended production altogether, due, among other reasons, to the losses stemming from the runaway production of *Cleopatra*. The unions were, of course, concerned that, when Fox resumed production, they might leave California for good. When Darryl F. Zanuck returned to Fox from a stint as an independent producer he met the AFL's Film Council and reassured them that Fox did have plans to return to southern California. In commenting on his own runaway production work Zanuck contradicts Preminger, noting: "I have found from experience that it actually costs more to produce a feature motion picture outside the U.S. than it does in California, having regard especially to the quality and efficiency of our American production personnel."[43] While that statement seems designed to appease union officials, Zanuck also defended foreign location work for the sake of authenticity. He did, however, suggest that much of the location shooting could be done with second units rather than moving whole productions abroad. The combination of location work in Europe and studio work in Hollywood resulted two years later in Fox's all-time greatest hit, *The Sound of Music* (Robert Wise, 1965).

Hollywood never did run away from home completely; it did, however, implement business practices that not only helped it weather the storms of the post-Paramount transformation, but also established a precedent of outsourcing production that prefigured the widespread globalization practices of today. Yet, the recounting of Hollywood's model of industrial outsourcing is only the beginning of the story. In moving productions abroad, filmmakers essentially began developing the story of their own presence abroad. That is, they used the idea of the American living and working abroad, especially in Europe, as a platform from which to investigate the dynamic nature of the postwar relationship between the New World and the Old. We see the combination of the production paradigm with the new attitude about Europe in a runaway film about a princess who runs away.

2

How Rome Saved Hollywood

As we surveyed in the last chapter, Hollywood was faced with a multitude of problems in the early fifties: the industrial scaling back resulting from the Paramount decision, plummeting ticket sales, millions in profits frozen in Europe, and blacklisting at home. In this chapter, in order to illustrate how the decision to film on location in Europe served as a response to the industrial crises of the early part of the decade we will recount the production history of Paramount Pictures' 1953 blockbuster *Roman Holiday*. We will pay special attention to the technical and logistical problems that the decision to make the film in Rome entailed. The persistence on the part of both producer–director William Wyler and the studio on working through seemingly insurmountable technical difficulties suggests that they had much at stake in completing this project in Rome.

Roman Holiday was by no means the first runaway film. But its use as our first extended examination of a runaway film is appropriate for a number of reasons. While this production was not the first Hollywood project filmed in Europe, its extensive use of location shooting is notable. Furthermore, it was the first such film in which the postproduction work was completed abroad as well. *Roman Holiday* was one of the most successful and critically acclaimed films of the category under examination here, namely Hollywood films both set and filmed in Europe during the 1950s and early 1960s. In this film we see many of the narrative tropes that would be shared by other travelogue romances. In these ways, *Roman Holiday* sets up a production model that would be mimicked to one extent or another for the following decade, a model that enabled the Hollywood film industry to survive the most difficult period in its history. Finally, the fable of the runaway princess and the American journalist looking for a new story to tell resonates with the conditions under which the film was produced.

The Decision to Run Away from Home

In the case of *Roman Holiday*, as in most runaway films of the era, the decision to take the production abroad was based on the perceived convergence of aesthetic and financial interests. Plans for *Roman Holiday* began in 1951, when Wyler agreed to produce and direct the project given to him by Frank Capra, the acclaimed filmmaker and Wyler's former partner in the independent company, Liberty Films, which was acquired by Paramount in the late 1940s. According to Jan Herman, author of a biography of Wyler, *Roman Holiday* was not originally conceived as a runaway production:

> Paramount at first resisted the idea. 'No, no' Freeman told him. 'We've got the studio.' When Wyler dug in his heels, Freeman offered a compromise: Wyler could get backdrop shots of the city with a second unit. 'The rest we'll do here.' But, Wyler flatly rejected that proposal. He already had in mind scenes at the Trevi Fountain, the Coliseum, the Spanish Steps. He wanted to use a sidewalk café across from the Forum. Paramount finally gave in, provided that Wyler could finance the production with blocked funds the studio had in Italy.[1]

The confidence expressed here suggests the benefit of hindsight. The production correspondence, on the other hand, reveals that, while still the primary advocate of shooting the film abroad, even Wyler was at times skeptical about its feasibility. In the heyday of the studio system it is unlikely that such a project would even have been proposed. Location shooting would have appeared to be a recipe for an overextended production schedule and cost overruns. Projects were conceived to avoid the necessity of extravagant second unit shooting. But in 1952, with a significant portion of its capital frozen in European currencies, Paramount set up two European projects simultaneously. The other was *Little Boy Lost*, directed by George Seaton and starring Bing Crosby, which was shot in Paris and completed in Hollywood. But whereas the European settings presented in *Little Boy Lost* are almost entirely the result of rear projection and second unit work, the studio and Wyler finally agreed to film the actors in Rome, moving among and interacting with the grand settings of the Eternal City. This extensive use of location shooting, perhaps the most important experiment undertaken by the *Roman Holiday* production, was a drastic departure from Hollywood visual cultural practices to that point.

Wyler and the executives at Paramount shared a sense that Hollywood would have to offer something new to draw back its American audience. Indeed, given the limitations put on the studios in the wake of the Paramount decision, with the loss of their exhibition business and their powers over distribution in doubt, control of the aesthetic aspects of film was one of the few tools the studios had left at their disposal. Claiming the need to produce different effects, Wyler insisted on a film that would bring the audience to Rome. The point of the considerable efforts at location shooting was for the audience to know that the characters are in the Eternal City and that, were the spectator to go to Rome, she or he could enjoy a similar experience. Wyler saw his as an attempt to offer the audience a different relationship to the image on the screen. The film begins with an intertitle that will serve as a model for dozens of films of the era to follow: "This film was shot entirely on location on the streets of Rome, Italy."

Other commentators frequently cite the success of Italian neorealist films in order to explain the Hollywood studios' openness to the practice of location shooting and the grainier aesthetic properties it would entail. In his study of the ideology of the American film industry, *A Certain Tendency of the Hollywood Cinema, 1930–1980,* Robert Ray describes the anxiety of the studios upon discovering the heterogeneity of their audience. Ray attributes this discovery to the emergence of art house and cult cinema in postwar America.

> With their harsh frankness about postwar realities, movies like *Open City, Shoeshine, Paisan,* and *The Bicycle Thief* had no possibility of widespread acceptance. But the discovery that there was an audience sizable enough to make even those bleak movies profitable unsettled the American film industry, which always thought of its potential market as uniform.[2]

While Ray is no doubt correct in noting that Italian neorealism caught the attention of the studio executives, it seems slightly overstated to claim that Hollywood had, at that moment, discovered a crack in the unity of their audience. To be sure, and even Ray's own work highlights as much, Hollywood understood the varied classes, races, and genders that constituted their audience. Instead, it was a strategy of the studios in the classical period to posit a unified spectatorship rather than to play to the realities of its differentiated parts. Arguably the most that the reception of early postwar Italian film in America suggests is that a portion of the audience wanted something different than what the Hollywood system was offering.

To claim that postwar Italian filmmaking caused a crisis of confidence on the part of Hollywood studios would seem to substitute a cause for a symptom. That is to say, the studios may well have been concerned that emerging art houses were peeling off a small percentage of cognoscenti. But, faced with the millions of Americans of all classes who were staying away from the cinema, the thousands going to art films would have caused minimal reaction on the part of studio executives. They had bigger matters to keep them awake at night. By the 1950s, the attraction of a few intellectual elites to foreign films was merely one small part of the larger problem of waning spectator interest in the standard studio fare. The cause, even in the eyes of the studios, was that Hollywood had indeed lost touch with its audience. Neither the studios nor the critics could predict the kind of film that would entice potential moviegoers to buy tickets. Ray argues quite convincingly that the "implicit arrangement between the industry, audience, and objective situation of America—upon which the Classic Hollywood had depended—was breaking down."[3] The studios feared the loss of their status as providers of mass entertainment. Ray quotes John Houseman's fear that "most of us face this harassing dilemma that we are working in a mass medium that has lost its masses."[4] Yet, many scholars have suggested, that loss is just as attributable to William Levitt's houses as the art houses.

To be sure, however, as their audience dwindled in the late 1940s and early 1950s, the studios did become more attentive to even the slightest cinematic successes by any would-be competitors. Not only did they wish to ward off any further incursions into their rapidly decreasing audiences, they also sought the secrets to the success, however limited, of these films, which in their eyes, managed to reach audiences in spite of or perhaps indeed because of their apparent directness and simplicity. In short, by the early 1950s, Hollywood was searching desperately for a new contract with its public. They may not have seen neorealism as the answer to their problems, but its birthplace was destined to be one of the first places they looked.

Once the studio bosses agreed that the film could be shot on location, the *Roman Holiday* production took on a new role for the studio. The studio went beyond its more common practice of simply shooting the film abroad and shipping the undeveloped rushes back to Hollywood. It developed into an experiment in the outsourcing of much production and all postproduction labor. Not only was the entire film shot in Italy, either on the streets of Rome or in the Cinecittà studios, but the entire editing and sound dubbing was completed there as well. The studio was committed to maximizing the percentage of the budget that used frozen funds. Months before Wyler began production, a Paramount executive team traveled to Rome to set up a studio outpost there.[5] They bought equipment and film stock in England with their stockpile of frozen pounds sterling. In fact, the interest in buying the film stock with these funds explains why the film is shot in black and white. Being an American product, Technicolor film stock was only payable in dollars.[6]

Wyler's insistence on location shots helped convince Paramount to experiment with a new aesthetic for *Roman Holiday*. Perhaps it was Wyler's reputation for exceeding his budget that convinced them to make use of the less expensive production facilities and labor available in Italy. If the experiment worked, it would allow for a more extensive and efficient use of the studio's frozen lira. If it failed, the loss would not tax the strapped studio as much as it otherwise would.

Running Away from the House and Home

The attempt to retrieve foreign profits and to reduce production costs tells only part of the story of *Roman Holiday*. The production seems to have been responding to other headlines that dominated newspapers in southern California and the rest of the United States as well. The resumed congressional inquiries into Communist Party membership in the film industry, which had effectively subsided since the last presidential election year of 1948, were again creating a community crisis in Hollywood in 1951, a crisis that is very much a part of the *Roman Holiday* production history.

The history of the effects of the House Committee on Un-American Activities (HUAC) on the film industry has been thoroughly documented. Larry Ceplair and Steven Englund's *The Inquisition in Hollywood: Politics in the Film Community, 1930–1960* gives a broad overview of the Hollywood studios' confrontation with leftist politics from the organization of trade unions during the Great Depression to the waning days of HUAC in the late fifties. Victor Navasky's *Naming Names* concentrates more specifically on the moral implications of cooperating with HUAC and the impact that "friendly witnesses" had on both the congressional actions and the film community. More recently, Jon Lewis has made the convincing and therefore disturbing argument that, far from doing damage to the studios, as many histories of the era have claimed, the blacklist actually saved the studios.[7] Lewis argues that the studios' collusion with HUAC helped them curb their union troubles and, over time, reestablish control of the entertainment marketplace. In short, Lewis believes that the congressional hearings provided the studios with an easy way to control skyrocketing personnel costs at a time when box-office receipts were plummeting.

While there seems little doubt that the studios benefited from collusion with the congressional investigations, Lewis perhaps overstates their value in the makeover that the Hollywood studios underwent in the 1950s. It was a necessary but alone insufficient piece of the puzzle. To be sure, the HUAC investigations hovered over many productions of the late 1940s and early 1950s. Blacklisting certainly relieved the studios of a few high-priced contracts and, more importantly, cowed many of the trade unions into submission. Yet, at the same time, it also interrupted some of the long-established modes of production, especially in script writing, the filmmaking subfield hit most heavily by the congressional investigations. As we will see in the case of *Roman Holiday*, it made getting script rewrites nearly impossible. Lewis takes the example of the Hollywood Ten to illustrate his point about how the studios used the blacklist to trim their budgets. But a closer look at the full impact of the congressional investigations into political activism in Hollywood provides a more complicated story. For the studios, the political whirl in which they found themselves was certainly more of a problem than a solution.

On November 24, 1947, Congress cited the ten "unfriendly" witnesses for contempt of Congress. That same day fifty members of the Motion Picture Producers Association (MPPA) met at the Waldorf Astoria hotel in New York City to discuss the congressional investigations. Despite the protests of, among others, Louis B. Mayer and then RKO chief, Dore Schary, the MPPA produced what became known as the "Waldorf Statement." The statement served as the founding document for the Hollywood blacklist by announcing that "We will not knowingly employ a Communist or a member of any party or group which advocates the overthrow of the government of the United States by force or by any illegal or unconstitutional methods."[8] Moreover, despite having risen to their defense a month earlier, the MPPA condemned the group that would be from that point forward known as the "Hollywood Ten," saying, "We will forthwith discharge or suspend without compensation those in our employ, and we will not re–employ any of the 10 until such time as he is acquitted or has purged himself of contempt and declares under oath that he is not a Communist."[9] With this manifesto the Hollywood studios attempted to liberate themselves from congressional investigations by sacrificing eight screenwriters and two directors.

Had the 1947 hearings and subsequent industry response been the end of the story, Jon Lewis's argument about the function of the blacklist in Hollywood's renewal might well be more convincing. At the very least, the studios gained a short-term reprieve. However onerous its methods, HUAC hardly represented the greatest threat to the Hollywood studios' survival during the period of its existence. Congress was attempting to influence an industry that was, as we now know, going through a dramatic shift in its business practices, market orientation, and scope. HUAC's intervention was merely the seediest part of the transition from "Classical Hollywood" to "New Hollywood." Large demographic shifts, tax laws, the Paramount decision, and the rise of television can each be said to have been as influential as the apparent benefits of the HUAC investigations in the twenty-year shift in modes of production that mark the difference between Hollywood practice in the studio era and the 1970s.

If HUAC and the subsequent blacklisting of leftist Hollywood professionals cannot be given sole credit for the studios' revival as entertainment conglomerates, they can certainly be credited with bringing together the talents that created *Roman Holiday*. In 1952, the American Legion, which was freelancing as a Hollywood blacklisting organization, asked Paramount about Lester Koenig, an associate producer with whom Wyler had a close working relationship and who was working on *Roman Holiday*. Koenig had proven uncooperative with HUAC in his first testimony before the committee. Paramount's Frank Freeman was forced to respond to the Legion's James O'Neil in a letter dated June 9.

> One of the conditions of employment of Mr. Wyler by Liberty, and a condition Paramount accepted when they acquired the stock, was he would have a right to select his assistants and also any writer he desired to work for him. . . . At the time Paramount acquired the stock of Liberty, William Wyler had as one of his assistants a young man by the name of Lester Koenig. Mr. Koenig was under contract to Liberty on an annual basis . . . When [his] renewal took place, none of us here at Paramount had any knowledge or idea that Lester Koenig had ever been a member of the CP, for had we such knowledge we would not have permitted the renewal of the contract.[10]

From this letter we can infer a number of things. First that the studio's practice of hiring director–producers was providing a useful mechanism to shield themselves from HUAC demands. Secondly, they were anticipating other questions about those hired by Wyler. The letter also suggests something that might explain the haste with which the film was put into production. It continues,

> When in New York I explained to you the problem that confronted Paramount in connection with Lester Koenig and the urgency of getting the picture *Roman Holiday* started and completed. To accomplish this, the services of Lester Koenig in helping William Wyler to coordinate and bring together the elements necessary to complete the work were essential. The failure to have him do this could have seriously jeopardized the whole venture.[11]

This letter was dated shortly after Wyler and Koenig had left the country for Rome. Moreover, it is clear that it was preceded by a conversation with O'Neil. Sensing that the Legion was out to cause trouble, it seems likely that Wyler and crew would have been in a hurry to get out of the country. Notes from a production meeting on March 11, 1952, reveal that few basic decisions about *Roman Holiday* had been made. Not only was the script incomplete, Gregory Peck had yet to have been hired. Audrey Hepburn had not yet made her famous screen test. Unit producer Henry Henigson, who would run the Rome operation, had not yet been contacted. Wyler and crew were not even certain that they would take the production to Rome. Yet, three months later all of the principals were in Rome and production had begun. The pressure would have likely only increased had the Legion caught the other reference to Wyler's discretion in choosing a writer.

Vigilante blacklisters such as the Legion and *Daily Mirror* columnist George Sokolsky had been after Wyler since his founding of the Committee for the First Amendment (CFA) with John Huston and Philip Dunne. Shortly after the 1947 HUAC hearings, Sokolsky responded to Humphrey Bogart's combined public denunciation of Communism and participation in the trip to Washington to support the Hollywood Ten that had been sponsored by the CFA by pushing Bogart to go further. "You show first-rate manhood in taking the people who admire you into your confidence. Now do something for your country that is really constructive. Tell us who suggested and organized that trip."[12] Anyone slightly connected with Hollywood knew that Wyler, Huston, and others had organized the protest. As was done in the HUAC hearings, Sokolsky was merely baiting Bogart for a public betrayal.

The production correspondence of *Roman Holiday* reveals a bit of coyness regarding the credited screenwriter, Ian McClellan Hunter. "We intend to proceed with our preparatory work based primarily on the socalled [*sic*] 128-page Ian Hunter script," writes Henigson in an early letter to Wyler.[13] The use of the term "so-called" adds another layer of confirmation to a story that has long been open. Hunter, another leftist activist who would eventually be blacklisted, functioned as a front for his good friend, Dalton Trumbo, one of the Hollywood Ten. While the script was apparently put together by Hunter and John Dighton, it was based on a story by Trumbo.[14] Judging by his own published letters, Trumbo never seemed to have stopped working for the studios after having become among the first to be blacklisted by them.[15] If blacklisted actors such as Larry Parks or John Garfield or directors such as Edward Dmytrk had difficulty finding work, screenwriters could and did go quickly underground using both pseudonyms and fronts. When allowed to choose writers, it would appear that Frank Capra provided such work for

Trumbo. Wyler, who would have known the genesis of the *Roman Holiday* story and screenplay, was also sympathetic enough to those who had been blacklisted not to have shied away from the risk. For, by the time the film went into production, Ian Hunter was also running from a subpoena and was subsequently blacklisted.[16] Capra, when he himself came under fire, claimed ignorance of the script's genesis. Henigson's highlighted reference to the "so called . . . Ian Hunter script" suggests that many of those involved were at the very least aware that Ian Hunter was a front.

It is difficult to tell whether Wyler himself ever faced the prospect of a subpoena. But, as his wife, Talli, told biographer Jan Herman, "It was all very unpleasant, even though he knew he was lucky to be leaving."[17] The production correspondence does suggest that Wyler was happy to leave the country in 1952 and was in no hurry to return. Herman also notes that

> leaving the country provided a tax shelter. The federal government had created an income tax loophole known as the 'eighteen month law.' It exempted Americans who remained outside the country for eighteen months from having to pay tax on their foreign earnings. 'That's why we stayed away as long as we did,' Talli recalled.[18]

Wyler remained abroad for close to two years. Fellow CFA cofounder John Huston also happened to have done a string of runaway productions from 1951–1960, a period of time in which the director lived in Ireland. (Huston's return to domestic production came with *The Misfits* in 1961.) Given the string of coincidences it is difficult to say whether these directors chose to leave the country because of the runaway production trend or they chose to participate in the runaway trend in order to leave the country. Both directors were autonomous enough in their careers to be able to make the choice.

Trumbo could not make that choice. The U.S. Department of State refused to grant him a passport, thereby preventing him from moving to Europe, where screenwriting work may have been easier to find. Instead, in the hope that he could at least cut his living expenses, Trumbo and family moved in November 1951 to Mexico City and remained there for three years.[19] Ian Hunter temporarily fled the revived HUAC to Mexico as well. Indeed, by the time Wyler was given the *Roman Holiday* script, neither Trumbo nor Hunter was still in the country. The reconstructed credits that appear on later copies of the film as well as the DVD refer to a story by Dalton Trumbo with a screenplay by Ian McClellan Hunter.[20] The Internet Movie Database includes, under screenplay credit, "Ian McClellan Hunter (front for Dalton Trumbo.)" For my purposes, whether Hunter played any role in the actual writing of the screenplay does not matter, for both Hunter and Trumbo were, by then, working under blacklist conditions.[21] Because of both Trumbo's exile and the general difficulty that production companies had in conducting follow-up meetings with blacklisted writers, the screenplay that Wyler took with him to Rome was little more than a first draft.

The Challenges of Runaway Filmmaking

When *Roman Holiday* began filming on location in Rome in the summer of 1952, the difficulties of making a film outside the rarified environment of Hollywood quickly became apparent. The production correspondence reveals much about the director, the audience, the differences in conditions between Hollywood and Italy, and the pros and cons of runaway productions. It is a scenario that would play out repeatedly in the following decade, as Hollywood established procedures for producing films abroad.

A long letter from Henigson to Wyler, sent to the director months before Wyler left Hollywood for Italy, shows the kinds of apprehensions Henigson harbored about the experiment. Henigson already had some experience with the Italian film scene, having run the Rome production of *Quo Vadis* for Metro. The letter gives an account of his exploratory journey to Rome to work out the bureaucratic details of setting up the *Roman Holiday* production. He begins his assessment of the working conditions in Rome with an ominous warning. "Willy, Italy is not an easy place to work in any sense of the word."[22] Henigson was obviously exasperated by the conditions he found. His primary complaint centered on the quality of the labor force. "Our business here does not attract the better element, even though we do pay premium scales to persons who are immediately associated with us."[23] When he found people with the right technical skills, they often lacked the language skills to communicate with the non-Italian speaking Hollywood staff. Wyler's native fluency in French and German was to be of little use.

Henigson was clearly worried whether everyone involved in the *Roman Holiday* project understood what effect making a film almost entirely in Italy would have on the resulting production values. Henigson had no experience with the Italian labs and a skeptical attitude in general about industrial professionalism in Rome. He continually sought reassurance from Paramount that they understood the quality concerns he was expressing.

In a letter sent just over two months before filming began, Paramount executive Frank Caffey assures Henigson of Paramount's plans. "As you know it has been the intent of the Company to do the picture entirely in Rome with the quality that we can get there."[24] Yet having been hired due to his involvement with *Quo Vadis*, a film with a huge budget and high production values that seemed to be the current trend of the day, Henigson seems to have had difficulty understanding what Paramount was trying to pull off. The diminished production standards that Paramount insisted it was willing to accept simply did not fit with what Henigson understood as his role. Two days later Caffey again reminds Henigson of the financial arrangement in place. "As you know, it was and is the intention of the Studio Management that ROMAN HOLIDAY would be made entirely in Rome within the confines of the Italian economy."[25] That he continually queries the studio as to whether or not they understand the implications of their decision indicates that Henigson was not comfortable with the arrangements. His disagreement seems to have stemmed from a lack of confidence in the technical reliability of the Italian photo labs. Caffey's May 21 letter continues with a confirmation

> that we would accept the differences in photographic and laboratory quality there as compared to Hollywood of which we were well aware. A number of pictures made in Italy were screened, and it was decided their quality was sufficiently good for our purposes. This was a decision rendered by Messrs. Freeman, Hartman and Wyler.[26]

Henigson had hoped that a recent visit by technical consultant Frank LaGrande to Rome to assess the facilities would build a case for sending the film back to Hollywood for processing. The correspondence indicates that the LaGrande visit did not produce the results Henigson intended. They decided to continue with the plan to have the film processed in Italy. Caffey writes to Henigson:

> As before stated, unless you have any serious objection (which in view of Mr. LaGrande's accord with us on the telephone it is not likely you will have) we would like to complete all work in Rome, including the making of final dupe dissolves, wipes, main and end titles, or any other effects.[27]

Thus, upon being told that Paramount was not expecting Hollywood quality, the consultant agreed that the production could be completed with the facilities at hand, albeit not without compromising studio production standards.

Concerns about the photo labs persisted throughout the production phase. At one point Wyler complains of an entire reel of shot film having been ruined. Yet it is noteworthy that the studio remains persistent in its goal of keeping all costs payable in frozen currency. In effect, this is to be a production on which almost no dollars are to be spent. The film's expenses were entirely cordoned off from the studio's stateside budget. Just as in the 1920s, when changing forms of financing directly contributed to shifts in modes of production, it is evident in *Roman Holiday* that the financial arrangements played a significant role in a new division of labor.

Despite having built a financial buffer between itself and the production, the studio still shows evidence of having been heavily invested in the picture, at least in terms of the ways in which it was staffed and financed. Yet, the production correspondence suggests that the studio was just as interested in running a clean experiment regarding the feasibility of completing whole pictures with the resources available in Italy. The stakes were far higher than securing a positive outcome for one production. If the production and film were successful, it would encourage more use of such cost-saving measures.

Another letter from the Hollywood production team, this time from Jacob Karp to Henigson, reveals exactly what kind of film Paramount was looking for. In response to fears that Wyler was scaling the production up beyond Paramount's parameters, Karp implores Henigson to press upon the director the studio's original plan.

> While we understand Willie's desire to secure as fine a picture as possible, I think you ought to keep emphasizing the fact that there is a cost element involved and Willie understood all the time that, as you say, he was going to make this picture based on the Italian economy, consistent with the type of picture that had been made in Italy before, which he had seen and with which he was satisfied.[28]

Paramount's intention could not have been stated more clearly. They were sending Wyler, an independent-minded director, to Rome to do a film, whose production values mimicked those of the Italian films that had been getting so much attention in the United States in the late 1940s. Executives perceived in the work of Roberto Rossellini, Vittorio De Sica, and others a model for inexpensive production that appealed to their sense of budgetary restraint. Karp pushes the point further when he urges Henigson to continue to impose economy on the picture. "I am sure it is not at all necessary for me to repeat that our objective is to have as fine a picture as possible; however, with conditions at the box office as they are today, the element of cost is a major consideration."[29] That is, rather than poignant tales of hardship and the legacy of fascism in Europe, Paramount seems to have taken cost savings as the primary message of the neorealist wave of films that were so well received in Hollywood.

Because of the many technical pitfalls of runaway productions, Henigson expressed further concerns about the state of the shooting script. The filming conditions and personnel restraints led Henigson to ask for more preproduction work to be done on the script in Hollywood. As Henigson writes to Wyler on April 12, 1952,

> The Italian element can only intelligently function from an Italian translated copy of the script. Scripts intended for foreign production should be much more fully written than they usually are when intended for production at home. The translation should be so detailed that even the foreigner who is forced to work by it will have in his mind a very clear picture of our intention.[30]

Despite this admonition, this was a script that would arrive in Rome underdeveloped and would never be fully written, presumably impeded by the blacklisting of both Trumbo and Hunter and their exile in Mexico.[31]

A letter from Karp to Henigson in July 1952, over a month after shooting had already commenced in Rome, continues to press for the current version of the shooting script suggesting that the one with which they were working had grown out of proportion. This had implications not only for the shooting schedule but also for the film's finances. In order to have the Italian government unfreeze "Paramount Lira" Italian officials had to approve the script. While the initial script by Ian Hunter provided the film's basic structure, Wyler still needed many of the scenes to be rewritten, and he could not turn to the writer of the story or screenplay. The lack of an adequate script to gain Italian approval threatened to shut down the production. Three weeks into shooting, some funds were finally unblocked.

But the Italian authorities demanded a final script before they would allow the film to leave Italy. Karp's letter to Henigson on July 21, 1952, points to the problem rather succinctly:

> Realizing, as I do, that it may be that there will be no completed script for Government approval before the picture is actually finished, is it your intention to have the Government approve the picture, or will you eventually have to have the script approved? You will remember that you and I felt it completely unwise to leave it up to the Government to approve the picture.[32]

The choice to which the letter refers was to either have the Italian authorities approve the screenplay, thereby precluding the need for further review, or to wait and have them pass on the final cut of the film. In other words, either the production staff had to work with the Italian officials in preproduction in order to get the screenplay approved or they had to risk a total rejection of the film on the part of those officials once they viewed the final project. Presumably, Karp's implicit fear stems from the idea that the government could hold the whole project captive after so much had been invested. The studio bean counters were beginning to get nervous. For their part, the officials in Rome only seemed concerned with how the city and its public officials would be portrayed.

In a letter written to studio executive Don Hartman over a two-week period from July 26 to August 9, Wyler attempted to assuage the studio's concerns that the production was spinning out of control. The letter suggests that the script had already undergone one review by the Italian authorities. "As you know," Wyler writes:

> the Italian government objected strongly to certain sequences and it was essential to do considerable rewriting. In the heat of many physical preparations for the production, I did not have sufficient time to get that portion of the script (which deals with the adventures in Rome, with the Roman people), in the best possible shape.[33]

The alleged concern that Italian officials registered about an earlier version of the screenplay seems to have focused on the portrayal of figures of religious and governmental authority.[34] Wyler and Henigson would arrive at a solution that tied them even further to their Italian contemporaries.

In searching for help in narrating the street scenes in Rome, Wyler employed Suso Cecchi D'Amico (one of the screenwriters for *The Bicycle Thief*) and Ennio Flaiano (story author for *Open City*). Merely bringing these noted screenwriters onto the project appears to have convinced the Italian government that the Americans were cooperating with the local film industry and thus allowed the production more access to frozen funds.[35] This is somewhat curious, given that the neorealist films and filmmakers themselves enjoyed little approval from the Italian government. Yet, the contributions provided by D'Amico and Flaiano certainly do little to signal neorealism. If we are to find a connection to Italian filmmaking, the "rosier" realism of the comic films of Luigi Comencini provides a more useful comparison.[36]

Every Italian represented in the street scenes of the final version of *Roman Holiday* is a comic figure—the cabbie, the hairdresser, the neighbor with the rifle. They are all likable but ridiculous. Oddly enough, even depictions of Italian authority, in the case of the police who arrest the three adventurers for reckless driving are rather Keystone Cop-like. Moreover, the court in which they land for reckless driving is easily duped. Perhaps the bureaucratic elites in the censorship office had a sense of humor, at least in regards to the portrayal of simple-minded working class Italians. Alternatively, we might speculate that the Italian government was much happier to see a lampooning of street life in Rome than they were to see the desperate scenes of suburban impoverishment that De Sica and Rossellini had provided.

Wyler ran into further difficulties in adjusting to the physical conditions inherent in doing the kind of location work upon which he had insisted. He complains about location work in Palazzo Brancaccio, where the early scenes of the grand ball were shot. Interestingly enough, it is here where both the studio and the director fail to understand the production techniques they had hoped to emulate. For despite all of the discussion regarding making films like the contemporary Italians, Paramount and Wyler were clearly attempting set-ups and coverage according to southern Californian standards rather than those of southern Italy. Wyler describes the scene:

> Four walls, none of them wild [removable] no way to rig platforms for lights, makeshift installations of every sort, and to complicate matters, mirrors everywhere. For sound, we had to close all doors and windows, and with the lights on, the temperature rose a degree a minute—on some days we hit as high as 120 degrees![37]

Here again, the theory of neorealist production values collides with the reality of Wyler's attempt to maintain Hollywood production norms.

The constant comparison to his Italian contemporaries haunts Wyler. He claims that Rossellini, De Sica, and others enjoyed, at least in one respect, easier work conditions.

> Now we are shooting on the streets and, in this regard, I must point out to you that no Italian company shooting in the streets has ever worked under conditions comparable in any way to ours. The reason for this is Gregory Peck. . . . Where he shows up, it is an absolute madhouse. Other Italian producers and directors have told me that they are now encountering difficulties shooting in public places because people think Gregory Peck may be working in their picture. The police are absolutely helpless, as the people of Rome have a very great sense of independence and will not be pushed around. They live on the streets and they own them.[38]

The production solved the crowd control problems by replacing the police, who were guarding the location, with "so-called 'group leaders' of extras."[39]

Wyler started writing this letter on July 26 and then did not return to it again till August 7. With the mid-August deadline approaching for Hepburn's contracted return to the States, the studio sent a flurry of anxious missives about the conditions of production. Without having received the letter that was started on July 26, they did not have Wyler's explanation of the various production delays. When Wyler picked up the correspondence again, he had to further quell the studio's fears that the project was not progressing. In his continuation of the letter he defends himself against many cables and letters expressing concern about the project and his ability to complete it. He again attempts to make Hartman (then studio chief and the only person at Paramount with whom Wyler corresponded) and the others understand the conditions under which his crews were working, including continuing problems with film processing.

Yet, Wyler was apparently remarkably sanguine about the technical problems the production continued to encounter. He expresses confidence in the film-processing lab despite several serious breakdowns. "They did ruin part of several days work because the machine broke down while the negative was being developed. . . . We made retakes, then *they* were ruined!"[40] Audrey Hepburn recalled that the ruined takes were of the scene on the Spanish steps. "It was a complicated scene to get because of the background. So we spent hours at it. It took us two days to get that one shot. Then the film was ruined in the lab . . ."[41] For a director known for shot perfectionism and an occasional hot head, Wyler's practical attitude on this occasion is noteworthy. Obviously, even the mistakes were a part of some greater plan.

Wyler and his staff gradually adjusted to the real conditions of filmmaking in Rome. Confronted with poor quality of the sound facilities at Cinecittà, Wyler chose to forego almost all process shooting. He writes to Hartman, "I hope you understand that putting the proper sound tracks throughout the picture is going to be a long and difficult operation . . . most Italian pictures are really made twice—once the picture and then the sound."[42] Thus, once shooting begins outside, the production begins to share some of the conditions of contemporary Italian cinema aesthetics, at least in terms of overcoming the technical difficulties of on-location shooting. Wyler explains how they overcame some of the sound problems. "Here it has been necessary to shoot scenes and parts of scenes entirely silent, sometimes even without a guide track due to the fact that we had to work with concealed cameras."[43] Having no guides meant that meticulous editing work would be required to synchronize sound and image. This, Wyler claims, would not be so difficult to accomplish, since Italian technicians were used to this kind of work. But, he expresses doubt that they would complete the work with the proper quality. "I don't think they do it as meticulously as would be required for American audiences who, I believe, demand perfect matching sound and picture."[44] The studio declared their desire from the start to make a picture that looked like contemporary Italian productions; yet Wyler felt it necessary to explain that he would have to undertake tremendous efforts to be sure it did not sound like one as well.

Most noteworthy in Wyler's July 26 defense of the production to the studio is the fact that, despite schedule overruns, retakes, and increased costs, Wyler claimed that the picture remained on budget. "This latest estimate which I judge is about correct is still well under the anticipated cost as of the time I left Hollywood. From this standpoint, the decision to make the picture here was correct."[45] Moreover, Wyler declared the street filmmaking experiment had been a success. "The values that have been and will be gotten on the screen should also justify that decision which you and I both supported."[46] Wyler and his staff felt confident that they had created a useful model for runaway productions. As they were wrapping up postproduction, Wyler sent a telegram to the studio in which he suggests that *Roman Holiday* had turned out quite well and that the studio should send someone to Rome immediately to set up other productions at greatly reduced costs.[47]

Despite the considerable difficulties they had encountered, the studio and Wyler understood the *Roman Holiday* experiment to have been a success even before the film premiered. The early worries about the acceptability of the production values achievable in Rome were overcome. They had all learned how to utilize Roman resources to make a picture that could also best exploit the backdrop that the Eternal City provided, and they did so at bargain prices. Paramount and the other studios would repeat and vary this experiment in Rome, Paris, and elsewhere for the decade to come. Yet, *Roman Holiday* would remain among the most radical attempts to both shoot and complete a Hollywood film abroad.

Industrial Allegories

The *Roman Holiday* production wore many hats. All of the various and conflicting conditions of production certainly would not have led any film industry expert of the time to predict a successful and enjoyable film. Yet, *Roman Holiday* defied all expectations, becoming both a critical and financial success. The production history underpins a reading of the film as something more than the light romantic comedy that it initially projects. How do these various experiments in which the production of *Roman Holiday* seemed to be taking part help us arrive at an understanding of the film, both in its historical context and as it has evolved today?

David Bordwell, in an attempt to provoke a more careful attention to film form, insists that in order to explain continuity and change within film styles, we ought first to examine the circumstances that impinge most proximately on filmmaking—the mode of film production, the technology employed, the traditions, and the craft routines favored by individual agents. More "distant" factors, such as broad cultural pressures or political demands, can manifest themselves only through those proximate circumstances, in the activities of those historical agents who create a film. The zeitgeist can't switch on the camera.[48]

The *Zeitgeist* may not be able to operate a camera, but it often haunts the issues, big and small, critical to the construction of a film. Attention to cultural attitudes and sociopolitical narratives of the moment drives the screenwriters', producers', and directors' efforts to keep a film relevant to contemporary audiences. The *Zeitgeist* may not have constructed the traveling shots that permeate *Roman Holiday*. But the "cultural pressures and political demands" as well as the economic constraints with which William Wyler and crew worked in Rome are anything but "distant" from the technological and production choices they made.

Robert Ray's study of the connections between Hollywood hits and the ideological environment in which they were produced can serve as an interesting guide for our study of *Roman Holiday*. Ray argues that *Casablanca* (Michael Curtiz, 1942) is a typical product of its moment, both in its thematic construction of the dangers of American isolationist tendencies and in its deployment of the continuity strategies of Classical Hollywood in order to insure that the audience directs its identification towards the protagonist, Rick Blaine. Moreover, as Ray points out, "the power of *Casablanca's* ending . . . derived from the coincidence of ideological need with official morality."[49] The film managed to suture the audience's desire for a happy ending to the wartime ideological need for filmic wives to hold to marital commitments under the conditions of war. This combination resulted in a hit in 1942 for Warner Brothers and the development of a cult following in the postwar years.

Ray's treatment of *Casablanca* is also interesting because it makes the argument that the filmmakers presumed to understand who their audience was and what it needed. Frank Capra's *It Happened One Night*, of which *Roman Holiday* is certainly a form of remake, functions with a similar confidence. Made during the heart of the Depression, *It Happened One Night* employs a similar strategy of identification building with its protagonist, Peter Warne, played by Clark Gable. The audience watches his transformation from a conniving and insubordinate journalist to an honest and lovesick suitor, while his paramour, heiress Ellie Andrews (Claudette Colbert) undergoes considerably less of a change. The film organizes its identificatory structure such that the audience would side with Warne and reject Andrews' intended husband, the playboy King Westley (Jameson Thomas). Capra and Company presumed that an audience of people exposed to the economic hardships of the Great Depression would be most invested in seeing that the financially strapped Warne marry well. Arguably, the film exhibits tremendous confidence both in its mode of address and in its presumed interlocutor.

A comparison of the 1934 Capra film set on the American eastern seaboard with its counterpart nearly a generation later, set and filmed in Rome, allows much more room to speculate about what the filmmakers may have imagined the about the 1953 audience and its desires. The narrative parallels between the film and the conditions out of which it rose motivate an initial reading of *Roman Holiday* as an almost purely self-referential film regarding the process by which it was made. As such it becomes a tale about a man who leads an attractive young woman and a photographer around on a tour of Rome in order to create a story that he hopes to be able to sell. While this reading accurately recounts the plot, it hardly accounts for the rich array of factors influencing the production. It does, however point to a similar reading that may well provide more explanatory force.

The Cold War, American ideological expansion, shifting class and gender consciousness, and domestic consumerism are narratives that influenced both how the film was constructed and received. The characters participate in these varying discourses as well. They preach free trade, enjoy the fruits of consumer culture, defeat the "security state," tolerate the inefficiencies, and bask in the charms of the Eternal City. Moreover, as a film that was to be so important for the studio's establishment of runaway productions, it tells a story of its own conditions of production. For the act of running away to attempt things impossible under the constraints of one's own domestic surroundings surfaces both in the film's production history and its story.

Roman Holiday opens with a typical Hollywood convention for establishing a contemporary setting, namely a newsreel story of the young Princess Ann (of an unnamed, non-British royal house) and her European tour. In order to establish the film's comic undertone, the sequence cuts to Ann losing her shoe while receiving a contingent of international dignitaries. Joe Bradley (Gregory Peck) does not appear until fifteen minutes into the film, after Ann has suffered a nervous fit, been given a sedative, and subsequently endeavors to escape the confines of her royal duties for what appears to be a lively street life below. The sequence portrays Princess Ann as being held captive by her duties and by her guardians, who reign over her life, if not her kingdom, with a bureaucratic efficiency.

Most of the shots of Princess Ann in the opening sequence are medium shots in which some other object frames her, whether it is the outline of a carriage or a balcony.[50] The bedroom sequence in which she is eventually given her sedative culminates this framing device by containing the image of Princess Ann with the ornate headboard of the bed. When she moves from the bed to the window, she remains bound by the frame. Until she jumps out of the back of the delivery vehicle that ferries her away from the residence in Rome she is confined to a series of boxes. By contrast, in her adventures through the streets of Rome, she is framed in longer shots, thereby liberating her from the spatial confines of her royal life and integrating her into the locales she visits.

In essence, the escape from her royal framing is then the entrance into "runaway" filmmaking as well. The princess breaks out of the studio-produced scenery and into the streets of Rome. It is a Roman holiday both for her and the industry. Each breaks out of the box in order to construct a different image for herself.

While the experience of the "runaway" princess parallels the studio's attempts to escape the increasingly troublesome confines of film work in southern California, studio outsourcing is not the only condition of production that makes itself known in the film. A trace of the blacklisted conditions under which the screenplay was written is visible in Joe Bradley's relationship with his newspaper employer, Mr. Hennessy, played by Hartley Power. Oversleeping (in the same room as Ann, whom he discovered suffering the effects of a tranquilizer on the streets of Rome) and showing up late for work, Bradley arrives at his wire service job with Mr. Hennessy glaring down from above. Hennessy berates Bradley for showing up late for work. When Bradley sees a newspaper with a picture of the supposedly ailing princess and realizes she is currently sleeping in his apartment, he quickly makes sure she will be unable to leave and then reenters Hennessy's office. The ensuing conversation suggests that Bradley, a writer living abroad on the modest means provided by Hennessy's news service, works below market conditions for the news service. He dreams of returning to the United States where he will be able to take up life as a legitimate writer free of financial woes. He is only able to make a living wage by peddling sensational stories, and he is clearly already in debt to Hennessy for hundreds of dollars. Bradley makes a hefty bet with Hennessy that he will land a personal interview with the princess, which, due to the fact that she has gone missing in Rome, will be necessarily scandalous. The treacherous conditions under which Bradley begins his pursuit of the story mimic the kind of risky story chasing Trumbo, Hunter, and all of the blacklisted writers had to undertake in order to continue working.

This doubly self-reflective reading provides an interesting take on the film's denouement. Bradley bets his boss that he can come up with an exclusive interview, with pictures, with Princess Ann. After enlisting his photographer friend Irving (Eddie Albert) he then joins the stray princess on a series of adventures through the streets of Rome. Of course, a sentimental attachment develops. Once Ann returns to her royal duties, Hennessy shows up at Bradley's apartment expecting a story. Irving arrives with photos as well. The only thing preventing Bradley from gaining financial independence, being allowed to return to the United States and earn a reasonable living as a writer is his unwillingness to betray the princess. Whether we want to attribute screenwriter intentionality or not, the screenplay sets up a situation with which its creator(s) in Mexican exile could certainly identify. It would, in fact, seem unimaginable for Trumbo, Hunter, or Wyler, at that point in time, to create a sympathetic character who would ultimately betray a friend for professional advancement.

This is, of course, a film historical reading, one that requires information not available to the historical spectator about the identity of the screenwriter, the fate of blacklisted workers in Hollywood, and insider knowledge about production decisions. It is hardly a view of the film that would be shared either by historical or current audiences. But the reconstruction of the ideal spectator to whom the film might have spoken is not only a problem presented to us over a half-century after its release. It parallels a problem with which the film itself seems to struggle. If Capra's forerunner, *It Happened One Night,* exhibits a confidence in the identity of its spectator, *Roman Holiday* displays ambivalence if not an outright confusion about its interlocutor. That is to say, do we root for the two to get together? If so, what would be the costs of that union? Would the princess abdicate? Are we to hope that Joe Bradley and Princess Ann would marry and that Bradley as consort would become essentially a kept man? Or might the film have been constructed to reveal that Bradley has some claim to great wealth and perhaps title, thereby legitimating a relationship? While the film sets up the possibilities for all of these endings and all of them seem like the kind of endings on which the film might have relied in the classical era, *Roman Holiday* backs away from any such conclusion.

Roman Holiday does not provide the fairy tale happily ever after. Princess Ann returns to her duties. However constrained her decision may be, Princess Ann chooses to reassume her duties rather than to have them forced upon her. She is stronger and more autonomous, but we do not expect this to solve all of her problems. Joe Bradley, having had the opportunity to free himself from his abusive work conditions, is more indentured to his boss at the end of the film than he was at the beginning. The production history grounds a reasonable reading of Joe Bradley as a man more interested in facilitating and protecting Ann's freedom than in betraying her for the sake of financial security. The protagonists' adventures come to an end when, upon returning to Joe Bradley's apartment, they hear a report of the concern expressed by the people of Ann's kingdom about her supposed ill health. Ann is called to return to her duties, duties that are represented at the beginning of the film as belittling and restrictive. Ann is no longer a princess, but a woman called back to perform her part in the national family. Bradley, her liberator, recognizes this duty as well and facilitates her return to the royal "home." Here, the film introduces a feature that will become common to the travelogue romances, namely that the women usually choose "home" over "holiday."

The film's ending marked the one aspect of the film that garnered considerable negative commentary. Although the ending was a bit of a risk for the filmmakers, it is hard to imagine them being able to construct a scenario in which the princess and the American Joe would come together. The difficulty is fundamentally ideological: How would screenwriters have been able to construct a scenario in which an American male agrees to an essentially subservient position of prince consort to an old European monarchy at a time when the United States was working hard to sell its theory of bourgeois democracy to the world?

Viewed differently, the bittersweet ending suggests the different stakes *Roman Holiday* places in the love story than does its 1934 predecessor. Whereas the odyssey on which the characters embark in *It Happened One Night* functions as a plot device with which to stage a romance, the brief suggestion of sexual chemistry between Bradley and the princess only works to insure that he will not betray her trust. That is not to say that Wyler's film does not set up a passionate encounter. But, when, at the end of the film the princess offers Bradley her veiled declaration of affection and gratitude, *Roman Holiday* reveals wherein the real attraction lies. At the closing press conference of her European ambassadorial mission, where Bradley and Irving wordlessly confess their real identities and promise to keep her secrets, the princess is asked which of the cities she has visited has been her favorite. At first, Ann begins to deliver the noncommittal answer that her duty requires, but then declares firmly, "Rome." Ann's fling is with the city, not with Bradley. Just as in dozens of travelogue romances that will follow, she discovers freedom, adventure, sexuality, consumerism, and a strengthened sense of self and independence in the cobblestone streets of the Eternal City.

Roman Holiday's Reception

The *Roman Holiday* experiment was an unqualified success for Paramount. The plan to finance the film using mostly frozen funds worked. The film was greeted with enthusiasm by the critics and was a success at the box office, earning $10 million in its first two years.

Roman Holiday received unanimously positive reviews. Moreover, the critics responded to exactly those things that the filmmakers hoped they would. The press kit handed out at the premiere emphasizes authenticity as one of the film's greatest assets.

> "Roman Holiday" filmed entirely in Rome, has as its background many world-famous landmarks, some never before seen in a motion picture. For example, the Embassy Ball sequence, which opens the picture was photographed inside the Palazzo Brancaccio, the first time a motion picture company has ever been permitted to enter the famed 18th century palace.[51]

Reviewers pick up this pitch and acclaim the wonderful backdrops presented in the film. Al Hine in *Holiday* notes the location work and ties it to a trend: "Without straying from his story, Wyler also lets his scenes serve as a kind of informal travelogue. This seems to be a trend of increasing popularity in pictures . . . Wyler gives you wonderful glimpses of Roman streets."[52] While Hine certainly offers the kind of review that the studio sought, no critic responded as perfectly to Paramount's and Wyler's intentions as the *Los Angeles Times* critic, John I. Scott.. "During the trio's tour a veritable travelogue of Rome is presented. In this respect, Wyler has outdone even the Italian film directors."[53] It is as if Scott had been copied on the production correspondence. Wyler and Paramount had succeeded in convincing critics that they had created an authentic travelogue film experience, one that was ahead of the trends of the time.

We have some evidence of how audiences reacted to the film in the response cards filled out during previews of the film in Southern California before the film had its Radio City Music Hall premiere.[54] Before delving into the preview cards for *Roman Holiday* it might be interesting to reflect on this particular kind of audience, the roles they are given in the production process, and the role they presume for themselves. Previews are lab tests conducted in order to determine the effects films produce. The producers not only scrutinize the written responses received after the lights come up, but also the responses elicited during the screening. Does the audience laugh where the filmmakers hoped it would? Are audience members silent during the serious moments? So the preview audiences are used to measure both affective and reasoned responses to the film. The response cards evince a notion that the audience members presume for themselves a set of roles ranging from technical advisor to acting coach, from critic to fan club member.

The preview cards for *Roman Holiday* reflect some dissatisfaction with the ending, but much praise of the film's setting. While most of the comments run along the lines of "scenery good" or "Scenes of Rome very good," others parsed quickly what the location work meant for the industry. "More pictures like these & won't stay home to watch television." In fact, the scene of the actors sticking their hands in the "mouth of truth" became the one that previewers cited the most when referring to both the films comic potential and its "authentic" interaction with the city.

However, the overwhelming majority of the responses offered on the preview cards expressed an appreciation of Audrey Hepburn. In fact, of the three previews for which I read responses, Hepburn did not receive a single negative critique. Comments such as "Audrey Hepburn wonderful . . . great actress" or "the new star Miss Hepburn was very good and herself." While these previewers may not offer the subtlest critique, they certainly know what they like, and the critics matched their praise. Al Hine again picks up the mood that is expressed throughout Hepburn's critical reception: "She is the most exciting young actress to come along in many a year."[55] Howard McClay gushes in the *Los Angeles Daily News* that "Miss Hepburn leaves her personality stamped on the screen."[56] Critics were universally unreserved in their responses.

Such responses were certainly gratifying to the executives at Paramount, who were confident that they had a star in the making as soon as the rushes started returning from Rome. These not only indicated that they had an actress with the charisma that leant itself to broad appeal, they had an image of a woman that differed wildly from that being sold by the other studios. Twentieth Century Fox's major films of that year were *Gentlemen Prefer Blondes* (Howard Hawks) and *How to Marry a Millionaire* (Jean Negulesco). Both starred Marilyn Monroe, alongside Betty Grable and Lauren Bacall in the latter film and Jane Russell in the former. Audrey Hepburn's entrance into the star economy arguably shifted the beauty paradigm proffered by Hollywood and propagated by other media outlets. By the time the film premiered, despite having had only a short Broadway run and no other Hollywood film to her credit, Audrey Hepburn's name appeared above the title and in the same sized letters as Gregory Peck's on the cinema marquise.

If Paramount had found in Audrey Hepburn a marketable star, they also developed with *Roman Holiday* a formula in which to package her. No star would come to be associated with the travelogue romance as would Hepburn. She offered a screen persona that could animate at once American optimism and European sophistication. She would go on to play American women seeking romance in Europe in *Paris, When it Sizzles* (Richard Quine, 1964) and *Funny Face* (Stanley Donen, 1957), as well as a Parisian out to hook an American playboy in *Love in the Afternoon* (Billy Wilder, 1957).

As *Roman Holiday* was not the first runaway production, it was also not the first travelogue romance. Nor was it the first to combine the new mode of production with the storyline of American–European love. What makes the production history and the film itself interesting to this project is the consolidation of both the new mode of runaway production and the story of the contemporary American–European romance. The studio clearly understood the location work in Rome, the development of Audrey Hepburn as a star who could be inserted plausibly as the European love interest, and the compelling story line of love in and with the Old World as a formula that could be repeated, reworked, and repackaged.

Conclusion

Roman Holiday was a runaway film in every sense of the word. It was a production financed almost entirely with frozen foreign currency. It was shot entirely on location, using next to no rear projection in a studio to depict an outside location. Moreover, as did many runaway productions, it provided work for Hollywood professionals who were either blacklisted, on the verge of becoming so, or simply inclined to leave the environment created by HUAC. That ideological background saturates the story of a man who, in the end, is simply unwilling to betray a friend, despite the economic hardship this refusal would cause him. The story of a princess turned common tourist for a day launched the career of Audrey Hepburn, a career that would ride on a series of similar stories and settings. Both she and the film created a model that other productions and other studios strove for a decade to reproduce.

This story of a rich but troubled princess who runs away from the confines of her realm in order to experience the liberties of the Eternal City animates the intentions of an industry looking to do much the same. At the same time, this inverted Cinderella story of the princess who wants to become a tourist consolidates a narrative line about the fantasies of sexual and consumerist adventures abroad which become a Hollywood staple for the next decade. Ultimately the film's final shot of a proud Joe Bradley growing ever larger as he walks directly into the camera suggests that *Roman Holiday* was above all a fairy tale that Hollywood needed to tell itself. Most importantly, by sending a production team abroad to shoot a film at radically reduced costs and producing a new visual culture of location shots and actors visibly engaging in exotic locales, Paramount created a production model that would enjoy great success and help the studios weather the industrial transformations of the postwar era. Rome would save Hollywood.

3

Foreign Affairs

Metaphors of Transatlantic Relations

T he example of *Roman Holiday* reveals how important Europe had become for the Hollywood studios as a location helpful in reducing production costs. Of course, Europe was not the only site for runaway productions. Crews fanned out globally, from Pakistan (*Bhowani Junction*, George Cukor, 1956), to Egypt (*The Ten Commandments*, Cecile B. DeMille, 1956), to Kenya and Tanzania (*Mogambo*, John Ford, 1953 and *The Snows of the Kilamanjaro*, Henry King, 1952), to Barbados and Grenada (*Island in the Sun*, Robert Rossen, 1957). Nevertheless, Europe remained the primary location for Hollywood runaway filmmaking in the 1950s. By the middle of the decade studios had invested millions in the technical capacity of Cinecittà, making it the obvious location for a variety of films, not only ones set in Rome. Although much runaway work was also done in London, Paris, and Munich, the same factor that drove filmmakers in the early part of the century to southern California motivated their move to central Italy, namely the climate. Central Italy best mimicked the weather conditions of southern California. In short, Rome came to function as if it were just another outpost in the Los Angeles sprawl.

In the course of establishing this industrial presence in Europe, Hollywood studios also consolidated a set of narrative assumptions, about the continent in general and some countries in particular. As film producers developed more and more scripts that had European settings, they began to populate these stories with certain types of characters. Equally as frequently, films begin to use certain places in similar ways, creating an imaginary geography of Europe as an amorous playground.

While we have established why these films are set in Europe from an industrial perspective, it is quite another matter to investigate what function Europe has in the context of the narrative itself. If film producers wanted to take advantage of cheaper labor costs by producing in Europe, they had numerous choices as to how to populate the films they produced. They could have made films set in America and found backdrops that could double convincingly as American locales. They could have made films about the European theater of World War II, using the actual locations of the battles. They could have simply made films about Europeans, using European backdrops. Or they could tell tales of the European–American encounter, using the one of the most easily marketable genres available, namely the romance.

Hollywood producers, of course, used all of these strategies. The Sergio Leone "spaghetti Westerns" offer examples of European–American coproductions that use European locations to depict American settings.[1] From *Battleground* (1949) to *Saving Private Ryan* (1998) Hollywood filmmakers have employed European locations to depict the Allied invasion of Europe in World War II. The costume epics, whether *Quo Vadis* (1951) or *Ben-Hur* (1959), certainly fit the bill of the telling of European tales in Europe. But the stories Hollywood told about contemporary Europeans always included an American love interest. This chapter is the first of three that uses the romance to show how Hollywood negotiated the new and complicated relationship between the "New" and the "Old" World in the postwar era.

The four films under discussion in this chapter, *September Affair* (William Dieterle, 1950), *Indiscretion of an American Wife* (Vittorio De Sica, 1953, a.k.a. *Stazione Termini*), *Summertime* (David Lean, 1955), and *Interlude* (Douglas Sirk, 1957) investigate the contours of relations between Americans and Europeans. Courtship, sex, and return, all common tropes of many melodramas and romances, here take on a metaphorical quality. Not only do they function as stages in the love stories played out in the streets, canals, and train stations of Europe, they also display how these films investigate what ought to be America's relationship with Europe. We will attend carefully both to the question of the identity positions of those who form the relationships and to how the films construct the stakes of the relationships. If we can accept the notion that the romantic players occupy ideological positions, then we would do well to trace what constitutes those positions. At the very least, each of the narratives offers a love story between a man and a woman, in most cases where each is identified to some extent as either European or American. As the characters work through the conditions of their relationship, the intensity of their belonging to one set of cultural values or another becomes tested.

One of the most common tropes of any romantic narrative is the love triangle. In its simplest form, the love triangle tends to pit one potential lover against another for the affections of a third. Often, however, an idea, action, or duty occupies this contentious space rather than a person. Nevertheless, in almost all cases, the apex of the triangle, that is, the person whose affections are being sought, must choose between the two, each of whom often represents both a love interest and an ideological commitment of a kind. As we sort through the various love triangles presented in these films, we will find the American characters confronted with choices that indicate their attitudes toward their country and the hegemonic value structures of the time. The decision as to which lover to take, keep, or pursue will be determined heavily by their domestic concerns.

Each of the four films in this chapter shares a primary plot point, namely they all tell the story of an extramarital affair. As such, each of the films begins with a structure that will force a choice. Each insists upon the return to America as the death knell for the affair. Thus the films, in varying degrees, link the relationship solely to the conditions of being abroad and force a choice between Europe and America. As Max Horkheimer and T. W. Adorno noted regarding Hollywood attempts at explaining everyday life: "The film can permit itself to show the Paris in which the young American woman hopes to still her longing as a desolately barren place, in order to drive her all the more implacably into the arms of the smart American boy she might well have met at home."[2] Whether in Paris, Rome, Venice, or Munich, the films establish these relationships as impossible, if only to make sure that the character appreciates her fate back home in the States.

All four productions exhibit unusual tenacity in their desire to depict the affairs as having been consummated. This resolve can be best verified through a reading of their correspondence with the Production Code Administration (PCA), headed until 1954 by Joseph Breen, to which various drafts of their screenplays were submitted. In each instance, we will notice the predictable resistance of the Breen office to both the overt nature in which the extramarital sexual affair is presented as well as the scripts' failure to punish any of the characters for what the PCA considered immoral behavior. The story of these films' relations with the PCA reiterates what we already know about the waning influence of the Breen office. But the PCA files of these productions also reveal how everyone involved came to understand implicitly the larger ideological stakes at play in the films' salacious representations.

Runaway Sex and the Production Code

Thomas Schatz quotes a letter from PCA chief, Joseph Breen, to his ally, conservative Catholic publisher Martin Quigley, from November of 1949: "We are really having a desperate time of it. During the past month at least, more than half of the material submitted has had to be rejected. We have had nothing like this situation since the early days of 1934."[3] Breen's concerns were likely directed at the growing number of films developed by the studios to respond to adult tastes and themes. This was tied to the studios' various narrative and technical experiments to create new products to address shrinking ticket sales.

One of the films that must have caused Breen to sense that he was losing influence was *September Affair*. Hal Wallis, the longtime Warner Brothers studio executive, had become an independent producer working with Paramount. In September 1948, Wallis submitted a screenplay draft titled "September" by Fritz Rotter and Robert Thoeren to the Breen office for preliminary approval. After reading the script Breen found it unacceptable. He writes: "This unacceptability stems from the fact that this is a story of adultery without any compensating moral values or voice for morality."[4] The reasons for submitting such an early draft of a script to Breen was to gauge whether or not he could envision eventual approval. In this case, Breen not only rejected the initial script, he strongly discouraged Wallis from continuing with the project. The final film traces the story of a married man who engages in a long-term affair with another woman, after conspiring to convince his wife and son that he died in a plane crash.

Breen took exception to the film script because, as he puts it, "throughout the story, the adulterous situation is 'taken in stride,' by both parties. It is not condemned, but, rather condoned; it is made to appear quite casual and, thus, right and acceptable; and there is no indication anywhere of the punishment which the Code calls for in treating a subject matter of this kind."[5] Breen's comments reveal the moral template that the PCA had always sought to impose upon film narratives, namely that immoral behavior, if depicted at all, must lead to negative consequences.

Some have suggested that, after 1945, the PCA replaced its obsession with sexuality with attention to communist sentiments. While Breen may well have become more interested in policing Cold War loyalties, his reaction to the "September" script indicates that he had not entirely given up his sexual censorship agenda. "The major difficulty of the story, as I read it, is that the adulterous situation is treated quite casually as a 'romantic interlude' and not as a serious breach of morality. . . . The element of adultery under the Code must be shown to be wrong."[6] This certainly reads like a letter from someone intent on enforcing prohibitions against representations of adulterous sexuality in Hollywood film narratives. Yet, subsequent discussions about the script and eventually the film reveal considerably more bark than bite.

Film historians have suggested that the Code was generally quite useful to the studios in the 1930s, providing an element of respectability needed to establish and maintain a middle-class spectatorship in America. Indeed, the PCA was a suborganization of the MPAA and thus a joint creation of the studios themselves. It would seem that it is likewise true that, once the Code was no longer commercially useful, it was also no longer enforceable. That is to say, if it was put in place to help ticket sales, once it was perceived as inhibiting sales, it lost its relevance. Thus, in the late 1940s when the studios began to respond to market segmentation and make films specifically for an adult audience, they were increasingly willing to defy the Code. This was rather easy, given that the Code always depended on a combination of voluntary compliance and the threat of the withholding of PCA approval. Once the studios could no longer control what was projected on the screens, the seal of approval did not mean nearly as much as it had before. Now-independent theater owners could, if they wished, screen non-PCA approved films and the MPAA could do nothing about it. While this relationship is easy to see in retrospect, it appears to have taken years for producers to decipher the role the PCA would play in the post-Paramount decision world.

Had the correspondence ended with Breen's letter of September 10, 1948, the subsequent appearance of the film would have indicated that Breen had lost his censorship authority overnight. Such, however, was obviously not the case. After the initial exchange between Breen and Wallis, the screenplay's coauthor Robert Theoren was dispatched to work with the PCA in rewriting the script in order to receive Breen's approval. Theoren responds with a gracious if not sycophantic letter in which he claims to have addressed all of Breen's concerns. "Mr. Wallis is sending you the revised script of 'September'. I am very happy to say that the necessary changes, which I approached with considerable apprehension, did not hurt the story. If you promise not to tell anyone (it might hurt my standing with the Screenwriters' Guild) I might even say that they have improved upon it is some respects."[7] The revised script transforms the role of Manina's mentor, Madame Salvatini, from a mere witness of the relationship to a moral siren. It also allows for Catherine, David's wife, to interject her belief in the sanctity of marriage. And finally, Theoren claims to have situated the end of the relationship in a tragic atmosphere.[8] Whatever Theoren's interpretation of the story, the main change Breen sought, namely the punishment of the adulterers, does not take place.

The force of Breen's response to Theoren's revisions, which he directs at Wallis, suggests that Breen understood that the nature of his role was changing. What he lacked in censorial power had now to be made up for in rhetorical force. He had obviously lost the battle on this script. Certain that Wallis was intent on producing a film about an extramarital affair, Breen turned his attention to the details of the script. His intent appears to have been to make the dialogue as awkward as possible, thus reducing the intimacy between the characters. He asked Wallis to strike every use of the word "darling." He also sought to have every kiss between the two adulterers expunged.[9] His strategy seems to have been to allow the affair, but to disallow any suggestion that the couple actually likes one another. It is the last evidence of correspondence between Breen and Wallis before the film went into production. Few of his suggestions were adopted.

In her book on the early years of the Hollywood censorship, Lea Jacobs narrates how the Production Code came into being and demonstrates what its early limits were.[10] Among other things, she documents the rise of Joseph Breen to power over his predecessor, James Wingate. A sign of Wingate's weakness that is said to have caused his downfall was his concentration on minute aspects of the script while ignoring the greater plot themes in play. Jacobs quotes MPPDA staff member Alice Ames Winter as noting:

> How, for example, can you raise the question of a seduction scene that colors a whole drama even though it is not shown in actuality while the censor is thinking only about the elimination of the word "lousy" and is not in the least sensitive to the fact that the audience is compelled to do its own dirty thinking on inferences it cannot escape.[11]

If the attention to the trees and not the forest was a harbinger of Wingate's downfall, we might just as easily take it as a sign of Breen's decreasing power. He could not prevent the making of a film about an unpunished extramarital affair, but he could try to make sure that they did not say "darling" to one another.

Breen's next intervention in the process again focused on a single word and came as Wallis attempted to register a new title for the film. Breen objected to the inclusion of "affair" in the title.

> We, in the office, are definitely of the opinion that such a title should not be approved for this particular picture, which is the story of adultery. To refer to this adulterous relationship as an *affair*, and to tie it up with the word *September* seems to us to be rather offensive.[12]

If we are to assume that Breen understood "September" to have been referring to one's mature years, it is unclear why that made the relationship more offensive than it otherwise might have been. Nevertheless, he goes on to express his exasperation with this project. "We have not yet seen the picture, but we have had considerable difficulty with the script."[13] Clearly, his suggestions went unheeded.

J. A. Vizzard, the PCA official assigned to review the film, seems still willing to criticize the film's main themes in his scathing review of it. He faults the film's conclusion for failing to properly condemn the preceding set of events. David is let off too easily.

> In this very ease and simplicity lies the problem. We are asked to believe that all David has to do is snap his fingers, kick the adultery into a bucket, and turn right around and take up his family life where it left off. We are asked to believe that the light is burning in the cottage window for him, and that when he walks up to the door finished—*but not repentant*—an ever-loving son and an understanding and forgiving wife will be waiting there with open arms to bring him back into the bosom of his family.[14]

Like Breen, Vizzard wants David to pay. And he finds the film makes excuses for David's behavior.

> The problem is complicated by arguments which are steeped in sophistry. It is urged upon us that this is the story of the preservation of a family. It is urged upon us that he should not be asked to return to a home in which he is serving out a sentence. It is urged upon us that the reason the affair is called off is because, having established a family, David has established too many roots in the past, which cannot be overcome. The vested interest he has in the family and work surrounding it, triumph over a 'vacation from decency.'[15]

Breen remained dissatisfied with the film's content and its title. Yet, Wallis persisted in keeping the film's adulterous story intact and in renaming the project "September Affair." Some of the final correspondence between Breen and the producers in this matter suggest that Wallis succeeded in convincing Breen over the phone that he was going to run this film with or without PCA approval and that Breen's final approval of the film was a face-saving gesture more than it was a shift in censorial priorities. In the end, over the objections of Joseph Breen, Hal Wallis produced *September Affair,* a film in which the adulterers suffer no consequences for their actions. In fact, both stand to profit from them. Manina plays a masterful concert in which she converts the pending end of her love affair into the passion needed to convey the Rachmaninov piece with which she debuts. David will embark upon a dam building project in Italy, which stands to bring him even more stature and wealth.

The encounter with Breen downplays the role of foreign displacement in this film. It is clear that the point of contention between the producer and the censor lay in the former's desire to produce a film that is up-front about illicit themes. Breen did not seem to notice or at least care how the affair was staged. Arguably, he would have reacted the same if the couple had commenced their dalliance in Nebraska rather than Naples. If, as some film historians have suggested, after 1945 Breen did indeed turn his critical eye toward international ideological questions, such as the Cold War, then that shift is not yet evident in his reaction to *September Affair.*

The PCA's reaction to David O. Selznick and the production of *Indiscretion of an American Wife* suggests that, by 1952, Breen was beginning to understand not only his diminishing role, but also the ideological value of sexual representation. Nevertheless *Indiscretion of an American Wife* seems, in many ways, to be the film that Joseph Breen was trying to get Hal Wallis to make in *September Affair.* It is the story of a housewife and mother from Philadelphia who carries on a brief affair while on a visit to Rome before eventually returning to her familial duties. Breen's correspondence with Selznick regarding the film suggests again that the PCA concentrated on the smallest of details without attending to the overriding theme of marital infidelity. There is little doubt that the indiscreet American wife perceives her own actions to be wrong and is working hard to escape the affair.

Much of the PCA attention is directed toward the scene in the Pullman car in which the couple is arrested for indecency. Breen insists that the film will not suggest that the two were actually caught in the sexual act, or that the relationship ever entailed one. He offers a suggestion to Selznick that the film explain their arrest as their not being allowed "in these cars."[16] The very cordial exchange between Breen and Selznick suggests that the latter had taken a different approach with the PCA than did Hal Wallis. Yet, the film itself leaves little doubt what happened in that scene. The insinuations and the actions that follow certainly highlight rather than elide the notion that the couple was caught *in flagrante.* In the end, when the couple faces the precinct chief in the train station who is to decide whether or not they should be prosecuted for their acts, he agrees to let it go as long as Mary agrees to get on the train and leave. It seems, at the very least, unlikely to the viewer that the acts that the police and the precinct chief are taking so seriously are confined to the couple having committed trespassing.

In a memo sent to Selznick in Rome when the film was already in production, Breen reiterates his reading of the script that "we believe it is your intention to indicate that a sex affair does *not* take place."[17] Either Breen was an absolute naïf or he had, by 1952, chosen to wink and nod at the obvious depictions of sexual encounters. The film leaves little doubt that this was a sexual liaison. Yet, Breen raises only marginal objections, instead choosing to believe that the film will not suggest that they have consummated their affair. Obviously, a viewing of the film would not have provided Breen with the outcome for which he claimed to have hoped. Yet, there are no indications in the files of a protest on his part.

For Joseph Breen and the PCA 1952 was a difficult year. That spring the Supreme Court handed down what has become known as the "Miracle" ruling. This less-than-miraculous decision ruled that film, including Roberto Rossellini's *The Miracle,* was protected under the First Amendment, thus effectively shutting down the New York State film censorship board. While this did not directly affect the PCA, which was an industry-run entity and not a governmental agency, it removed the threat that was behind the founding of the Code twenty years earlier, namely that of government-imposed censorship. Immediately film producers began developing a new relationship to the Code restrictions.

So, what are we to make of Breen's engagement, or lack thereof, regarding the portrayal of extramarital sexual affairs? As we shall see regarding the PCA's treatment of *Summertime* and *Interlude*, the Breen office was still willing to go through the enforcement motions with filmmakers. The gradual relaxation of PCA restrictions coincided with Breen's gradual replacement by the Englishman Geoffrey Shurlock. The new PCA director was confronted early in his tenure with the eroding influence of the Code. Producers were beginning to release films without the Code seal and experiencing few, if any, negative consequences.[18] Therefore, the PCA under Shurlock's leadership sought to maintain whatever influence it might still enjoy by adopting a much more pragmatic and conciliatory attitude about portrayals of sexual situations. That flexibility would be necessary when encountering the British adaptation of a Broadway play designed for American distribution.

Summertime is based on Arthur Laurent's play "The Time of the Cuckoo." A screenplay adaptation commenced shortly after the play premiered in October 1952. It tells the story of a middle-aged woman who goes to Venice looking for love and finds it in the arms of a married Venetian. By January 5, 1953, Breen had read the play script and passed his judgment as to its potential for PCA approval. "The basic unacceptability of this story stems from the fact that it is a treatment of adultery without any recognition of the fact that adultery is a violation of the moral law—that it is a sin—that it is wrong."[19] Calling upon the film's various arguments for adultery, which will be discussed at greater length below, Breen insists rather strenuously that the play is not suitable material for the screen, especially not with a PCA seal. "All of this adds up to an extraordinarily vocal argument in favor of adultery, and I am sure you can realize that this is in violation of the very heart and intent of the Production Code."[20] Two years later, when the film is in postproduction and Shurlock has succeeded Breen, the new PCA chief introduces his critique of the film by way of quoting from the Code. "The Code problem presented by this picture arises from the fact that the Code states quite specifically, 'Adulterous and Illicit Sex, sometimes necessary plot material, must not be explicitly treated or justified or presented attractively.'"[21] Shurlock then refers to a set of cuts proposed to remove the suggestion of condoned adultery from the film, to which the filmmakers supposedly agree.[22] Curiously enough, the production company clearly held secondary negotiations with the Legion of Decency, which demanded cuts beyond those stipulated by the PCA.[23] Yet all of the material Robert Blumofe, who was handling the film for United Artists, agreed to cut remain in the film.[24] The film appeared with the PCA seal of approval.

One wonders why the players would go through such machinations to pretend both enforcement of and compliance with the Code, if all sides understood it to be little more than a ruse. Yet, it is clear that both sides have something at stake in continuing to play their roles. United Artists was not willing to risk a boycott from the Legion of Decency.[25] In this case, where the star salary of Katharine Hepburn was at stake, they were perhaps unwilling to court controversy. Shurlock, on the other hand, maintained the need to at least remind filmmakers of the stipulations of the Code, even if he was powerless to enforce them. It seems at least likely that producers may have been deferring to the PCA not as a censor of inappropriate materials, but rather as indicator that the materials were salacious enough. Had Breen or Shurlock failed to respond it would have indicated the need for more direct sexual portrayals.

Ross Hunter's production of *Interlude*, directed by Douglas Sirk, provides us with another opportunity to observe the PCA's attitude toward the treatment of adultery. The coy relationship between Geoffrey Shurlock and film producers remains evident a year later when the PCA reviewed the shooting script of *Interlude*. Their only intervention at the time that they approved the final script was to make sure that sacrilege is avoided. "We assume, of course, that there is no intention to suggest or infer a sex affair in the Sacristy."[26] While approving script changes offered a few weeks later, Shurlock again only makes perfunctory comments about the nature of the relationship between the film's two main characters, Tonio Fischer and Helen Banning. "We presume of course that in your finished picture there will be no suggestion whatever of an illicit sexual relationship between Fischer and Helen."[27] Shurlock's comments notwithstanding, he understood quite well the nature of the narrative. *Interlude* offers yet another story of a young woman traveling to Europe for sexual awakening. If anything, Shurlock dedicated his efforts to making sure that the characters did not enjoy their sex too much. "The fact of an illicit affair having taken place seems to be further pointed up on Page 12D, where Helen is described as 'completely radiant, completely happy.'"[28] Enjoyment, we can presume, would suggest that the film condones the relationship.

Contrary to Spurlock's wishes, the finished film again leaves little doubt that a sexual relationship occurs. But, afterwards it has Helen tell her would-be American suitor that she is a bad person, not worthy of his affections, presumably because she is not as virginal as her parochial schoolgirl wardrobe would suggest. This display of shame does not necessarily function to condemn Helen for her sexual actions. Rather, in the context of the narrative, it propels her decision to return home to America.

The difference between sexual morality and ideological position takes on significance as we study the ways in which each of these films negotiates the characters' entrances and exits from their adulterous affairs. When we study the conditions in which the Americans choose to exit their extramarital affairs, we will see that, in each case, the affair serves to consolidate their desire to return to America, which, in each case, becomes ideologically more significant than the fact that illicit sex has occurred. Ultimately, the sex functions only as a signifier of the fact that the characters require their American homeland to remain morally anchored.

Tourism, Lost Selves, and Sex

The fuller story of *September Affair* to which Breen reacted so strongly is that of a successful American industrialist, David, who takes a holiday to Europe, presumably to escape a loveless marriage. On the airplane returning home he meets a young pianist, Manina, who is on the way to make her American concert debut. When the plane is forced to land in Naples due to mechanical problems, the two decide to take advantage of the brief stop to engage in some spontaneous tourism. Upon returning to the airport to resume their trip they find the plane has just taken off, leaving them behind. Since they must wait a few days to catch the next flight they decide to visit Capri, where they discover growing feelings for one another. Again returning to Naples, they read in the newspaper that the plane they were supposed to be on went down, killing all on board. The newspaper reports them to be among the casualties. This allows the characters to escape their obligations and begin a relationship together. They establish a household together in Florence, devising a scheme to live off of David's previous wealth. Eventually the realities of their previous lives begin to invade their new one together. They finally make the journey to America where the two part. Manina resumes her music career and David reassesses his commitment to his marriage and family.

What does it mean to set a film about adultery in Europe? In *September Affair*, Italy provides a fantasy space for two lovers looking to start a new life arguably unavailable in the United States. In fact, having it set in Europe may well have been the film's only redeemable feature in Breen's eyes. The adulterous temptations and a desire to recast oneself in a new life while forgetting the old one are temptations created in a foreign country. They are associated with Italy and are negated by the characters' return to America.

The film constructs Italy almost purely as a fantasy location. To be sure, this fantasy is not without a certain amount of the trappings of tourism. Unlike many of the other films in this study, all three participants in the love triangle are American, though the film is quick to disassociate Manina from America and an American background. She has been living in England since childhood. David and Manina both use Italy as a backdrop against which they can re-create themselves. It is where Manina journeys both to become a concert pianist and to avoid becoming one. That is to say, when she decides to stay with David in Naples for a few days, one of her stated reasons is that she wants to escape the stressful preparations for her American debut. For David, Italy functions as the stage for his midlife crisis. Having built a business and provided for a family, he travels to Italy on a quest to escape or at least remold his American middle-class male identity, one to which he makes frequent reference. When asked why he came to Italy, he replies "I came to Italy to get some distance from me." He comments to Manina that while she may like the person she sees on Capri, it is likely that she would find him a bore were she to meet him at his country club.

September Affair works to preserve Italy as a fantasy space ideologically as well. If we are to presume that the film's story takes place contemporaneous to its making, then both David and Manina are old enough to have been affected by World War II. We are told that Manina has lived abroad since 1938, presumably living in London, where her American passport was issued. Thus, she would have survived the Blitz and deprivations of the war. David, we are to presume, is in his mid-forties, having spent the last sixteen years building up a successful manufacturing business, one that would have been founded in the middle of the Great Depression. As a manufacturer, he likely would have been spared the draft so as to convert his factory to the needs of the war effort. He appears to be a designer of pumps, big and small. In the beginning of the film he diagnoses the plane's defective fuel pump from his seat and later in the film he proposes a massive dam project. His attitude and skill set mark him as the bearer of the New Deal's hopes for a modernized, engineered society. Both characters have lives that are only marginally tied to Italy, thus preserving the locale as the scene of their life together.

The film also insists on a visually pristine construction of the Italy fantasy. One of the constant features of the Hollywood romances made in Europe is the combination of the travelogue and the feature film. The travelogue is itself one of the oldest genres of the cinema, having been deployed shortly after the advent of the medium to attract audiences with moving images of exotic locales. *September Affair* integrates this nonfiction, ethnographic film into the feature film, placing fictitious characters in exotic locations among real people, albeit through process shots. The film contains numerous shots that linger on the faces of real child street musicians, vendors, or beggars. While not taking the location shooting quite to the extreme that the *Roman Holiday* production would three years later, it was Paramount's most extensive European location shoot to date. But, in order to preserve Italy as a pristine background, director Dieterle makes extensive use of rear projection, with only occasional actual interaction on the part of the actors with the locale. In the production files, it is clear that the shooting in Italy was considered second unit work, with equal time spent on location and in the southern California studio. As such, the film creates an image of Italy that, unlike *Roman Holiday*, more readily approaches the Hollywood continuity standards of the moment and thus keeps the image of Italy uncomplicated by the interference of actual Italians.

This carefully constructed illusion is deployed to simulate an amorous experiment. The question this experiment intends to resolve is whether or not one can start life anew by leaving the country. Likewise, it sets up a scenario that will doom the relationship in this film and many to follow, namely a relationship constructed under the conditions of a life of leisure. The film removes both of the characters from their identities, which are tied closely to their vocations. Upon setting up household in Florence both of them gradually resume their passions. Manina spends hours practicing piano, and David embarks on an engineering project larger than anything he has undertaken before. They are firmly middle-class individuals ill equipped for the life of leisure that their economic status could afford them.

Thus, the film situates Italy as an experiment station, liberated from the troubles of real Italian or American existence. However, this liberation remains incomplete, since the characters make use of the wealth David accumulated in his old life in order to create their new one. Madame Salvatini, Manina's musical mentor, makes note of this inconsistency in their plan. It is eventually the source of its undoing. It allows the David's old American life to intrude upon their new Italian existence, thus compromising the separation upon which the latter depended. The minute the intrusion occurs, the Italian fantasy begins to crumble.

Ultimately, the narrative that is played out in *September Affair* restricts itself to David's fantasy. He is the one hoping to begin life again with a younger woman. Although Manina introduces him to the title song, as the middle-aged male looking for renewal, he is the one meant to identify with its lyrics referring to someone in the autumn of life. When the affair ends, Manina resumes her intended international musical career seemingly unimpeded. David is left to consider how he might resume his American life, with his American wife, American son, and American business.

A film that contains such blatant ideological international discourse offers powerful suggestions for allegorical interjection. As stated, David Lawrence is a character who has spent the years, closely corresponding to the advent of the New Deal, building up a successful industrial empire. With his own material needs and those of his dependents secured, he looks toward new challenges, hoping to separate himself from the binds of his purely domestic relationships and create new internationally grounded ones. The film is set in an historical moment in which America itself turned its attentions from securing domestic prosperity to building relationships with Western European nations in order to sustain broader American economic and ideological interests. His plan to bring electricity to an underdeveloped valley in Italy resounds of the Roosevelt era Tennessee Valley Authority project, as well as insinuating the then-new Marshall Plan. In fact, one of the factors contributing to the demise of the relationship is that it hinders him from doing the work about which he is so passionate. Because he has severed his home ties, he is unable to call upon his former contacts and resources to take up the massive development project he has conceived with an Italian acquaintance. The story implies that he cannot contribute to the rebuilding of Europe without maintaining relations at home. In the end, *September Affair* is a film about learning how to establish new relations in Europe while sustaining domestic tranquility.

September Affair has not fared well in cinematic memory. It does not appear frequently in the repertoire of the classic films presented on the cable television movie channels. I would argue, however, that it is important as a foundational film of a genre that does survive. In it, Europe, most often Italy, emerges as a location where a different life is imaginable, one in which the economic and social pressures left behind in America are replaced with a sensuous landscape and sexual liberty. The freedom of the foreign affair comes with a moral judgment. The European life of leisure, while alluring, emerges ultimately as inferior to the American values of work and progress. America remains a symbol of duty that one flees and to which one must eventually return.

"It Was You, It Was Rome, and I Am a Housewife From Philadelphia"

As the above quote suggests, *The Indiscretion of an American Wife* builds its plot around the dynamics of the American–Italian encounter. Mary Forbes' (played by Jennifer Jones) purpose for being in Rome is to visit her sister and family. Despite anchoring her visit to Rome in a family, the film also depicts her as a tourist. It is in this role, as she is visiting the Piazza di Spagna, that she meets Giovanni Doria (played by Montgomery Clift). The search for a new experience, associated with tourism, is immediately sexualized. It is as if the mere visit to Old World wonders is a form of foreplay that will lead innocent American women to compromise their virtues. Mary asks Giovanni for directions to the American Express office and finds herself sitting in a café with him for three hours. An affair ensues, which Mary attempts to end by abruptly leaving Rome. The story then consists of the couple's last hour in the train station as they negotiate the end of their relationship.

The product of a failed cooperation between Selznick and De Sica, *The Indiscretion of an American Wife*, like *September Affair*, treats the protagonist's marriage directly. Neither Mary Forbes nor David Lawrence attempts to conceal their marital status from their lovers. The primary difference in the story lines lies in how these two characters perceive the future. David had asked for, but was not granted, a divorce before starting the affair. That is to say, Catherine Lawrence knew of his intentions to leave the marriage. The act of deceit in *September Affair* involves David and Manina's faked deaths, which is carried out and later confessed without penalty for either. Mary Forbes, on the other hand, has much more to lose. The entire tension of *The Indiscretion of an American Wife* stems from Mary's fear of exposure and shame. Herein lies the moral difference that may have assuaged Joseph Breen's censorial sensibilities.

Seduction in and by Rome dominates both the style and narrative of the film. The mise en scéne provides a foreboding atmosphere for a cautionary tale about romance in Rome. The opening sequence's depiction of the bright and active new main train station soon gives way to a film dominated by close-ups of faces expressing anxiety, anger, and betrayal. Given that the film introduces Mary's maternal sentimentality before it introduces Giovanni, we are to presume that the audience should root for her return to her American family. But the film suggests equally as much that this "indiscretion" involved much more pleasure than pain.

The fear that the illusion of Mary's marital fidelity will collapse provides the film's suspense, more so than the question of whether she will climb on the train in the end or stay with Giovanni. Her husband and child are presumed to believe their familial situation is still secure. Both the presence of Mary's young nephew, Paul, in the train station and the couple's citation for public indecency after they are caught presumably making love in an empty rail car threaten to reveal the fragility of her American family idyll. In the end, she does manage to escape with the illusion of her marital virtue intact, thus allowing the film to sustain the fantasy of both sexual adventure and American middle-class marital respectability. In contrast, it paints a relatively unattractive picture of the life Mary and Giovanni would lead, were she to stay in Italy. The future that they discuss together is one in which she would become an Italian wife, still a housewife, but without the dishwasher and other modern appliances, and with a husband who will make sweet love but who will also scream and hit (things associated with lower-class behavior, things that we're supposed to believe do not happen in middle-class Philadelphia). The lesson appears to be: Your life might be dull and unfulfilling, but it is still preferable to the passion and drama Italy has to offer. Rub the gilding on the fantasy just a bit and it flakes off, and the Americans run home again where, even if things are not perfect, at least modern creature comforts help to ease the pain.

Italy would play out for Mary, with the effect of rendering her Italian tryst harmless. It stands as vacation sex, but nothing so appealing as to actually present a threat to her domestic life. When pressed by Giovanni to explain why she responded to his advances, Mary cries, "It was you, it was Rome, and I am a housewife from Philadelphia." Europe presents sexual opportunities unimaginable in her own social context in America. When she is prepared to leave Giovanni and end her sexual adventure he inquires: "What am I to you . . . some old guide book you don't want anymore?" Despite Mary's protestations, it would seem that Giovanni's suspicions are justified.

Indiscretion of an American Wife might be read as an antidote to *September Affair*. The latter offers Italy as an appealing fantasy posing a genuine threat to an established American family, whereas the former makes no such attempt. We do not fear that Mary will decide to stay with Giovanni in Italy, only that her Roman dalliance will be exposed. In fact, the film is quite forgiving of Mary's adultery, identifying with her goal of concealing it.

Despite the bluntness with which *Indiscretion of an American Wife* treats the transatlantic choices Mary faces, it leaves behind traces of regret. Mary is, to be sure, sentimental about her daughter and husband. But the film leaves the viewer with the sense that she would prefer more alternatives. Her "indiscretions" seem less that she had an illicit affair in Rome and more that she desires something other than her comfortable American life.

This attempt to avoid, escape, or replace a suffocating domestic existence is the shared plight of all four American protagonists in these films.

They justify their European adventures with the desire for something more than their domestic fates offer. David Lawrence fakes his own death to escape the wife who will not grant a divorce. Jane Hudson of *Summertime* is a middle-aged, single, career woman who expresses no desire for marriage, seeking instead sexual and romantic adventure she cannot find at home. Helen Banning in *Interlude* uses her adventure abroad to forestall the inevitable wedding to some nice boy back home. While this attitude toward marriage is hardly uncommon in 1950s culture, what interests us here is how it is tied to the European travelogue romance; for none of these four films contains a story line that would plausibly set up a marriage between an American and a European.

Europe in these films functions as a world apart, a sexual sphere unconnected to American realities. Americans travel abroad and experience an immediate shift in status.[29] Not only do they engage in affairs that would have been unimaginable at home, affairs that disappear when they return to their American consciousness, they also ascend in social status. They move from an America where they are situated in the work-a-day middle class to a place where they can enjoy the luxuries of the leisure class.

"She Came To Venice As a Tourist— And Went Home a Woman!"

Summertime presents the story of an American tourist, a single woman approaching middle age, Jane Hudson (played by Katharine Hepburn). As the film begins Jane arrives in Venice by train. She checks into a small hotel run by an attractive widow, Signora Fiorini. Two American couples, the frumpy, elderly McIlhennys and the newlywed, young, and fashionable Yeagers, also occupy the hotel. The McIlhennys are in the midst of a whirlwind tour of Europe, and the Yeagers are in Venice to reinspire Mr. Yeager's failing art career. Jane is a physically and socially awkward single woman, prone to falling into canals and to excessive drink. A young homeless boy with miraculously good English skills accompanies her on her tours through the city. During her visit to an antique store, she meets up with Renato de Rossi, the proprietor of the store, whom she had encountered briefly the evening before. A romance ensues, which is made more complicated by Jane's fear of sexuality and her discovery that Renato is married. In the meantime, Jane learns that Fiorini and Mr. Yeager are having an affair, thereby confusing her attitude toward love and marriage even more. Her yearnings for romance and Renato's continued advances allow her to overcome her apparently prudish ways. In the end, she not only learns to enjoy love, but also finds the gracefulness to know when it is time to say goodbye. The film ends with her pulling away on the train waving to her vacation lover.

In *September Affair* and *Indiscretion of an American Wife* the violated marital contracts were made in America. *Summertime* and *Interlude* present us with European marriages. No matter how troubled the marriages in the former two films are, they remain active relationships tied to the present. *Summertime* and *Interlude* treat marriages, especially European ones, as historical bonds, a part of a long, dark Old World past from which the husbands (in both cases played by Rossano Brazzi) are trying to escape. It is an ancient institution, an entangling alliance, an attachment to history unable to respond to modern situations.[30] Jane's encounter with Renato in *Summertime* thus becomes an encounter with the set of stereotypical assumptions Americans carry with them about Europe and Europeans. At the same time, the film attempts to counter this Old World gothic with a New World naïveté.

David Lean's adaptation of the Arthur Laurents play is at once an artifact of arcane views of female sexuality and a noteworthy attempt to break through the era's supposed sexual conservatism. The reference in the above-quoted tagline to Jane having been "made a woman" again clearly relates to the industry's larger goal of attempting to sell salaciousness. Thus, the film packages the promise of sex with the allure of European travel. Not only does the tagline, and for that matter the film itself, offer the connection of sexuality and tourism (a connection at least as old as Casanova), it supplements a set of fantasies about, to paraphrase Freud, 'what the woman tourist wants.' The film is a prototype, in many ways, both of the travelogue romance and of the running narrative of Europe as an Oz-like sexual playground, wherein nothing is real, and one can go home again with a click of the heels.

Upon arrival in the small hotel that will be her Venetian home, Jane Hudson expresses both her joy in having arrived and the set of expectations she constructed for herself on her journey. The film establishes Jane's initial prudish demeanor by having her attribute these expectations to a third party. A conversation with Signora Fiorini reveals four different versions of tourism that she imagines for herself for her trip to Venice. She says to her hostess:

J.H.: "I met a girl on the boat coming over—in America every female under fifty calls herself a girl—anyway, this girl on the boat was waiting.

S.F.: For what?

J.H.: She was coming to Europe to find something, it was way back in the back of her mind, past seeing things and getting culture, that was here [gestures to the front of her head], buying perfume cheap about here [gestures slightly further back], letting loose for once

> about . . . well we won't go into that . . . but way back, way, way back
> in the back of her mind was something she was looking for.
>
> S.F.: What?
>
> J.H.: A wonderful, mystical, magical miracle.
>
> S.F.: No! To do what?
>
> J.H.: Beats me! I guess to find what she'd been missing all her life.
> Well, I'd better take a shower.

The film plays through a panorama of tourist experiences, most of which are introduced in this speech. Her tour should allow for unmediated experience, that is, the ability to encounter Venice herself, not through travelogues, pictures, or secondhand tales. Tourism is to serve as a consumer fantasy of purchasing everything, including experience, at bargain prices. Moreover, Jane hopes that her Venetian holiday will be an adventure, one that will allow her to let loose, become someone she is not at home. Lastly, she seems to hope for something beyond tourism, that is, a situation in which she is no longer a tourist of her own life. Her magical experience will be one in which she participates in the world of which she has up to now only taken pictures. Her statement to Signora Fiorini becomes her travel agenda, her answer to the Freudian query regarding female desire.

If the displacement of her fantasies into the third person is meant to provide her with a prudish distance from them, it seems also designed to display a certain girlishness, as if fantasy were merely the realm of a child. Moreover, it establishes the fact that she is alienated from her own life. She has yet to engage in that which will insure her happiness.

Sociologist Pierre Bourdieu would claim that Jane's first expressed desire, "getting culture," indicates a middle-class desire for the acquisition of cultural capital to supplement her bank account.[31] While I believe that "cultural capital" does, in fact, describe the goal of much American tourism to Europe in the 1950s, the rest of her dream suggests something far less objective than the notion of "cultural capital" implies. It is clear that Jane's trip is motivated in great part by the desire to claim to have seen some of that which still constitutes the foundations of Western culture, a bit of canonical experience still useful in legitimating oneself in the American middle class. But, the desire to stabilize or even improve her class standing does not constitute her entire motivation for journeying abroad. In fact, the film never shows the cultural acquisition part of her trip. We do not see her in museums or churches. It merely makes mention of such activities to motivate occasional movement through the city on her part. The answers to her satisfaction and the plot's motivation lie elsewhere. She is a tourist in search of a variety of experiences.

The most lampooned version of tourism offered in the film is that in which the McIlhennys are partaking, namely tourism as consumerism. The film depicts in the Midwestern retired couple an unabashed version of the ugly American tourist. Their packaged tour price includes everything, thereby prescribing all possible experiences. The stops along their tour are organized according to consumerist acquisition opportunities. They function as a contrast to Jane's tourist agenda. They harbor few expectations from their journey other than the opportunity to claim to have taken it once they arrive back home. Jane and the McIlhennys meet on the ferry from the train station into the city. The latter are portrayed as loud, indiscreet rubes chewing their way through Europe. They, of course, also seek experiences. But such encounters are all contained within the prepackaged trip they purchased in Kankakee in which each minute of their trip is arranged, save two hours a day for "I.A.: Independent Activity." Jane already has much in common with the McIlhennys. They represent a dismal, ridiculous future she must avoid. The jaded and troubled Yeagers mark the other dangerous end of the spectrum.

Jane is by no means immune to the allures of consumer cultural acquisition. At the beginning of the film, she appears intent upon observing Venice only through the lens of the 8mm movie camera she has brought along to capture her trip. Presumably she too will return home to the Midwest and force her friends and acquaintances through evenings of reenactment of her Venetian experience all neatly contained within the frame of her small format film. When Jane spies the red goblet in Renato's antique shop, she reveals herself as at least a moderate participant in tourist consumerism. Thus, the mediated tour and the consumer tour appear as part of the same symptom, namely Jane's McIlhennyesque inability to experience the city (and by extension, life) directly.

Jane Hudson's body, her class, and her behavior are problems that the film takes as its mission to solve. She begins the film gawky and out of place, speaking too loudly and consuming too much space. She is, by her own admission, socially awkward and bibulous. Her willingness to travel alone to Venice is taken as an indication of independence, and she expresses no particular intention or desire to marry or regret at not having done so before. Yet she clearly seeks companionship. An early sequence shows her staring out at Venice's beautiful cityscape unable to find the proper medium to access it. That is to say, she appears momentarily hesitant to deploy the experiential defenses of her camera, her liquor, or her humor.

Jane's constant observation of human intimacy, whether between couples or friends, depresses her. It is a form of existence she fantasizes about, but seems only able to monitor. Indeed the fantasy functions to lift her from her depression. Shortly after her second encounter with the handsome shopkeeper, she writes a letter to her friends back home wherein she fabricates a relationship with Renato, which has yet to materialize, but about which she has already begun to dream. While her exact age is never mentioned, the film operates with many assumptions as to what it might mean to be an unmarried middle-aged woman. In fact, the story depends heavily upon her age and marital status in order to motivate her actions. It attempts to legitimate the eventual affair through the suggestion that Renato's offer of his affections is somehow generous. He is able to seduce her by insinuating that, at her age, she may not have many more opportunities for sexual satisfaction and that she would do well to accept something less than her ideal.

The primary tension in the development of the romance between Jane and Renato stems from Jane's prudishness. In fact, at times her sexual reluctance seems to extend to the mere suggestion of sexuality in others. Early in the film, when sitting in a café on the Piazza San Marco she films couples as they walk by, as if even in matters of love she were merely a tourist left to watch everyone else. She promptly stops her filming of the square once she realizes she is filming men scoping out women. It is the first of many depictions of Jane as afraid of her own desire. We are left to presume that she does not want to have to explain such scenes or her interest in them to those to whom she will show the film. In other words, it appears that she fears sexual discourse of any sort. Shortly thereafter, when she realizes that Renato is observing her, she promptly attempts to pay and leave. The entire sequence cements our view of her as a prude.

The film treats her sexual inhibition as a fault, as a refusal to experience the real Venice. Renato captures her in his gaze at the Piazza San Marco. He overtly schemes to get the name of her hotel and promptly shows up there, assuming that she shares his intentions. The film's experiment depends on her accepting these gestures as appropriate and choosing to enter a relationship with a relative stranger who is married. Any resistance offered to Renato's charms is treated as hysterical prudishness. In the scene where she confronts Renato about his marital status, she explains that Americans take sex seriously, to which Renato responds: "Take, don't talk." That is to say, her problem is that she is too busy representing sex, talking about it, even observing it, such that she forgets to actually partake in it. He admonishes her to stop behaving like a schoolgirl:

> You come to Venice . . . you ride in a gondola, you sigh, you say 'ah Venice, it's so beautiful, so romantic. Oh, these Italians, so lyrical, so romantic, such children.' And you dream of meeting someone you want, young, rich, witty, brilliant, and unmarried, of course. But me, I am a shopkeeper, not young, not rich, not witty,

not brilliant and married, of course. But I am a man and you are
a woman. Don't you see? It's wrong. It's wicked. It's this. It's that.
You are like a hungry child who is given ravioli to eat. 'No', you say
'I want beefsteak.' My dear girl, you are hungry. Eat the ravioli.

JANE: I am not that hungry.

RENATO: We are all that hungry, Miss Hudson . . There is a noise in
your head. Be quiet. Let it happen. I want it to happen. I want it
to happen.

JANE: Do you think I don't?

RENATO: Then?

JANE: It just isn't the way I thought it would be.

RENATO: I'm sorry.

JANE: But, I come from such a different world and I am not going to
be here long.

RENATO: So, you want to only take home Venetian glass?

Even he suggests that their relationship is to be nothing more than a holiday
fantasy. The proper visit to Venice evidently entails casual sex with a handsome stranger. They kiss and she runs away again. But, his seduction has succeeded. Renato's analysis of her motivations stand as the accepted description
of her desires and fears. It is clear that she wants more than Venetian glass.

Sex transforms her. The morning after she consummates her relationship
with Renato, Jane returns to her hotel standing up in a gondola. Earlier in the
film, this shot would have set up a slapstick moment of her tumbling into the
canal. Instead, at this point in the film, it portrays her as graceful and victorious. She has now inserted herself into the scene rather than remaining a mere
observer of it.

Jane loses her loneliness and her virginity. She has become independent,
socially secure, and insightful. By the end of the film, she is no longer the
awkward woman that Leona Samish (the Jane Hudson character in Laurents'
stageplay) remains to the very end. In fact, this aspect of the play is praised by
one reviewer who bemoans its less central treatment in the film. He writes,
"In that [former] work Laurents had many shrewd things to say about the
American lady spinster and about the childish fear and selfishness at the
core of spinsterhood."[32] The assumption lying at the heart of this comment
about singlehood appears to consist of a woman's presumed moral obligation
to marry and raise children. While it is a bizarre reference in any case, it is
even more so in regard to Leona Samish. Not only does she express more
longing for a committed marital life than does Jane, she is also presented as
having a history of caring for her own younger siblings when their parents
died. In short, the play goes to an extreme to depict this woman as generous

and maternal. It is then hardly surprising that this reviewer would find no joy in the film's protagonist, especially if he reads her as ambivalent about the idea of marriage and commitment, rather than interested but unsuccessful.

Moreover, the film does not include the manifestations of financial inequality found in the drama. The play depicts Leona's willingness to subsidize her lover's black market habits in order to keep the romantic fantasy afloat. In the film, Jane's only bit of sacrifice lies in her choice to leave Venice rather than to stay and compete for Renato's affections. Even that choice is framed as self-preservation, or perhaps a wiser manifestation of her newfound sense of dignity, rather than an altruistic acknowledgment of Renato's familial commitment. Actually, apart from her dismay at having been initially deceived in that regard, she never does express concern about Renato's family ties. In the play, the fact that Italy did not allow divorce is mentioned. The film seems to either presume knowledge of this fact or purposefully leaves the conditions of Renato's marriage ambiguous.

Summertime can hardly be declared innocent of participating in the most retrograde gender politics of its day. All of the moral burdens of the relationship are placed clearly on Jane's shoulders while Renato's infidelity is treated as a private misfortune that he has to bear. His adultery is presented as a reasonable, human response to a failed marriage where divorce is not a legal option, yet he makes it clear that an extramarital affair by his wife would be a denigration of his manhood. Despite the film's conservatism, it depicts a middle-aged woman who supplements a life of material independence with a newly discovered sense sexual freedom. However tear-jerking the ending intends to be, it places Jane in a relatively autonomous position. She leaves Venice early because she wants to control how the relationship ends. Moreover, as we see over and over in the films of this era, Europe is merely a place to visit. To stay, as do the Yeagers, connotes a certain failure at home.

Much of the film is about the education of Miss Jane Hudson, a sort of *Bildungsfilm*. For it is truly *Bildung*, the notion of education, development, and transformation in one, that drives a great part of her tourist and romantic desires. This edification is not only sexual. In the first half of the film, hers is a body both out of control and underutilized. She is undignified. As the film continues, this condition does not disappear, but it improves. She may still occasionally lose composure, but she has the ability to regain it. The film treats her unmarried state as a comment on her inadequacies, her awkwardness in her own skin. Sexuality gives her grace, which, in the end, also gives her the presence of mind to terminate the relationship and her trip to Venice. A stronger sense of self becomes the souvenir that she takes home from Venice.

If, at the beginning of the film, Jane's consumerist tourism is measured against that of the McIlhennys, Signora Fiorini functions as the contrasting figure in her later transformation. Fiorini is approximately Jane's age and involved in at least two relationships, a long-term affair gone stale with an unseen Signor Faustino and an affair with the American artist living in the *pensione*, Eddie Yeager. Fiorini is highly charged sexually and, at one point, invites Jane along to dinner with her and Faustino, suggesting either that their relationship is so dull that a third party would be no interference, that the addition of Jane would add spice to the relationship, or perhaps that Jane might borrow Faustino for a while. Jane rejects the invitation out of hand, not understanding the offer.

So, what should we make of the film's insistent coupling of sexuality and tourism in Europe? I would argue that in the three films discussed so far, sex marks a certain kind of unreality. That is to say, the sexual encounter becomes part of the delirium of travel, perhaps the one part of the trip of which one is less likely to take pictures. The sexual encounter takes on value no greater than that of the excellent meal one enjoyed in Florence or the perfume bought in Paris. These films insist on Europe not only as nothing more than a tourist destination, but one that has no intrinsic meaning itself. The humans walking around the streets, serving one in restaurants, or with whom one occasionally sleeps are not real. They are merely extras hired to fill out the pictures we take home with us or the stories we tell about ourselves. As such, Europe is represented as not unlike current-day Las Vegas (where one can also encounter versions of Venice, Paris, or Ancient Rome). Europe and Europeans are not real. They are only in place for the temporary convenience and pleasure of the American tourist. For that reason, what happens in Venice, stays in Venice.

Reader, I Didn't Marry Him

James Powers' review in the *Hollywood Reporter* provides a workable outline of *Interlude*'s plot:

> June Allyson is the American girl who has come to work in Munich as an employee of the U.S. Information Service. Shortly after she arrives she meets the talented musical director, Rossano Brazzi, and in the incomparably beautiful setting of the Bavarian Alps, enters on an idyllic love affair with him. It is shattered when she discovers he has a wife who is apparently incurably mentally ill. Miss Allyson renounces her lover and prepares to return to the U.S. where there is an implicit promise of a happier future with her fellow-American, Keith Andes.[33]

Throughout the 1950s Rossano Brazzi established himself as the stock character actor of the European seducer in the travelogue romance. Within a twelve-month period, he played a young law student in *Three Coins in the Fountain* (1954), a castrated aristocratic war veteran in *The Barefoot Contessa* (1954), and the aging antique dealer in *Summertime* (1955). Shortly thereafter he took up the role of a successful conductor in the prime of his career in *Interlude* (1957). The recurrence of stars in similar roles is, of course, another identifying factor for a film genre. Regardless of the social status of his characters, by 1957 the appearance of Brazzi on the screen offers the necessary generic shorthand for the European male onto whom the American woman projects her desires.

Like many of the other European expatriate directors in Hollywood, Douglas Sirk's return to Germany was hardly an intentional sentimental journey. Sirk's own comments about the production suggest how little he was involved in developing the film on which he was to work in his native country. Flying to Germany immediately after wrapping the *Battle Hymn* (1957) production, Sirk claims to have had little to do with the preproduction of *Interlude*, which was one of his numerous remakes of John Stahl films from the 1930s.[34] *Interlude* reworks Stahl's *When Tomorrow Comes* (1939), which itself is an adaptation of James M. Cain's novel *Serenade*. The departures that the *Interlude* screenplay makes from the Stahl film and the Cain novel reveal the degree to which the European travelogue romance was taking on a distinctive form by the mid 1950s.[35]

The *Interlude* screenplay elides much of the sexual upheaval that underlies Cain's novel, offering instead a much more socially conservative transgression. The novel's main character, the failed opera singer down and out in Mexico, has been transformed into a successful conductor, Tonio Fischer (Rossano Brazzi), touring the great concert halls of Europe. In *Interlude* the conductor's wife is, at best a secondary character, who has gone blind and crazy. The threat to the marriage comes in the form of a virginal office clerk, Helen Banning (June Allyson), who has just arrived in Munich from Washington to take up a U.S. governmental post in the Amerika Haus. The change in the narrative perspective from that of the successful man to that of the woman who has fallen for him is necessitated by the generic conventions the film follows. This is the point where the film diverges from other versions of the *Serenade* story. *Interlude* is Helen's story of an ill-fated travelogue romance, molded as much along the lines of *Jane Eyre* as on *Serenade*.

Interlude reads like a slight resetting of *Summertime*. Brazzi as Tonio Fischer is again cast as an aesthetically sensitive European with a wife who does not satisfy him and Old World charms to seduce an unsuspecting American woman. But Tonio encounters an obstacle that Renato did not, namely competition for the affections of Miss Banning. A love quadrangle ensues, one in which the corners appear quite geopolitical.

Helen works in Amerika Haus, a cultural institution founded after World War II in larger German cities by the United States Information Agency to spread information about the United States and to foster cultural exchange. Its greatest function was as a library of American books and periodicals. The film shows Amerika Haus in this function, as a cultural institution capable of commanding the respect of the American and European cultural elite.

Orchestral music and its performance rituals generally connote Old World cultural heritage. While symphony orchestras exist on every continent with a permanent human population, they all generally function according to a set of practices bound in European tradition. Tonio Fischer is European, that is to say, neither German, nor French, nor Italian, but a bearer of the orchestral tradition. The film remains ambiguous as to his background and nationality. He is nothing more or less than a representative of Old World aesthetics and economics, namely an aristocratic symphony conductor who moves among European elites, the educated middle-class equivalent of a rock star. At one point in the film we see his recordings in a music shop window.

While these two characters work through their romance, each has another person with claims on her or his affections. Tonio is, of course, married to a beautiful, aristocratic woman, who for unexplained reasons has gone simultaneously blind and mad, thus setting up a gothic household into which the naïve Helen stumbles. The marriage is spoken of as a historic tragedy, one that prevents the kind and passionate Tonio from carrying on a normal life. Nevertheless, Tonio remains in the ancient villa that obviously belongs to her lineage, tying him inextricably to this ancien regime.

If Reni Fischer, the aristocratic woman confined to live in the memory of a previous grandeur, is Helen's cultural counterpart, Morley Dwyer plays opposite the worldly Tonio Fischer. Morley is a representative of the successful American middle class of the 1950s, namely a physician. He is portrayed as understanding, morally upright, and practical. He reveals that his stay in Europe is intended to provide him with a bit of cultural cachet upon his return home to the States. He desires the 1950s American dream of a suburban familial existence. He is suspicious of European decadence and counters it with petit bourgeois stability.

Helen's first conversation with her supervisor in the Amerika Haus reveals how commonplace the travelogue romance equation had become by 1957. As if to mark her as little more than a stock genre character, the supervisor, Prue Stubbins (played by Anne Wyatt), declares "Well, you look human anyway," before she goes on to describe her in strict generic terms. "Don't tell me why you've come. You were unhappy in Washington. You're ready to start a whole new, fresh, romantic existence." Prue enunciates this conjecture as if it could be nothing but clichéd. While Helen strives to deny this speculation, the subsequent story belies her denial. Prue's speech appears merely to confirm what the spectator knew before a word was spoken. She is a woman from Philadelphia who is in search of something, first by moving to Washington and then to Munich.

In almost every aspect, the film paints Helen as a dopey American, fascinated by everything and critical of nothing. She states in more than one way her New World belief that you can have whatever you want if you want it enough. She is costumed in little girl's clothing, wearing a series of frilly white gowns that resemble overgrown first communion dresses. The film constantly stresses the fact that this is a fantasy and that it can only be spun away from home. When pondering the reasons for Tonio's affections, she points out to him that she is an "average American girl," one he would not even make note of were this scenario playing itself out in Washington, D.C., rather than in Munich. Tonio insists that it is her simple and pragmatic attitude that attracts him.

Tonio represents exactly the set of Old World charms unavailable in American life, that which is most attractive about Europe for Americans. He occupies an elite position that Americans, with all of their economic strength, could never quite match. Thus, Helen considers entering into a relationship in which she will never be an equal, a fact that dooms the encounter. As we saw in *Roman Holiday,* it is simply unacceptable in the narrative economy of Hollywood in the 1950s for an American to be a junior partner in an international relationship.

Yet, Helen is in Europe, so this must be a tale of sexual self-discovery. That is to say, she can, and indeed must, have her affair with Tonio, if only to prove to herself that her fate is to return to her comfortable American identity. The transgression of middle-class American sexual norms may go unpunished as long as that transgression confines itself to Europe. The film inserts Morley into the plot to provide a reality check for Helen and to assure that she has a domestic fallback position. Toward the end of the film, when Helen appears to have chosen to stay with Tonio, despite his marital status, Morley lectures her about the false set of circumstances into which she has landed. After being told what a good provider he will be, Helen suggests that she is no longer a "sweet little girl." Morley then supplies the following mantra regarding dalliances in Europe that could be inserted into almost any of the films under discussion here:

Maybe you are the one who needs to look at things they way they are. Helen, in more ways than one, you are on foreign soil. What's happening to you is a delusion, a dream, a lovely nightmare. This couldn't happen back home in Philadelphia, not to you, not in a million years. You gotta wake up. Someday you will. You don't belong here.

Despite having just insulted Helen by suggesting that she would never have such opportunities for sexual adventure stateside, Morley goes on to confess his love. Helen then confides that she understands how unrealistic the scenario has become. "Sometimes I wish I had never come to Munich. I wish you hadn't either. We might have met back home on Chestnut Street, at a social gathering." This innocent mating ritual is uninteresting to her now. Yet, the film has staked its outcome on containing her.

Helen must realize that the fantasy is over. The final sequence has her enjoying another concert backstage when suddenly Reni Fischer joins her. They quickly move to a backstage room where Reni dresses down Helen for her class transgression: "You wretched office girl with your penny book dreams. You think you'll have a grand love, a big romance. What are you? What makes you think these things are possible for you?" It is the second time that evening that she has been berated for not belonging to the romantic class. Yet, Helen reveals her continued do-gooder compassion in that she escorts the mad wife home.

In the end, the film develops a Brontë-esque scenario that would allow legitimacy for her relationship with Tonio. Reni attempts to drown herself in a lake. But Helen, of course, goes in the water and saves her. Helen comes to understand that European relationships contain emotions that she is ill-equipped to handle. She sums up her own expectations, which differ a little from what her boss suggested at the beginning of the film.

> When I came to Europe, I don't know what I was looking for. I don't even know if I was looking for anything. I guess I was looking for the impossible. The notions you pick up as you go along, romantic book notions. It's horrible what happens when you want something too much.

Helen then confesses that she had considered not saving Reni. Her American dream of getting whatever one wants if one wants it enough confronts her European dream of desiring that which one should not desire. When she comprehends that things had become so complicated that they threatened her honest, American decency, she knows that she is out of place. Thus is the abject wife rescued and perhaps rehabilitated. Helen Banning is not Jane Eyre. She does not marry Tonio. Having saved the Europeans, the Americans grasp that continental relationships are far too gothic for their pragmatic New World perspective. Helen asks Morley to take her home. When he agrees to see her to her apartment, she counters: "No, I mean home, really home."

So, like *September Affair*, *Interlude* animates a romantic encounter abroad that must end, inevitably, with a redomestication of the American characters. We could read this as having broader allegorical implications, that is, of America not forgetting its identity and sense of moral superiority while establishing a more international image. Or, the film might suggest something slightly more direct such as: 'go abroad, do what you must, but return home ready to resume American values and norms.' Ultimately the two readings differ very little from one another.

Conclusion

These four films suggest that it is difficult to divorce the development of attitudes about Europe from attitudes the films project about America itself. Each film contrasts the decadent and sometime dark existence of the Old World with an America that is rational, functional, and transparent. David Lawrence in *September Affair* offers an example of American ingenuity and industriousness. Although he has amassed a wealth that would sustain him in the leisurely life he claims to want, he proves himself to be incapable of idleness. Whether diagnosing the mechanical failings of a plane or imagining large-scale infrastructure plans for a perceived underdeveloped Italian countryside, the film maintains an image of David as a functional bourgeois. It ties his class status to America, where he must return in order to realize the grand plans he has concocted for Italy.

Indiscretion of an American Wife presents the most painful associations with America. Mary Forbes claims the desire to return to a world that the film suggests has been less than fulfilling for her. Her Philadelphia life conjures up a combination of sentimentality and ennui from which she seeks respite through her European adventure. Her American life offers all of the creature comforts of the day without emotional sustenance.

Summertime and *Interlude* also offer notions of a stable yet unsatisfying America. The characters flee to Europe to escape a world that provides material comfort but lacks inspiration. The tourists supplement American virtues of normalcy, consolation, and reason with sexual adventure, knowing full well that they will return to their self-contained American lives. They can return because alongside the erotic awakening the films also represent Europe as burdened by a complicated history, whereas America stands as a beacon of progress. Remaining in Europe suggests that things will be done as they have been for centuries, while returning to America connotes engaging in the promises of the "American century." With each film having presented the contrast in similar terms, the characters can do little but return.

In each of the films considered in this chapter, the married state of one of the lovers prevents the lovers from uniting in the end. While these films may have something to say directly regarding marriage and marital law, the use of marriage in these films is also a metaphorical device of another order. We see in the films' combination of questions of marital fidelity and foreign affairs a set of inquiries about the character of the European–American relationship. In the 1950s the question remained whether or not the new relationship between the United States and its Western European allies was to be a brief affair or a long-term commitment. Europe was a continent to which America had both strong and complicated ties and from which many Americans, including a good number of runaway filmmakers, had fled. It was a place capable of tremendous beauty, cultural sophistication, and, at the same time, incessant internecine conflict. It was a place torn between alliances to American and Soviet interests. Americans understood that keeping Europe on its side in the Cold War was going to be a difficult courtship. The question was, insofar as attention and resources were necessary to secure the affections of Western Europeans, would the courtship necessarily come at the cost of attention to domestic relationships and American integrity? Moreover, the recurrence in these European–American romances based on marital deception suggests, at the very least, that both a cultural and an economic gap existed that made full disclosure unlikely. Europe, as it had always been from an American perspective, remained a site of complicated marriages, Byzantine practices, and mad women in the attic. Domestic sanity, stability, and security remain the providence of the New World.

So, if the sexual sphere abroad only served to reinforce the values at home, what was that trip to Europe all about? Each film ultimately turns on the same conceit: The European tour was not real. It was a mere intermission in the driven lives of productive Americans. As such, the American extramarital dalliance abroad as depicted in this set of films provides a premise with which we will work even more in the next chapter, in which we will study a set of characters who are again removed from a mundane domestic reality into one in which they behave as they otherwise never would in order to experience things otherwise unavailable. Whether Manina Stuart, Mary Forbes, Jane Hudson, or Helen Banning, these women are ultimately Alices in a European wonderland in which strange and stimulating things occur to release them from the boredom of a summer's morning.

4

Tourists with Big Cameras

Widescreen Runaways and Class Mobility

All of the major Hollywood studios participated in runaway productions. The cost savings this particular mode of production offered were soon well understood, as was the appeal of Europe as a film setting. Each studio seems to have developed a strategy for the kinds of stories and the production modes that would be employed. In this chapter, we will explore how first Twentieth Century-Fox and then Paramount attempt to expand, quite literally, the scope of the travelogue romance. Working by then within established story lines, the studios sought to further enlarge their audiences by combining romantic European settings with their new widescreen formats. We will trace the combined use of the new widescreen formats, the economic appeal of Europe as a tourist and filmic location, and the association of Europe with consumer opportunity, high fashion, and the power to create a new class identity.

Twentieth Century-Fox deployed its newest technical innovation, CinemaScope, and the travelogue romance to create its romantic melodrama hit of 1954, *Three Coins in the Fountain*. In 1955, Paramount sent Alfred Hitchcock to the French Riviera to shoot *To Catch a Thief* in the studio's own widescreen format, VistaVision. In 1957, after both widescreen processes and travelogue romances are firmly entrenched, *Funny Face* combines them to sell a different kind of tourist experience, namely one centered on fashion. And fashion itself becomes a fantasy vehicle by which characters transcend previous class positions. In all cases we see both the aesthetic and ideological consequences of the conditions of production abroad and the deployment of new film technology. In the end, these films use Europe as a site of self-reinvention and endless consumer opportunity (and, frequently, self-reinvention *through* consumer opportunity).

Widescreen Technologies and the Studios

On September 30, 1952, Fred Waller, a longtime inventor who had always worked at the margins of the film industry, premiered a film called *This is Cinerama* introducing his new widescreen film process. Both the new technology and the film produced to introduce it changed the industry overnight. Despite Cinerama's many obvious limitations, such as exorbitant start-up costs and focus difficulties, *This is Cinerama* was a great hit, one that motivated the motion picture studios to expedite the introduction of their own widescreen processes, which had been under development for some time. As John Belton describes it, the film "demonstrated to an economically troubled film industry that considerable popular demand existed for a new kind of motion picture entertainment."[1] For Twentieth Century-Fox, the problem was slightly more acute than at the other studios. When given the opportunity, years before, to buy into Waller's project, Fox's research department dissuaded Fox president Spyros Skouras from doing so. Immediately after the premiere of *This is Cinerama* Skouras intensified Fox's development of the studio's own widescreen process, which would become known as CinemaScope. Thus, in 1953, with the studio facing a hostile takeover from New York businessman Charles Green, Skouras was compelled to prove to the shareholders that he had a plan for saving the troubled film company. Skouras called a press conference on February 3, 1953, to announce that all future Twentieth Century-Fox productions would be shot in widescreen format.[2] This gambit on a process that was still in development forced the studio to be the first one out the door with a usable wide format technology, one that also included a Stereophonic sound track. In developing their process, Fox called upon an older technological device, the anamorphic optical system developed by French inventor, Henri Chrétien. Although the patents on Chrétien's device had expired, Fox contracted to purchase the actual lenses that the French optician had developed, thus giving the troubled studio a few months head start on its competitors in the development of a widescreen process that could be distributed widely.

When Fred Waller introduced his new device for creating and projecting widescreen cinema, he chose, among other things, to present a travelogue. John Belton describes the film:

In Europe, the audience is treated to ballet at La Scala, a gondola ride in Venice, the gathering of the clans (complete with bagpipers) in Scotland, a bullfight and flamenco dancing in Spain, and the Vienna Boys' Choir, returning to La Scala for the finale from act 2 of Aïda.[3]

Cinerama was a technology designed to increase the sensory experience of the cinema. Belton quotes a *New York Herald-Tribune* article claiming that *This is Cinerama* caused so many inquiries at "the State Tourist Office of Italy about the festival of Venice that a painting depicting the scene in the film was installed in the office window."[4] Cinerama's goal, demonstrated by its opening images of a roller-coaster ride, was to plunge the spectator "into one of the most visceral motion picture experiences ever created."[5] Because of the technical limitations of this original widescreen process, foremost among them being considerable difficulties in maintaining sharp focus, travelogues became an ideal genre for the new cinematic medium.

It was inevitable that one of the studios would attempt to combine the foreign locales of the runaway production with the widescreen wonder of the travelogue. By the time *Roman Holiday* premiered in the summer of 1953, Twentieth Century-Fox was already in production in Rome with *Three Coins in the Fountain*. Ever since Wyler and company had opened production on *Roman Holiday* in 1952 the industry was abuzz with Paramount's experiment. Meanwhile, across town, Twentieth Century-Fox was already premiering a film in widescreen format. *The Robe* (Henry Koster) opened three weeks after *Roman Holiday* on September 16, 1953, followed in November by *How to Marry a Millionaire*. Directed by Jean Negulesco and starring Lauren Bacall, Betty Grable, and Marilyn Monroe, *How to Marry a Millionaire* became Fox's first widescreen romantic comedy. *The Robe* and *Millionaire*, both filmed in Hollywood studios, were big hits, successful enough to overcome their high production costs. Thus, Fox was confident in having found an attraction strong enough to draw people back to the movie houses.

Outsourcing production had, by then, become another part of the industry's survival package, one that Twentieth Century-Fox had yet to fully exploit. Having committed itself entirely to CinemaScope production, then, and having seen both the box office and operational appeal of *Roman Holiday*, Rome and the Cinecittà studios provided the best possible setting to take the new medium on the road. Thus, Jean Negulesco and crew headed to Cinecittà in the summer of 1953. Their formula for *Three Coins in the Fountain* called for a filmic event in which the splendors of the Eternal City would be revealed in Stereophonic sound with Technicolor on the wide screen.

"For Travelers Who'll Miss Rome This Summer"

If the *Roman Holiday* production had to answer a set of questions regarding how to make a film suitable to Hollywood standards using Italian film resources, Italian lira and a screenplay written by blacklisted screenwriters, the *Three Coins in the Fountain* producers were responding to different concerns. The technical apparatus, including the anamorphic lenses, stereo sound, and Technicolor film stock, would not allow Fox to run the postproduction experiment as Wyler had. On the contrary, *Three Coins in the Fountain* was an expensive production in which almost the entire crew was imported from Hollywood. This film had to make a case for widescreen filmmaking in general and CinemaScope in particular. Moreover, it had to show that this could be done outside the comfort zone of a Hollywood set in order to take advantage of both the lower costs and the grand vistas available in Europe. Rome was merely the most readily exploitable backdrop in the battle against television, a medium that was still basically tied to the studio.

While it may seem obvious that Twentieth Century-Fox would combine a number of the most dominant Hollywood trends of 1953–1954, namely runaway film production, travelogue romance, and their new widescreen technologies, it was a difficult combination in practice. CinemaScope's unreliable focusing required delicate light configurations to make it work. But the appeal of runaway production and location shooting was undeniable and appeared to be growing. The success of the early runaways appeared to stem from an authenticity that the films purported to offer. Whether or not this could have been achieved if the productions had been filmed on the lot is immaterial. *Roman Holiday* announces in the opening credits that the entire film was shot in and around Rome. The characters obviously walk up and down the Spanish steps, ride a Vespa through the streets of Rome, and stick a hand in the Mouth of Truth. To be sure, all of these effects could have been created on the lot or through process work. But, the film's emphasis on authenticity succeeded, as did the new outsourced mode of production that Paramount and Wyler developed.

As one of the most direct descendants of *Roman Holiday*, *Three Coins in the Fountain* obviously remains in dialogue with the Wyler film. At the very least, one could count numerous identical location set-ups. Both are, in essence, Roman holidays. In fact, many of the initial reviews of *Three Coins in the Fountain* refer to it as a journey to Rome. As the review in *Newsweek* put it, *Three Coins in the Fountain* is "pleasant for travelers who'll miss Rome this summer."[6] This comment is important for our reading of the film. It suggests that something slightly more might be at stake in the

CinemaScope experiment being waged in the film. *Three Coins in the Fountain* is not only supposed to be a film with pretty pictures of Rome, its CinemaScope effects are meant to function as a portal, allowing the spectator to experience Rome with more immediacy than the cinema had theretofore been able to provide.

Technical exploitation subordinates all other aspects of *Three Coins in the Fountain*'s production. In a fashion not dissimilar to the ways in which the new motion picture medium was deployed in the late nineteenth and early twentieth century in the service of colonialist ethnographic enterprises, the film sets out to 'capture' Rome with its new medium. As the reviewer for the *Dallas Daily News* put it: "Director Jean Negulesco acted as if he had never seen Italy before. When the story gets in the way of the tourist spots it doesn't have a chance. Fortunately this Cinemascoped Baedeker is fascinating."[7] The reviewer is right in noting that all script decisions appear to have been based on how best to exploit and highlight the features of the wide screen.

The film opens with the wonders of Rome captured by CinemaScope in a three-minute travelogue accompanied by the film's hit theme song, performed uncredited by Frank Sinatra. After the credits finally roll, we see a woman who could easily have worked as an Audrey Hepburn double, Maggie McNamara, in the role of Maria Williams, walking through Rome's then-high modernist main train station (Stazione Termini is, of course, the setting of *The Indiscretion of an American Wife*). Maria is met by Anita, the woman she is meant to replace in the American government office in Rome. Maria's initial tour through the city serves as a plot device to motivate even more travelogue cinematography, as the new roommate experiences the widescreen splendor of the Eternal City, including a necessary visit to the Piazza di Spagna.

Darryl Zanuck, head of production at Twentieth Century-Fox, often used the phrase "audience participation" to refer to the notion of a heightened realism that would draw the spectator into the cinematic illusion. In fact, since the late 1940s he had been obsessed with the growing trends in recreation. It is clear that the switch to widescreen cinema coincided with his belief that movies had to engage audiences in a more active role. "Entertainment is something others provide for you," Zanuck claims, "while recreation is something you provide, in some measure, for yourself."[8] Zanuck's advocacy of a participatory cinema was designed to shift film into the 'recreation' category. In a letter to his fellow studio head and former boss, Jack Warner, Zanuck expounds on the technological leap made by the anamorphic over current practices. "From the standpoint of 'audience participation' alone it is like looking at the first talkie and trying to compare the sound with what we have in pictures today."[9]

Yet, this enthusiasm appears to stem from a certain novelty of the new shape of the image, rather than from the range of technical capabilities exhibited in the new process. For, what the first versions of CinemaScope provided in image width, it gave away in terms of depth of field.

The technical limitations of CinemaScope present a particular narrative problem for the sequence that establishes the characters' motivations in *Three Coins in the Fountain*. The two women, joined by their third apartment mate, Frances, visit the Trevi fountain. In order to keep the depth of field necessary to depict the throwing of coins into the fountain, the camera holds back, using a medium-long shot to depict a conversation that, in classical Hollywood practice, would have been shot at medium or closer. The sequence cannot resort to established Hollywood conventions, such as a medium shot–countershot in order to both capture the melodrama of the dearth of romantic choices these women face and the fountain in the background. As such, the act of tossing coins into the fountain, which symbolizes the desires and motivations of the three protagonists, remains visually subservient to the splendor of a Roman tourist site without the editorial punctuation that one might expect.

The drive for visual splendor again comes into conflict with the need to serve the melodrama's narrative requirements in a sequence a few minutes later depicting Anita and Maria descending the steps at the Piazza di Spagna. The shot is practically a repeat of the set-up of Peck and Hepburn at the same spot in *Roman Holiday*. The real difference is in the shot quality. The anamorphic lens used by Negulesco and company cannot keep both the women and their background in focus to get a close enough shot to provide the visual information for the dialogue being depicted. In order to cover this dialogue, Negulesco resorts to a process shot with a transparency of the Piazza di Spagna in the background. Given the previous shot of them descending the (curiously empty) steps, the cut is rather jarring. In order to shoot the intimate conversation between Anita and Maria about the former's unfulfilled love life, the film has to sacrifice a bit of its hard-fought authenticity. This brief scene reveals the hurdles to be overcome for these two characters to find husbands and is therefore integral to the film. It may be the only example in the film where the needs of the narrative prevail over the desire to exploit the medium.

If Spyros Skouras staked his career as president of Fox on introducing and establishing CinemaScope, it was left to Zanuck to determine how to make films with the new process. Zanuck's monitoring of the dailies of the first two widescreen productions caused him to set some studio policies that would carry over to *Three Coins in the Fountain* as well. In his production memos regarding *The Robe* and *How to Marry a Millionaire*, Zanuck warns against too much camera movement, this presumably stemming from the concern regarding the anamorphic lenses' ability to maintain focus. Camera movement remains limited throughout *Three Coins in the Fountain*. Most of the movement comes in the form of slight pans in outdoor shots depicting car travel. Moreover, the film sets up a rigorous rhythm whereby, at least for the first hour, it alternates between studio-shot indoor and location outdoor scenes, thus giving the spectator ample opportunity to visit Rome through the anamorphic lens.

In a message to the production staff of *The Robe* Zanuck writes, "I am now more than ever convinced that the *greatest value* in a camera angle is to try and keep the people spread apart if there are only two or three people in the scene so that the *entire scene* is constantly filled."[10] His memo of the same day to the production staff of *How to Marry a Millionaire* elaborates the point: "If people are spread out filling the screen then we are putting on film an effect that we cannot get on the old 35mm."[11] It is noteworthy that Zanuck reserves his comments about the rushes he was seeing primarily to the camera work, noting only in passing the quality of the acting or the development of the story being told. For a studio mogul known for his control over filmic storytelling, the absence of comments about the depiction of the story is informative. At this point in his career, Zanuck had clearly placed his priorities elsewhere.

Even before Fox's widescreen conversion, Zanuck seems to have made some determination about the efficacy of certain cinematic conventions. In a memo to all Fox directors, Zanuck suggests that they curtail severely the number of close-up shots they attempt.

> I think the two best examples are *Twelve O'Clock High* [Fox, 1949] and *Father of the Bride* [MGM, 1950]. They contained minimum set-ups and practically no close-ups, yet you always had the feeling that the people were close to the camera and that everything that should be seen could be seen . . . If you get a chance, look at *Twelve O'Clock High* again. You will be amazed that at least sixty percent of the picture is told in master scenes without close-ups.[12]

Negulesco, the epitome of a staff director at Fox, one who had influence over most of the early CinemaScope productions, clearly follows Zanuck's suggestions about close-ups in *Three Coins in the Fountain*. The film contains none.

Whole sequences of *Three Coins in the Fountain* appear created merely to exploit the new medium. This, in turn, requires the screenplay to then explain the visuals on display. One example of this is early in the film, when

Maria first enters the apartment she will share with the other two women. The sequence (clearly shot in the studio) begins with Anita opening the door to the apartment in "Villa Eden" with a stunning view of the city. As Anita leads Maria into the flat, the camera pulls back to reveal a spacious, colorful modern apartment with a combination of modern and antique furniture. Throughout the film, the mise en scène, whether location determined or in the studio, is designed to capture Rome as a combination of the ancient and modern. As Anita calls out to Frances, the other roommate, the sequence employs both Zanuck's desired spread of the mise en scène and the other technical development that accompanied CinemaScope, namely directional Stereophonic sound. As the three move to the balcony table overlooking a tremendous view of the city, the sound is designed to pick up the spatial differences among the figures on the screen.

The need to display the range of CinemaScope's capabilities requires *Three Coins in the Fountain* to put on an opulent display. This leads the film into troubling ideological territory. Secretaries in a U.S. government agency, we are led to believe, can live like royalty. As the *Dallas Daily News* reviewer notes: "Life in Italy (on American exchange) must be a lot of fun, especially since CinemaScope makes no effort to capture smell." Putting aside the reviewer's insinuation that Rome is unduly aromatic, his comments suggest that a colonialist message was a broadly noted part of the reception. Having designed a set that could best exploit the splendors of the wide screen, the film must explain how these characters could come to live in such luxury. The answer given depends heavily upon the state of postwar American imperialism in Europe. The reference to the exchange rate and the greater economic power of the United States explains not only the opulence in which these working women live, it also goes far to elucidate the relations among the American characters' with their Italian hosts. This is a world in which American secretaries are invited to cocktail parties alongside Italian royalty but are prohibited from dating Italian coworkers. The film depends on a colonial mindset, in which to be American is to be a member of the elite, in order to both project a cinematic opulence and to motivate the melodrama played out on the screen. Europe is little more than a beautiful playground on which Americans perform their hegemonic self-actualization.

Three Coins in the Fountain has not aged well. That is to say, over fifty years after its production, the spectator strains to see how the film managed to achieve any commercial success. This is not only because its ideological positions are so troubling, but also because the current viewer simply cannot recreate the wonders and novelty of the widescreen process. While widescreen projection certainly still exists, Fox's "Miracle Mirror" screens are long gone, and the film is hardly likely to show up at the local IMAX theatre. Instead, we are left to imagine how the spectacle of the then new cinema technology cast a spell over the spectator such that she could ignore the underdeveloped screenplay. But, if we put the film back into the context in which it was made, we may better appreciate how this film managed to draw at least some moviegoers back into the theater.

Having staked its entire future on widescreen productions, Fox explored every possible device to ensure that its productions would draw an audience. The combination of widescreen spectacle and salaciousness resulted in such success in Fox's *How to Marry a Millionaire* that the formula seemed ripe for further exploitation. While *Three Coins in the Fountain* was still in production, studio executives considered capitalizing on another big seller of the time. In the fall of 1953, the most controversial book on the *New York Times* "Bestseller List" was the second volume of Alfred Kinsey's description of sexual practices in America, *Sexual Behavior in the Human Female*. Production files for *Three Coins in the Fountain* suggest that the studio was working to exploit both the popularity and the scandal of the Kinsey report. Though the final title of the film remained tied to that of the John Secondari novel, this title was the result of substantial deliberation.[13]

Zanuck, like Hal Wallis and David O. Selznick, had begun to see the Production Code as irrelevant. On May 7, 1953, Zanuck wrote a note to producer–writer Philip Dunne in which he contemplates what he believes to be necessary in order for a film to attract an audience. After laying out all manner of quality films, he analyzes why some achieved box office success and others did not. It is not a difficult formula.

> This report does not necessarily prove that a picture must have sex to survive or become a big hit. It indicates, however, that more pictures with this content are successful than any other type of picture. It indicates that even a heavy, downbeat, depressing story can be lifted if it contains really strong, violent sex situation.[14]

This comment obviously aligns Zanuck's attitude with the other film producers discussed in Chapter Three.

Zanuck suggests that the Breen office might well have been an easy front to circumnavigate by this point in time. In February 1954, Columbia studio executive Jerry Wald inquires about Zanuck's recent work with the PCA. Wald complains of having felt hampered by what he viewed as an obsolete code. Zanuck expresses support for the PCA, noting one could put almost anything past them, but points out the greater danger. "What infuriates me is the pressure groups and censorship groups both here and abroad. This is where we should carry our fight."[15] Here Zanuck refers to the Legion of

Decency, Catholic dioceses, and other independent organizations that would rate, ban, boycott, and otherwise influence cinema attendance.

A letter in the Fox archives at UCLA library from the PCA reveals both the diminished influence the Breen office had on production and Fox's intent to exploit the Kinsey report to attract an audience.[16] The letter responds to a request from studio executive Harry McIntyre's office to register *Behavior of Three Females* as the title for the film. The PCA asked Fox executives to withdraw their request for the title. Fox held out on rescinding their registration of the title until finally settling on *Three Coins in the Fountain.*[17] But by this time the production was far enough along for them to have known that the other title would have been a stretch to fit the screenplay that was being filmed. While Fox was clearly interested in selling sex along with Roman vistas in *Three Coins in the Fountain*, it appears that, due to the need to quickly produce enough films to fulfill its promise of 100 percent widescreen release, it did not have time to follow up on this idea.

While Zanuck was apparently willing to provoke the sexual censors' ire, Fox, arguably more so than any other studio, emptied its slate of all films that would have any political connotation, at least any that would offend the anticommunist American Legion. This decision was not unconnected with the studio's decision to fill their schedule entirely with widescreen films. Zanuck admits as much in a letter to Elia Kazan on July 15, 1954, responding to the latter's dismay at Fox's dropping *On the Waterfront.*

> Actually the advent and debut of CinemaScope was responsible more than anything else for my final decision against the property. At that time I felt that since we had overnight committed ourselves to a program of CinemaScope 'spectacles' I had no alternative but to back away from intimate stories even though they were good stories.[18]

Thus, Zanuck admits that the move to CinemaScope meant a foregrounding of spectacle over story. Zanuck goes on to discuss in the letter how much time he had spent with Kazan and writer Budd Schulberg developing the property. Moreover, just the year before, shortly before the conversion to widescreen programming, Kazan and Zanuck had worked together on the anticommunist runaway production, *Man on a Tightrope.* Schulberg and Kazan had both named names in HUAC testimony and were thus cleared by the studios. But Kazan, because of the extent to which he cooperated with HUAC and his public defense of his actions, remained a controversial figure in Hollywood.

Fox's move away from politically sensitive subject matter (and, arguably in the case of *Three Coins in the Fountain* toward absolute political insensitivity) is bound with the other issues facing the studio as well. Six months before the decision to convert to CinemaScope, in an earlier letter to Kazan regarding *Man on a Tightrope*, Zanuck claims "people are going to the theatre today to escape lectures, propaganda, politics and the constant talk, talk, talk, which they get on television."[19] Twentieth Century-Fox, under Zanuck's creative control, navigated the difficult terrain of both competition with television and the atmosphere of political censorship by resorting to material with high visual impact and minimal narrative content.

Thus, the adoption of CinemaScope at Fox can be seen as a reaction to the politics of Hollywood in the early fifties. Certainly HUAC did not drive Zanuck and Skouras to the decision to switch to a total widescreen production schedule. But, once they switched, they could justify restricting their properties to only those that could best exploit the spectacular aspects of the medium. The highly charged urban dramas, films noir, or other scripts that played to either side of the Cold War struggle in Hollywood could simply be turned down categorically as inappropriate for the new techniques required by CinemaScope. As Zanuck explained it to his producers and executives:

> It is our conviction that almost any story can be told more effectively in CinemaScope than in any other medium but it is also our conviction that every picture that goes into production in CinemaScope should contain subject matter which utilizes to the fullest extent the full possibilities of this medium.[20]

This stated policy of the studio then is a passive aggressive move away from heavily scripted dramas, of which Fox's quasi-social-realist dramas, such as *Grapes of Wrath, Gentleman's Agreement,* and *Pinky,* had been a part, toward films that were to be scripted around and for the scenery.

Class Mobility in the Eternal City

Three Coins in the Fountain constructs a fantasy about three working women in Rome who remain single because the only marriageable men must necessarily be in the position to occupy the same fantasy. Murray Pomerance has referred to *Three Coins in the Fountain* as a "voyage film," which he considers a prototype of the "elevator" film.[21] In an elevator film, a portal through which someone is allowed to travel connects independently existing worlds. Using this portal, like an elevator in an upscale department store, one steps out of the familiar. When the doors open again, a very different realm lies before one. According to Pomerance, exemplars of the elevator film include science fiction films such as *The Fifth Element* (Luc Bresson, 1997), *Total Recall* (Paul Verhoeven, 1990), or *eXistenZ* (David Cronenberg, 1999). Pomerance claims "the conceit of an elevator story is that everything we look at is doubled, thanks to the action of a mystifying and omnipotent portal by means of which a voyage has been made to introduce this new vision."[22] *Three Coins in the Fountain*, in which the magical portal is simply the plane or boat the American character takes to Italy, is part of the prehistory of these other films of reality displacement, a prehistory that includes *The Wizard of Oz*.

This particular gesture of escape through a technological portal is made by more than just the narrative of *Three Coins in the Fountain*. A "voyage . . . made to introduce a new vision" describes remarkably well the Negulesco-Twentieth Century-Fox widescreen production itself. The widescreen camera was used as a magical portal, designed to transport the viewer to another place. Arguably, this is precisely the point of Darryl Zanuck's "audience participation." CinemaScope was not designed to transport us into some other universe, as much as it was to provide access to another part of the world we already inhabit, to make our world bigger and more visible. CinemaScope presents Rome as it has always been; only now the American audience is able to see it in 140-degree vision without having to step on a boat or plane.

The widescreen view of the world not only alters how the audience sees the monuments of Rome, it also alters the diegetic world that the secretaries inhabit. *Three Coins in the Fountain* offers a dreamy narrative in which Americans get to live like princesses, marry princes, and bask in Old World luxuries, all on a clerical salary. This opulent widescreen world is made possible diegetically by the voyage to Rome. The film's opening sequence, with Maria arriving in Stazione Termini, functions as an embarkation on a new life.

The story line for *Three Coins in the Fountain* offers up a set of contradictory interpretive possibilities regarding how one might read its treatment of the American–European relationship. Here, as in all the travelogue romances, Europe is approached in romantic terms. The three women are unabashed about the fact that they have come to Rome in hopes of finding husbands, but are frustrated by the economic and class distinctions they discover there. Wealthy Italians, we are told, are not going to "waste their time with secretaries and Italians who work at the agency are too poor." They are too high on the Italian social ladder for some desirable mates and too low for others. On the one hand, the film and its characters enjoy economic power and social access that is available to them in Rome but not at home. On the other hand, these secretaries move about Rome refreshingly disrespectful of the ancient class structures of the Old World, living out the myth that Americans are not class conscious.

The postwar social world in Rome and the Americans' place in it are presented in colonialist terms. Women from modest American backgrounds live a life of luxury based primarily on the weakness of the local Italian economy.

On the strength of their American passports alone, they find themselves at parties with the old, moneyed families of Rome. But while the Roman elites, represented in the character of Prince Dino di Cessi (played by Louis Jourdan), are willing to flirt at parties and even have romantic flings with pretty American secretaries, they do not take them home to meet their mothers. The amount of cultural capital requisite in a mate has not been affected by the strength of the dollar. In contrast, those Italian men with similar levels of education, the Italian coworkers at the agency, represented by Rossano Brazzi's character Giorgio, are too poor to support the American women in the material style to which they have recently become accustomed. Obviously, working for the agency is not as good a deal for the local population as it is for the Americans.[23]

The colonialist overtones in this portrayal of American–Italian relations originate in the John Secondari novel *Coins in the Fountain,* from which the screenplay was adapted. The novel goes even further in describing the conditions under which its cast of American expatriates populates Rome. Maria and Anita are employed by a U.S. federal agency known as the United States Distribution Agency. While the exact function of the agency is never discussed, its very name suggests a power relationship more aligned with colonialism than an alliance of political equals. In the film *Three Coins in the Fountain* the power relationship is made even more distinct. Anita informs Maria early on that American agency employees are not allowed to fraternize with the native employees. Anita's subsequent relationship with Giorgio causes him to be fired for breaking the rule. No reason is given for the rule, but Italians, even aristocratic ones, are generally represented as primitive sexual predators. Meanwhile Mr. Bourgoyne, the head of the agency, is depicted as a benevolent patriarch, whose only interest is to protect his young American female employees' virtues.

The troublesome ethnic politics of the film gain notice in only one prominent review of the period. The reviewer from *Time* suggests ironically that

> Hollywood should re-examine the film before exporting it to Europe, where it may set back Western amity by 20 years. Two of the girls work as secretaries in a U.S. Government agency, which, as a matter of policy seems to regard most Italians as strictly colonial inferiors. When Actress Peters starts to run around with Actor Brazzi, who plays a lowly Italian translator, her boss and his wife react as if she were bound on miscegenation in the Deep South.[24]

The justification for this attitude comes from its function in adding tension to the plot. It is a cheap device for creating forbidden love.

If class boundaries are the problem the film sets for Maria and Anita, Yankee pragmatism and egalitarianism provide their solution. The women regard class boundaries more as inconveniences than immovable barriers. While Maria and her friends accept the description of Dino as an aristocratic playboy, one who could only ruin a girl's reputation rather than offer the possibility of marriage, they see it as a challenge rather than a prohibition. If Maria's class difference is all that would stand in the way of making her a marital candidate, they will simply scheme to get around it. If Giorgio's class inferiority is meant to be taken seriously, Maria's serves as more of a joke that can be performed at the expense of the aristocracy.

This too is a kind of cultural clash between the Old World and the New. Dino's class status is displayed through his cultural sophistication. The sign of this sophistication is his apparent ability to appreciate modern art. Maria presumes this is nothing more than a performance, one for which she can rehearse. She and her friends contrive to claim that her family too is part of the American cultural elite, namely owners of a museum. While she is aware that there is a difference between her father's roadside collection of Indian artifacts in Oklahoma and Europe's great halls of art, she does not let the difference stand between her and her desire to prove herself a worthy marriage candidate. Moreover, the film takes her position as well. The humor derived from these scenes comes from the contrast of the plucky American girl insinuating herself into a stuffy European aristocratic family. As in most of the travelogue romances, the physical and cultural distance between Europe and the United States makes her deception possible. At first, the audience roots for her in her attempt to fool the aristocrats. Yet that game has to end as soon as the film suggests that Dino's intentions are sincere. After meeting his mother, the gesture that, we are told, is the next step toward a marriage proposal in Italy, Maria must come clean about her deceptions.

Anita's romance with Giorgio offers a contrasting, yet equally American, attitude about love and class. Their relationship is constructed along much more sentimental terms. Giorgio, a low-paid translator at the agency and part-time law student, is a hard-working, honest fellow from a humble, rural background. When Giorgio and his large and boisterous peasant family pick Anita up for an outing to the country in an old truck with no brakes, she (unlike Mr. and Mrs. Bourgoyne) does not turn her nose up at them. In fact, Anita seems to be so charmed by Giorgio's family that she allows the relationship to develop further. The only thing that stands between them is Bourgoyne's sanction against 'going native.' In true romantic fashion, the dedicated lovers flout this rule.

The third romance of the film does not emphasize class difference and mobility, as do the first two. Rather, it offers a rendition of a trope that we encounter throughout the travelogue romances, namely the necessity of returning home. The third secretary, Frances, works for John Frederick Shadwell, a well-known expatriate American novelist, who has spent most of his life in Rome. Shadwell is a Jamesian character with European sensibilities and class standing. Frances herself has lived abroad and worked for him for fifteen years. (The film, which is supposedly a contemporary drama, does not explain how Frances and Shadwell managed to survive in Rome during the Fascist and war years.) Shadwell is diagnosed with a terminal illness, the only possible treatment of which is to be found in the United States. In the end, his decision to marry Frances (the decision seems to be all his) is at the same time a decision to return to the States for treatment. Thus, the film finds a way to bring home the lost Americans.

Shadwell has a final function in the narrative, one that somewhat undermines the class pragmatism of the two younger secretaries. While both Maria and Anita were capable of initiating their desired relationships, the film leaves it to Shadwell to bring them to their happy end. Once Frances has convinced him that she wants to be his bride despite knowing of his infirmities, she also prevails upon him to fix the relationships of her two friends. In the end, it is Shadwell's status as cultural patriarch that allows Dino to see that Maria's simulations of culture were actually acts of love. Shadwell presumably also convinces Bourgoyne not to punish Giorgio and Anita for their real affections.

Interestingly enough, of the films under discussion here, *Three Coins in the Fountain* is exceptional in setting up romances between Americans and Europeans that are designed to neither end in Europe nor to be easily shipped home. Yet, the fact that Maria and Anita will now be entering permanently into Italian families does not diminish the impression that the film's happy ending is a victory for American values. Unlike Henry James' *The Ambassadors*, in which American characters try to find a place in European hierarchies, in *Three Coins in the Fountain* the Americans find their place by infiltrating, undermining, or ignoring Old World class boundaries.

Yet the fantasy of egalitarian Americans who are above class wears thin as soon as we ask why the American characters chose to go to Europe in the first place and why the American audience is so happy to go along with them. Pomerance sees in the choice of travel to a different world an inherent critique of the one left behind.

> If I'm willing to leave my current social position to go to another that is not characteristically augmented . . . but simply different while being equally real, indeed even cheaply real, then my present social

position must be seriously problematic. In what inheres the appeal of films that offer us an imaginary possibility of leaving this social life for something coexisting yet banal?[25]

The fantasy world offered by *Three Coins in the Fountain* quickly asserts the notion that being an American in Rome allows for at least signs of a high-class status (sports cars, designer apartments and clothing, etc.) that were unavailable to these women in America and that can be transformed into good marital prospects. For the viewer, the filmic trip to Rome provided the chance to see how the other half lives and what the other half gets to see on their holidays.

As Nicholas Ray's 1956 melodrama *Bigger than Life* portrays so brilliantly, the maintenance of the high-end consumer lifestyle becomes a legitimating factor in middle-class America. Given the prevalence in Ray's film of European travel posters on the walls of the characters' home, Europe and a European experience belonged to the cultural capital that was expected of the consuming middle class. Acquisition of both the cultural capital and the actual money to enable one to buy into the 1950s domestic fantasy of prosperity became a tremendous burden, one not as easily achieved as the historical myths of the decade would indicate.

If the picture of the 1950s offered by *Bigger than Life* links success with acquisition of cultural capital and consumer freedom, *Three Coins in the Fountain* limits its marker of success to marriage alone. By placing these working girls in a situation where their consumer needs are easily met, the film suggests that their only real problem lies in finding husbands. In more than one instance it threatens the women characters with the potential of old maid status, thereby urging them ever more urgently to accept marriage at any cost. In the end, each is expected to be satisfied with matrimony under troubling circumstances. Maria will marry into a class and culture for which she is in no way prepared. The same is true of Anita, who will obviously be living under considerably more humble conditions than the opulence in which she dwells at the film's beginning. And Frances will marry a man who will likely die within a year, giving her merely the title of Mrs. Shadwell, without any long-term prospect of love and companionship. Yet, in all three cases, we are meant to see the outcome as successful.

The widescreen format allows *Three Coins in the Fountain* to simulate the fantasy of a Roman holiday in the highest technical fashion of the moment. While the characters depicted are working abroad rather than touring, the spectator, to whom the fountains and monuments of the Eternal City are so gloriously revealed through the anamorphic lens, is made into the most stereotypical form of the consumer tourist. The notion of the spectator as tourist reappears in Alfred Hitchcock's first work with the widescreen format, *To Catch a Thief.*

Sun Scream: Alfred Hitchcock and the Anxiety of the Tourist

Alfred Hitchcock's *To Catch a Thief* (1955) is one of the director's least-discussed films. This lack of attention likely has to do with the discourse that has evolved around much of his other work. In fact, studies of the director, along with those of Douglas Sirk, Nicholas Ray, and John Ford, constitute the foundation of auteurist film inquiry of Hollywood directors, which, in itself, occupies a central role in the foundation of the academic inquiry into cinema. Even the many psychoanalytic treatments of Hitchcock's filmmaking have not strayed far from the assumption of Hitchcock as author of a unified body of work. This unwavering disciplinary gaze has rarely, however, lingered long on Hitchcock's journey to the French Riviera in *To Catch a Thief.* The director, in his interviews with François Truffaut, dismisses the film as lightweight and is reluctant to talk about it.[26] In the seminal work on Hitchcock's films by Robin Wood, which in its current edition extends to well over 400 pages, the film is mentioned only twice. For a film produced in the middle of the director's career in between two of his more-discussed films, *Rear Window* (1954) and *The Man Who Knew Too Much* (1956), one might expect that a bit more attention may have been warranted.

If we find it necessary to place the film within an aesthetic framework, the critic has recourse to a sort of New Critical normativity by simply categorizing *To Catch a Thief* as a lesser work. Less canonical Hitchcock projects, such as *Stagefright* (1950), *Under Capricorn* (1949), and *Torn Curtain* (1966) have certainly been accounted for in that way. Of course, unlike these noncanonical Hitchcock films, *To Catch a Thief* remains quite popular. This kind of categorization is, of course, susceptible to the accusation of confirmation bias. That is to say: 'Hitchcock films display certain characteristics, especially if we choose as our pool those films with such characteristics.' The fact that *To Catch a Thief* does not engage in the same project of uncanny exposition that has been the catalyst of so much of the psychoanalytic work on Hitchcock films and that the film eschews construction of a psychoanalytic symptomology so prevalent in Hitchcock's later works may well have a simple explanation. But, it is one that the director would have been loath to admit.

Alfred Hitchcock liked to imagine that his films constituted a genre in themselves, and *To Catch a Thief* did not, somehow, belong. If *To Catch a Thief* participates in a different discourse than much of the rest of the

Hitchcock oeuvre, which discourse is it? The film reminds us that Hitchcock was a fully functioning and successful member of the Hollywood studio system, one who paid tremendous attention to and benefited from the economic trends and necessities of the era. What disturbs the Hitchcock narrative is how easily *To Catch a Thief* fits into the generic filmmaking practices of the time. The film registers an apparent turn away from Hitchcock as producer of his own genre in favor of Hitchcock as producer of a genre film; seen in light of runaway filmmaking and the travelogue romance, the film and its production history fall readily into place.

What confounds Hitchcock devotees and bores his critics is their view of the film as little more than a vehicle to set Grace Kelly and Cary Grant in front of a beautiful French Riviera background. It marks a departure from the careful, close-up psychological studies for which the British-born director had become famous. The ubiquitous death drive so prevalent in other Hitchcock films is absent here.[27] In fact, the one murder depicted in *To Catch a Thief* goes further to illuminate the mystery than to cause it. In many ways, the narrative economy resembles the film noir tendency to search for historical truth. But of course the visual representation remains quite the opposite of the typical noiresque chiaroscuro. Instead, it adds A-list star power to the formula of *Three Coins in the Fountain*, organizing itself around exploitation of setting and glamour rather than the normally tightly constructed Hitchcockian visual narrative. Yet, this film, more than many of the films that share its production conditions, fronts the difficulties of the very trend of which it is a part. The production was itself a case of extravagant tourism made possible by asymmetrical economic conditions between the United States and Europe, and the film narrates a story that highlights those conditions.

A trip to Europe joined the list of recreational outlets increasingly available to the expanding middle class of the 1950s. In fact, by 1955 over one million Americans annually undertook a nonprofessionally related tour abroad, for the most part to Europe.[28] Not only film but also the popular press represented the European tour as a sine qua non for the ideal bourgeois American lifestyle. In a 1950s American culture obsessed with questions of taste, appreciation of European culture indicated a necessary legitimating discernment.

Educational travel became institutionalized with the founding of the Fulbright Commission, university and college study abroad programs, and even increased pressure on schoolteachers to acquire a cosmopolitan attitude through European travel. According to a 1954 article in *Scholastic*, a popular magazine for schoolteachers, Pan American World Airways conducted a survey that showed a boom in schools offering continuing education credit and even salary increases to teachers who agreed to travel abroad.[29] On the same page as this brief article are three different advertisements for European tours offering enticements such as "Escorted Tours . . . for discriminating people who want to enjoy carefree travel" and "Intercollegiate tours planned for cultural values." Being a part of the burgeoning white middle class in America meant, among other things, that one could represent oneself as properly acquainted with one's Western European heritage, whether one actually descended from it or not. In a domestic culture in which, among other things, the budding Civil Rights movement was beginning to have some effect, a European tour became a strategy of staking claim to hegemonic whiteness.[30]

The travelogue romance positioned itself as a value-added product to another consumer desire, allowing film audiences to experience faraway places that had recently come into the range of their imaginations. The advent of tourist class air travel in 1952 expanded the opportunity for travel to Europe to more Americans than ever before. The travelogue romances made in Europe depict actors physically engaging with famous locations that an increasing number of viewers had actually encountered. While the films may not have been able to bridge the entertainment–recreation gap, they at least display recognition of the spectator's expanded interests. The discerning Babbitt could point to the Forum and identify it as being in Rome and not in Florence, thereby displaying his worldliness.

The popular press not only encouraged the wave of travel to Europe, it helped one prepare for the trip. Film marketing employed this interest to sell runaway productions. One of the interviews Grace Kelly gave while publicizing *To Catch a Thief* picked up on her image as a seasoned traveler. Entitled "Grace Kelly tells how to travel light," the *Woman's Home Companion* article tells women how to present themselves properly while carrying the minimum amount of luggage.[31] Of course, the article itself is little more than a vehicle for presenting Kelly in a wide array of appealing fashions with which she supposedly travels. Nevertheless it underscores the convergence of heightened interest in European travel critical to the story of *To Catch a Thief*. Moreover, it served as a public relations device for a Hollywood practice, namely runaway filmmaking, that had attracted increasing amounts of bad press.

The U.S. government, in line with its general approach to postwar reconstruction, encouraged this popular interest in the European tour. Tourism by Americans to Europe was already a significant industry before World War II. By the 1920s, the population of those who could and would take a trip to Europe had already begun to expand from its leisure-class base. Increasing numbers of middle-class travelers began to seek out the sites of occidental cultural heritage. But the tremendous food and housing shortages of the postwar years threatened to inhibit the recovery of tourism. The wave of tourism to Europe in the 1950s was hardly accidental. As Christopher Endy puts it:

The revival of American leisure travel after the liberation of France quickly became part of broader foreign policy concerns for both nations. In a time of economic scarcity, French officials faced the problem of how far, if at all, they should subordinate domestic consumption for the sake of luring Americans and their badly needed dollars. [32]

While this balance was much more critical in the late 1940s than it was in the early 1950s, the tension between the needs of the French population and the desire to attract foreign currency remained throughout the 1950s. American officials encouraged tourism as a way to privatize the subsidizing of the French currency, whereas French officials had to balance their need for such subsidies with demands from their active unions to provide more food and lodging for the stressed French working class. Americans pushed the issue even further by pressuring the French tourist industry to adapt its services to fit the needs of Americans and their greater spending powers. American interference in the French hospitality industry caused a rift among hoteliers. Since the French viewed their operation of hotels and restaurants as a general part of the high culture that separated them from Americans, being asked to live up to New World standards was an insult.

An inevitable tension arose then between the tourists and the tourist industry workers. As the Americans gradually succeeded in convincing French hoteliers to accommodate American tourist desires, they assured that the workers of those hotels and restaurants would never be able to afford to go to them. Economic class came to the forefront as American officials demanded more material amenities for their own middle-class travelers at the price of the labor-intensive services that the French had been accustomed to offering before. Moreover, workers were being asked to be more flexible in work hours and to curb their frequent strikes to accommodate tourists, thus further irritating the Communist- and Socialist-led unions in France. In general, the encouragement of expanded tourism became a sticking point among American and French officials, French trade unions, and American critics of the Marshall Plan, all of whom staked out claims in the Franco–American relationship. [33] *To Catch a Thief* animates this discussion of tourism and its discontents.

Making films in Europe was not a marginalized industrial custom. As we have seen, it was one practiced by all of the major studios, employing many of the most prominent directors and actors of the period. For many filmmakers this form of professional tourism would have been seen as a welcome opportunity to escape the political pressures of HUAC red-baiting and the industrial anxiety brought about by plummeting cinema ticket sales, and it would have appealed to a sensed need for a new cinematic aesthetic. Production notes from *To Catch a Thief* indicate that, while the same was true for Alfred Hitchcock, he was less enthusiastic about the idea of filming abroad than was William Wyler. In 1954 his *Rear Window* had been a smash hit, as had Grace Kelly's first film with him, *Dial M for Murder* (1954). Unlike other Hollywood players who were still resisting the growth of the television broadcasting industry, Hitchcock signed on in 1955 to produce a series. This fit in well with a business model he had followed for a decade of playing Hollywood sides against each other for his own benefit. Thus, Hitchcock would not have had as much incentive to flee southern California as other filmmakers. Yet, Hitchcock clearly gave way to the priorities of Paramount studios, with whom he was then under contract, to seek ways to exploit their new widescreen format, VistaVision, the process being touted by Paramount as a competitor to Twentieth Century-Fox's CinemaScope. Moreover, the ability to finance films, in this case only partially, through the use of frozen currencies did much to decrease the film's production costs.

While Hitchcock had dabbled with 3D filmmaking in *Dial M for Murder*, *To Catch a Thief* marks his first formal experiment in widescreen cinema. This fact becomes important, because it exerted tremendous influence over how the director could set up shots and include visual information. According to studio correspondence, the director did not adapt easily either to the new technology or to the location conditions. Despite Paramount's advertised claims to the contrary, the earliest versions of VistaVision could not accommodate close-ups without tremendous distortion. Therefore, Hitchcock had to forego a principal tool in his construction of psychological drama. The normally claustrophobic shots of Hitchcock's earlier work were no longer appropriate in the new widescreen format. Conventions that an astute viewer had come to expect from a Hitchcock film, such as process shots and experimentation with deep focus became, respectively, much more difficult or impossible to set up. Since continuity editing of the classical Hollywood style often demanded that longer shots be left on the screen longer, Hitchcock was faced, at the cutting table, with significant constraints to his well-established editing style.[34] Thus, many of the tools that made Hitchcock films Hitchcock films had to be rethought in working with the new technology.

It did not take a Hollywood insider to reveal what Hitchcock's problems with the new camera were. John Rosenfeld of the *Dallas Daily News* opines: "The editing is drastic in spots and continuity dangles. Obviously Hitchcock had more footage than was practical. He was unable to cut it into his usual whole piece of suspense."[35] This failure to produce a film with his usual authorial markings likely explains why Hitchcock would henceforth eschew European location work, despite whatever financial advantages they offered.

To Catch a Thief reveals a director ill at ease both in terms of camera and mode of production.

Hitchcock eventually adapted well to the new widescreen technology and would go on to exploit it masterfully in subsequent films. If the new format proved, in Hitchcock's first experience, incompatible to his aesthetic, later films, such as *Vertigo* (1958) or *North by Northwest* (1959), reveal almost an obsession with the details of large format filmmaking.[36] Thus, *To Catch a Thief* reads as a failed trial run for subsequent successes.

In a correspondence between Hollywood and the Cannes production unit, Hitchcock expresses his ongoing frustration with working both on location and with the new technology. The unit producer, C. O. (Doc) Erickson, admits in his daily missives to Paramount Studios that the ambitions of doing a wide-format thriller on location in the south of France exceeded many of the technical capabilities available to Hitchcock and his crew. Clearly the producers intended to take advantage of the location for the sake of authenticity. However, the combination of a camera (the double-frame VistaVision format) with which Hitchcock had never before worked and the conditions on location made it impossible for the famously detail-oriented director and producer to create his desired set-ups. Erickson writes:

> I have talked to Hitch and Burks and Kelley [the two cameramen, rrs] about the problem of out-of-focus backgrounds and close-ups. As you probably know, Hitch feels very strongly about this point and insists upon shooting normal close-ups, but will be protected in all cases with a looser shot or a transparency background.[37]

The "looser" shots are the ones that finally make it into the film. Hitchcock's frustration stems from the inability to achieve a deep enough focus with the wide-format camera. This dramatically altered the style of the film away from the shot rhythm to which Hitchcock was accustomed. One short scene reveals how the editing and focal length differences conspire to alter the typical Hitchcock psychological effect. The scene takes place as a part of the larger sequence in which John Robie and Frances Stevens go on a drive through the countryside. The larger sequence is designed both as a showcase for VistaVision landscape shots of the Riviera coast and to stage a series of conversations that reveal Frances's need for dangerous adventure and consequent affections toward Robie. For Robie the primary motivation for the sequence derives from his attempt to predict where the next jewel heist will happen. As such, he is traveling under the guise of Mr. Burns, an American lumberman in the market for a villa in the region. The scene epitomizes the typical Hitchcock recognition–misrecognition situations the director often employed to establish the plot suspension. Frances is attempting to discover Robie's intentions at the same time that Robie seeks to unveil the person who is trying to frame him.

The sequence takes us through a series of medium tracking shots as the couple walks from the front to the back of the villa. These shots are interspersed with POVs of Robie scanning the villa. Frances thinks Robie is scoping the place for a robbery. As they reach the back of the villa, one such POV reveals a man in the distance descending the staircase from the house to the terrace. The countershot is a two-shot of Robie and Frances moving toward the camera. Their dialogue has him providing a seemingly accurate reading of her romantic motivations while his eyes appear to follow the movement of the man down the stairs. The sequence cuts back to reveal quite briefly that the man, whom the spectator cannot identify, has come much closer. It cuts back to the continued medium tracking shot of the conversation and finally back to a medium shot of the man, who has now met them at the bottom of the staircase. We now see that the man is Bertani, the restaurant owner who had claimed to be helping Robie. However the shot is at enough distance that it is easy to imagine that the identity of the man may not have been clear to the spectator upon one viewing of the film. VistaVision simply cannot achieve the depth of field required to provide the spectator the information required to build up and sustain Hitchcockian tension. The next shot, a tail on, match-on-action of Bertani walking away from the camera, dissolves what little tension the scene may have hoped to create to that point.

This scene would normally constitute a melodramatic high point. It portrays a shift in the plot where Robie discovers whose trail he must follow to clear his name. He discovers that the same people who had been his comrades in the French Resistance underground are now betraying him.

In essence, the screenplay contains all of the elements of the formulaic thrillers that Hitchcock had been accustomed to producing. What is lacking is the typical Hitchcock visual punctuation that would provide the necessary tension. This series of shots would have been followed in almost every other Hitchcock film with a series of shot–countershot close-ups that would signal recognition and betrayal. Absent these shots, which the studio correspondence indicates were attempted, Hitchcock must displace the dramatic tension elsewhere in the film. That displacement is most obvious in the car chase scene, the second one in the film at this point, which follows the scene just described. These large production numbers appear to be an attempt on Hitchcock's part to compensate for his inability to create suspense through the addition of action.

The experience with *To Catch a Thief* influences subsequent Hitchcock efforts. It was meant to be the first of two runaway productions the director would undertake. But Hitchcock and Erickson's experience on the Riviera caused them to return to the Paramount lot to shoot the remake of *The Man Who Knew Too Much*, another film about tourism gone awry. The technical limitations of runaway filmmaking and the director's inability to master them make *To Catch a Thief*, in formal visual terms, a failed model of the famous Hitchcock anxiety machine. When *To Catch a Thief* premiered in the summer of 1955, critics were unanimous in their dislike of the film but could not agree on what made the film fail. They concurred that, whatever it was that consti-tuted a Hitchcock experience did not apply here. A more interesting reading of the film is available if we view it, not as a "Hitchcock film" but as a runaway film and travelogue romance. By the time Hitchcock made *To Catch a Thief,* films shot on location and set in Europe had recognizable characteristics.

The emergence of the notion of the ugly American tourist is an obvious byproduct of the debates about taste and the nouveau riche that permeate intellectual debate in the 1950s. No one was more threatened by the growth of the middle class than those who had enjoyed that status for decades. "Estab-lishment" Americans turned to taste and cultural capital as the gatekeeping standards for bourgeois legitimacy. Everything from scholarly agendas to real estate covenants were set up to assure that financial security alone was not a guarantor to middle-class (or, for that matter, upper-class) status. As Jackson Lears has argued, "the dominance of New Criticism was itself evidence of the pervasive aestheticism of the 1950s—the tendency to make literature into a kind of surrogate religion."[38] In effect, taste became a guarded moral and aesthetic category that separated the enlightened from the barbarians.

Taste in travel became a test for whether the newly affluent American was eligible to belong to the social as well as to the economic class. Where did you travel and with whom? Where did you stay? What did you wear? The answers to these questions help negotiate who was in the club and who was not. This particular fear about who is minding the gates of entry into the middle class drives many of the melodramatic film narratives of the mid-1950s, including *Sabrina* (Billy Wilder, 1954), *All that Heaven Allows* (Douglas Sirk, 1955), *Bigger Than Life* (Nicholas Ray, 1956), and *The Man in the Gray Flannel Suit* (Nunnally Johnson, 1956).

Traveling abroad was meant to edify and socialize the American. The American version of this journey extends back to Thomas Jefferson's sojourn in Paris and is concretized in American intellectualism through the work of Henry James. For James, one's status as properly acculturated is most often tested in regard to one's appreciation for the aesthetic values of continental Europe. Harry Levin has noted of James's characters in Europe that they are "guided in the goings and comings by his seasoned knowledge of local topography."[39] James established an elite intellectual norm for tourists, wherein polyglottism and aesthetic appreciation were proper accessories. Taste in travel was determined by how well one responded to a foreign environment. One was meant to exhibit familiarity with local behavior without 'going native,' at least morally. (The exception to the Jamesian rule was England, which offered a greater set of shared values.) Moreover, the sophisticated traveler was to be able to rise above the inevitable misadventures of travel.

Decrying the ugly American tourist as lacking in these skills became a sport of the intellectual elite of the 1950s. Ogden Nash penned a poem entitled "Who Wants to Travel All Over Europe and See Nothing But a Lot of American Tourists? I Do," published in the *New Yorker* in 1955, in which he differentiates his longing for a European journey from that of imagined Texans who want to drive large American cars on St. Andrews Golf Course.[40] At the same time, it was a thinly guised expression of fear that the American middle class was losing the set of distinctions that defined it. The popular novelist Judith Krantz recognized the hidden agenda behind the stereotypification as expressing its perpetrators' need to feel "superior." Krantz offers a sympathetic reading of the petit bourgeois tourist's drive for cultural education in the face of American and European snobbery. "People don't seem to realize that there has been a revolution in foreign travel, and that of the many Americans departing every year, only a few are in the Eden Roc-Paris Ritz class."[41] Arguably, *To Catch a Thief* responds to this tourist culture of which it is also a part. Tourist anxiety explains the film more than any discourse one might locate in another Hitchcock film.

Of what then does the anxiety of the tourist represented in this film consist? Tourists fear being ripped off, swindled, or even not getting the proper bargain. This fear stems from the necessary class difference that lies at the heart of the tourist experience, especially the journey abroad for the postwar American. If this is less true now, with the global expansion of the middle class, it was certainly true in the 1950s, when American tourism to Europe still had a colonialist tinge to it. One went abroad to experience the general benefits of status, whether material or cultural, that one did not enjoy at home. The downside to that is, of course, that one's disjointed enjoyment rested entirely on the wealth one brought along on the trip. Thus, travel became the perfect realm for the nouveau riche. The tourist could expect the destination and her own arrival in it to provide the cultural capital as long as she brought the traveler's checks.

Even more so than *Summertime,* which we discussed in the last chapter, *To Catch a Thief* foregrounds its commentary on tourism. But it applies its critique primarily to the general institution of tourism rather than to individual expectations. The film's credit sequence opens with a shot of the storefront of a French Government Tourist Office window advertising trips to France.

The sequence creates a bit of geographical confusion within seconds, leading the spectator to conclude that the storefront shot is, in fact, nondiegetic. We are clearly not experiencing the POV of any particular character in the plot, for the sequence cuts with a sound cue from the storefront to a medium shot of a screaming, sunburned tourist with cream on her face. This is followed by a shot from outside a Riviera beachfront hotel and a soundtrack filled with similar screams, mostly in English, one in French, proclaiming the loss of valuable jewels interspliced with an image of a black cat walking away from the camera. Thus, we are thrown immediately into a tourism-related trauma and given a symbolic suggestion as to its source.

This rapid opening parodies the representation of theft. The victims receive no sympathy for the crimes committed against them. Rather, from the very beginning, the film portrays the tourist victims of a sophisticated jewel thief as tasteless and idle boors. The screaming tourist offers a standard of anxiety against which the film's main characters will be judged. In fact, these thefts function as little more than a plot device with which the film sets up the real crime, which appears to be class mobility. That is to say, in the eyes of at least his former working-class comrades in arms, the crime John Robie stands accused of having perpetrated appears not to have been ripping off tourists, but betraying his former leftist Resistance comrades. His participation in the decadence of the leisure class runs counter to the Resistance solidarity that evidently protected him.

Through mysterious means Robie has gained class stature while his comrades are consigned to serving those of the class to which Robie has ascended. Postwar conditions required the members of the Resistance, who had spent five years living outside the martial law imposed by the Vichy regime, to again submit themselves to legal norms. If Robie has broken this social contract and enriched himself in the process, then in so doing he has betrayed his working-class former comrades in arms.

As the story plays itself out, it becomes less a clash of right versus wrong than a class struggle between tourists and those who serve them. The film wavers in its sympathies toward the contending sides. The only side we get in this first sequence is that of a middle-aged, female, presumably American tourist with her hair up in rollers and cold cream on her face. Thus, the film creates an immediate link in the narrative to "the ugly American tourist." As Raymond Durgnat has described the scene:

> People who aren't qualified for 'life'—i.e. romance—are bound to end up losers if they're unrealistic enough to court it—and it isn't merely her appearance and age that are at stake—it's everything that is greedy and querulous in that face and that scream.[42]

The film punishes the American tourist who attempts to experience the excitement without the danger.

Once the theft has been presented, the camera pulls back to a long shot of men entering a car and driving off. The film then cuts to a helicopter shot of the car traversing the serpentine roads up a mountain. Thus, within seconds of the end of the opening credits, the film puts on display the capabilities of the widescreen mechanism with which it is experimenting. What we get is a panoramic view of the French Riviera. The film deliberately places itself in the ideal tourist's perspective throughout, providing the look and feel of a travelogue.

Studio files reveal the degree of difficulty the production unit had in achieving the panoramic shots that make up a significant portion of the film. The combination of a helicopter, which was at that time relatively rare aeronautic equipment, the need for good weather, and the VistaVision camera added considerably to the film's negative costs. Why was it so important? These shots were integral to the look the film was attempting to sell. They become the primary footage for the prerelease trailer, which gives little indication of the film's actual narrative. The film was sold as a VistaVision location film with stunning scenery and A-list cast and director. The producers apparently wanted a film that, more than anything, would appeal to the new taste for travel. Moreover, as I noted above, the wide-open shots of the French Riviera coast are also a substitute for the visual tension Hitchcock seemed unable to construct. Tourism thus replaces suspense.

To Catch a Thief takes on the questions of taste and tourism quite directly. Like *Summertime*, the film identifies varying typologies of the American abroad. The first ones to appear on the screen are the vulgar nouveau riche tourists who are among those being robbed of their baubles. Cary Grant's character, John Robie, is a much more complicated construction. He stands in for the American expatriate who populates so many Henry James's stories. Yet, despite the suave exterior that suggests a comfortable middle-class status, we learn quickly that his wealth was acquired as an adult, in fact as a jewel thief. His history of having fought in the Resistance suggests a political background, linguistic competency, and commitment that align him more with the Lincoln brigade fighters of the Spanish Civil War than with James's genteel leisure class. As such, one can read him as a kind of postwar Rick Blaine from *Casablanca*. When John Robie disguises himself as Burns, a lumberman from Oregon, the character makes sense only in terms of audience expectations of a recently successful businessman from the American West seeking to acquire cultural capital to adorn his fortunes. Hence, the disguise chosen by Robie to assimilate into the luxury hotel in the Riviera is that of a boorish, nouveau riche American.

Interesting contrasting versions of taste come in the mother–daughter duo Jessie and Frances Stevens, played by Jessie Royce Landis and Grace Kelly respectively. The mother owns up to the vulgar displays of wealth to which she feels compelled in order to present a class standing that would otherwise not be evident. The daughter, on the other hand, who has enjoyed a lifetime of the luxuries her mother's fortunes have allowed her, vacillates between hiding the fact that her family's money is their only claim to status and using her class awareness as a source of charm. Class difference and the performance thereof motivate these characters throughout the movie. Touring Europe is represented as a cultural obligation signifying that a degree of both financial wealth and cultural capital has been obtained.

The film toys with the struggles of the newly rich to legitimate themselves. Its climax is set at a costume ball in which the tourists attempt to outdo each other in their imitation of ancient regime splendor. Hence these newly rich hicks imagine themselves into the Old World aristocratic class replete with decadence and splendor that would have made the Marquis de Sade proud.

Jessie Stevens spans the class structure more thoroughly than do any of the other characters. Initially she is depicted as living up to the cliché of the tasteless rich American. But she soon embraces and parodies this position. Unlike the initial victims, Jessie turns the anxiety of the nouveau riche tourist on its head. In fact, by providing her with a self-critical awareness regarding her own taste and behavior, the film puts her in a position to solve the crime. She exhibits a willingness to pay the price of her (admittedly heavily insured) jewels for a bit of adventure. In fact, she derives enjoyment from the nervousness this causes other people.

The triangle that fuels the tension of *To Catch a Thief* depends heavily on the extradiegetic context of which the contemporary American viewer in 1955 would have been aware. As the reports in the popular press regarding travel abroad indicate, both class-consciousness and America's place in the world pervaded popular discourse. But that only accounts for part of the narrative economy in the film. The tension derives from a struggle among three parties, the old tourist–expatriate class, the new tourist class, and the French natives engaged in serving the tourists. The triangle pulls on mutual antagonisms among Robie, an expatriate American former cat burglar who atoned for his criminal activity by siding with the French Resistance during the war; his former comrades, who claim to believe him to be back to his old tricks, thereby getting wealthier while they wash dishes; and the tourists, who accuse him of stealing their jewels. This triangle forces Robie to declare loyalty to either one or the other group, thereby creating the suspense that holds the film together. Moreover, the film animates this conflict with a love triangle among Robie, Frances Stevens, and Danielle Foussard, the daughter of a former comrade of Robie's in the Resistance who has now become a waiter.

The native French population, which has been reduced to serving the Americans, is placed in between the protagonists and uses its position to play one against the other. We first encounter this class in the initial restaurant scene, one in which Robie's former colleagues in the Resistance accuse him either directly or indirectly of having reneged on his pledge to give up crime. They, in the meantime, have spiraled from patriotic freedom fighters to servants of those who were their fellow allies a decade earlier. The plot depends upon a certain assumed French–American tension. That is to say the film would not be understandable without the contextual background of postwar Franco–American mutual resentments, which newspapers in both the United States and France reported frequently in the ten years following the war. These resentments find animation in the relationship between Robie and his former allies.

The screenplay provides little motivation for the appearance of Frances Stevens, apart from providing Robie a seemingly unwanted romantic counterpart. On the other hand, Brigitte Auber, in the role of Danielle, the ingénue suffering from unrequited love for Robie, plays a crucial role. She narrates the political dimensions of the resentment felt by the former resistance fighters. In the end, she is a bit of a Gaullist figure, one who first causes and then lives off a sense of American betrayal.

The Stevens' first encounter with Robie, then under the disguise of Mr. Burns, occurs just after Jessie has displayed her quiet aggression toward the hotel wait staff. The success of his charm toward Jessie comes from his playing to her class sensibilities. The humor of the scene derives from his portrayal of himself as a wealthy but tasteless tourist demanding payment in full for a roulette table marker he drops into a woman's cleavage. Presumably enjoying his philistine behavior and the good looks she commented on earlier, Jessie invites him back to her table. There she marks him as similar to her late husband, Jeremiah, whom she praises in practical American fashion for having "had both feet on the ground." Her comment about preferring bourbon to champagne because the latter took too long to age invokes a stereotype of class difference regarding the appropriate appreciation of delayed gratification. All along, Frances's role is to be shocked and dismayed at her mother's boorish ways.

Durgnat praises Jessie as rising above the class stereotype with which the film begins. "The very actions with which she seemed, at first, to epitomize the crass vulgarity of the nouveau riche . . . are her, and perhaps Hitchcock's comment on 'the good life.'"[43] Her enjoyment stems from her ability to maneuver within and around class status. Underneath the surface version of unabashed consumer materialism indicative of social insecurity is a woman thoroughly enjoying the tensions that come with having only recently arrived in the leisure class.

The opposite is true of her daughter. Frances gives the air of a sophisticated adult woman, sovereign in her sexuality and polished veneer. But, part of the double entendres of the seduction scene comes when, after presumably giving herself to Robie, she discovers her jewels are missing. Her demand "Give me back my jewels!" suggests not only that her virtue and valuables seem to be closely linked, but also, having succumbed to Robie, she no longer is very secure in what either may have meant. This, as Durgnat suggests, equates "money with virginity in particular, and sexuality in general."[44] He points out that dialogue earlier in the same scene "coyly equates the warmth of worn jewelry with Frances's breast."[45] Her virginity, jewelry, and class standing are of a piece. Losing one seems to equate losing them all. Only Robie can restore two while providing meaning for the loss of the third.

To Catch a Thief offers more cultural parody of Americans than any of Hitchcock's more psychoanalytically driven films. While hardly speaking to real French or European concerns about the invasion of what they may or may not have seen as crass Americans, it points to the class issues that often accompanied participation in the tourist industry in postwar France. If the film participates in the construction of the travelogue romance, it does so while making clear the unstable conditions under which the American–European encounter occurs.

Upon visiting the set of *To Catch a Thief*, André Bazin was disturbed to find the legendary control freak, Alfred Hitchcock, curiously unengaged in the making of the film. The production files suggest that Bazin's observation may not reflect the whole of the shoot in Cannes. Albeit frustrated by a series of conditions to which he was not accustomed, including an incomplete screenplay at the commencement of shooting, French crew members' work habits, and a widescreen process that seemed incompatible with his aesthetic principles, Hitchcock received praise from the studio for his economy and precision, the work habits that had well served his reputation with Hollywood studio executives. Yet, it is clear that the control and camera work in *To Catch a Thief* failed to live up to his Hollywood reputation. Moreover, he was unable to fulfill the studio's desire for the film to be shot completely on location, a claim that had been used in the successful marketing of other contemporary runaway productions. The grand ball sequence had to be constructed entirely on a Paramount set in California. And, despite his own best efforts to replicate the Wyler experiment, he was unable to complete the film without frequent resort to process shots, which remain a staple of Hitchcock films.

The result of Hitchcock's and the Paramount crew's labors in the south of France was an entertaining film with brilliant costumes, alluring actors, and beautiful widescreen location footage. In short, *To Catch a Thief* became a quite typical Hollywood runaway film. It is only because of the Hitchcock imprint on the film that such a description sinks to the damnation of faint praise. The film, nevertheless, occupies an important position in the history of Hitchcock's films.

I started by asking why *To Catch a Thief,* one of Hitchcock's most commercially successful films, has slipped past the critical gaze. For both the director himself and the throngs of scholars who have created and attended to the Hitchcock aura seemed to have conspired to have us look elsewhere. What we have then failed to see, I would argue, is Hitchcock's own anxiety about *To Catch a Thief.* Hitchcock produced and reproduced a self-portrait that equated the director with his work. But Hitchcock apparently did not want to be identified with his work on this film. His obvious inability to master the medium and conditions of production reveal his dependence on formal studio conventions. Hollywood needed desperately to change the very look of the products it was offering. Hitchcock displayed a willingness to try to adapt quickly to new conditions. In this instance, however, he appears to have failed. In short, Hitchcock becomes the kind of tourist his film so compellingly parodies, unable to adapt quickly enough to his surroundings and conditions. He fails as a tourist because, like a Texan in a Taco Bell in Tuscany, he seeks to have everything as it is at home.

Citing Hitchcock's inability to master a certain mode of 1950s Hollywood production is not so shocking a conclusion unless you consider to what degree the entire academic enterprise of film studies depends on arguments of exceptionalism surrounding certain figures. The picture of Hitchcock changes significantly if we read this film not as an anomaly but as an integral segue from his classical Hollywood style to the late "psychoanalytic" Hitchcock. Fredric Jameson describes a vanishing mediator as a moment of surplus in a dialectical process in which the agent of change remains behind in the old form while a new content is being generated. Having completed its task, the mediator in the guise of the old form vanishes and reveals the radicalized content.[46]

We can read *To Catch a Thief,* then, as a vanishing mediator between two eras of Hitchcock production. It is, if you will, a summer vacation between Hitchcock's mastery of academy ratio and claustrophobia and the later fascination with widescreen format and agoraphobia. It is the last of his successful collaborations with Grace Kelly and therefore the beginning of the simulation of her in the bodies of Doris Day, Kim Novak, Eve Marie Saint, Janet Leigh, and Tippi Hedren. Thus, far from being a MacGuffin (that is, a distraction from the "real" Hitchcock), *To Catch a Thief* creates the conditions that will make Hitchcock the constant object of the disciplinary gaze he has become. Vanishing mediators only function properly by appearing as "aberrations or excesses" that must quickly be dismissed.[47] Perhaps therein lies the reason behind Hitchcock's and Hitchcock scholars' silence around the film.

Solving the problem of To Catch a Thief within the discourse of Hitchcock studies does not take us as far as does contextualizing the film within its industrial conditions. The film correlates directly to Three Coins in the Fountain, in which the industrial necessity of experimenting with new production technology sets up an ideological situation within the narrative itself. In the case of To Catch a Thief, the widescreen process is deployed to turn the spectator into a tourist and in Three Coins in the Fountain into a colonialist. (As the discourse on colonialism and tourism suggests, the difference is often slight to nonexistent.) In both cases the plot requires an explanation for the affluence necessary to properly exploit the range of the widescreen capabilities. In order to fill the wide screen with sumptuous excess, Europe must be contrasted as an economic other, whether colonized or criminalized. The consumer joys on display, whether travel, jewels, or clothing, are available only to the American characters.

From High Culture to Haut Couture in Funny Face

To the degree that the travelogue romances and other runaway films of the 1950s and 1960s survive at all in the memory of film viewers from the 1950s, they often do so as filmic fashion shows. The gowns, sportswear, and hats draped on the likes of Grace Kelly, Audrey Hepburn, and Elizabeth Taylor and put on display in front of fabulous European locations linger in the memory of historical spectators long after the film's story has been forgotten.[48] The advertising tie-in campaigns of both To Catch a Thief and Funny Face (Stanley Donen, 1957) suggest that the films were a part of a larger effort around the middle of the 1950s to create a certain kind of consumption pattern that included a European journey, high fashion, and romance. In fact, it would be difficult to re-create the impact of these films, along with Sabrina (Billy Wilder, 1954), Rhapsody (Charles Vidor, 1954), and countless other films made both in southern California and abroad on the fashion sensibilities of their female viewers without a simultaneous perusal of the fashion and women's magazines of the day. The pages of Vogue, Vanity Fair, and even Ladies' Home Journal insisted that a trip to Paris or London was a necessary accoutrement to stylish middle-class living. Even Rear Window (Alfred Hitchcock, 1954), a film set entirely in one room of a Manhattan apartment, ties together Grace Kelly, high fashion, and travel abroad as the proof of one's bourgeois legitimacy. In short, the films seek to establish themselves as required viewing for those interested in both European fashion and travel to Europe.

While both *Three Coins in the Fountain* and *To Catch a Thief* seek to offer themselves as authoritative texts on fashion, it is at best a secondary discourse. Paramount's 1957 production *Funny Face* establishes *haut couture* as the central relationship between Americans and Europeans, one that should trump all others. Moreover, the film draws clear lines regarding who is the proper consumer and what is proper to consume.

Funny Face presents the story of an American fashion photographer, Dick Avery, loosely based on Richard Avedon, the famous portrait photographer who served as a consultant on the film. Avery is a freelance photographer on contract with a notable New York fashion magazine run by Maggie Prescott. In order to create a theme for the presentation of the new fall collection, the magazine decides to choose a single model who can best represent the qualities they intend to portray. On the promise that she will get to go to Paris to see her favorite philosopher, the magazine recruits a young student, Jo, whom they encounter on a location shoot. While in Paris, she is wooed by the photographer and briefly by the philosopher of whom she is a professed disciple. After much slapstick and heartbreak, Jo allows fashion to triumph over philosophy, and she returns the affections of Dick.

Generically speaking, the film is structured as a musical comedy, with nondiegetic musical numbers occasionally interrupting the story. It is a reworking of a 1920s stage musical in which Fred Astaire starred with his sister, Adele. The now-familiar structures of the travelogue romance are revealed here, as well as in *An American in Paris*, to be easily combined with the musical. In Paris, Jo is turned from a mousey bookworm into a work of fashion art. In various location shoots she is photographed in front of the Arc de Triumph, as Anna Karenina at a train station, and as a modern-day Venus de Milo. Not only is Europe a site of self-discovery and sexual awakening for the young American, but there Jo can insinuate herself into the high culture that she had, up to that point, only observed from afar.

Jo's transformative encounter is more with the sights of Paris than it is with any particular Parisians. As in *To Catch a Thief*, her love affair is with another American, one who, though a fashion photographer, is not represented as particularly Europeanized. And, as in *Roman Holiday*, the Audrey Hepburn character's real romance is with the city itself and the transformative possibilities it entails.

Before departing for the City of Lights, the characters already polarize their notions about what the trip represents. A musical number inserted upon arrival at the airport then fills out these various meanings. The song is an ode to the combination of travel and romance. Each character hails a cab claiming to be headed for the hotel and each sets about discovering 'their' Paris. For Maggie, Paris is the capital of *haut couture*, feminine consumerism, and, as such, a defining part of her professional character. But this woman is not an empty-headed shopper. She is depicted as a self-assured feminist, who sees fashion as a form of empowerment. Thus, her trip to Paris takes on a sort of ambassadorial function, as she sells her sort of fashion politics to the world. Yet, when she strolls the Parisian boulevards, she remains little more than a giddy American tourist. For Avery, Paris is a playground. He has professional duties to perform in the city. But his work is merely a vehicle to allow him to change the setting of his *flaneur* existence. Presumably, he could be as equally entertained in Milan, London, or Tokyo. Jo's Parisian pretensions focus primarily on Paris' cultural and intellectual resources. Like many of the characters in the travelogue romances, exposure to the City of Lights will transform. While she has a cultist attraction to the famous philosopher, her intentions extend to the museums and intellectual atmosphere as well. Yet, as different as the sites visited by the three are, they are nonetheless strictly tourist renditions of the city rendered splendidly in widescreen format. "Bonjour Paris" ends with all three of them meeting by accident at the Eiffel Tower with the song's lyrics revealing the truth about their trip: "We are strictly tourists, you can titter and jeer, all we want to say is 'Lafayette, we are here.'" Thus, Paris is not the site of a functional bourgeois life, but the playground that Hollywood continued to depict Europe as being. In rendering Paris nothing more than a tourist site, the film announces that the actions and thoughts of the city's inhabitants need not be taken seriously. From here on out, the film becomes a widescreen catalogue for high fashion.

Funny Face sets up a competition between a contemplative and a consumerist life. The latter wins hands down. Jo is transformed into a doll whose freedoms are restricted and whose impact is based on how she looks rather than how she thinks. Jo continually avoids her photo shoots with the magazine crew to spend her time in Bohemian dives, where the locals wear nothing but black, smoke funny little cigarettes, and try to look deep. The "empathicalist" philosophy that Jo continually parrots is transparently absurd. When she finally meets her philosophical hero, their encounter is reduced to the philosopher's attempt to seduce her. He, and thereby also her intellectual ambition, is revealed as a fraud. Dick also betrays how little he is interested in her other than as a model. During a jealous tirade about the philosopher Dick spouts: "He is about as interested in your intellect as I am." The film makes no attempt to salvage her intellectual ambitions. Rather it assures us that they can be easily replaced with fancy dresses.

Whereas in *Three Coins in the Fountain*, European high culture is represented as something one can fake, in *Funny Face* high culture is itself fake. There is no point in learning French or studying obscure books, all one needs is a great dress and a fabulous backdrop, items readily available along the Champs d'Elysee. The European culture worth acquiring is that which one can buy.

The conventions of the travelogue romance in *Funny Face* allow us to see in general what function the European holiday is meant to perform in the lives of the characters. At the beginning of the film Jo is an enthusiastic student of philosophy who decries the fashion scene with which she is confronted as hollow and ridiculous. Paris represents a shrine to her intellectual interests, and she is therefore willing to participate in the inane modeling business in order to parlay it into an experience of some other form of authenticity. But this initial concession turns out to be transformative. When her own fantasies about "empathicalism" are shattered, she is forced to seek validation elsewhere. Even the modeling, which had initially provided her with the freedom and resources to support her academic enterprises, is only a medium by which she arrives at what we are to assume as her real desire. The last dress she models is a wedding dress. *Funny Face* remains rather tentative about whether she wants to become a wife or whether she just wants to keep the dress. The love ballad at the end suggests again that she has fallen in love with the consumerism as much as she has the man: "You've made my life so glamorous, you can't blame me for feeling amorous."

Conclusion

Widescreen processes, whether Fox's anamorphic CinemaScope or Paramount's dual lens VistaVision, provided studios the opportunity to participate in the American fascination with European travel by creating films that offered the spectator the best possible two dimensional simulation of actually being there. For the studios, widescreen travelogues were a product that could potentially stand up to the challenge presented by television. Here was a level of spectacle that the black-and-white home set could not match. For the spectator, a vicarious romantic adventure to Europe offered not just a fantasy of middle-class standing, but information that might actually help one to simulate or support one's claim to such a class standing outside of the movie theater.

Hollywood on Holiday: Gregory Peck during the filming of *Roman Holiday*. (Publicity still, *Roman Holiday*, Paramount Studios, 1953, courtesy of Photofest.)

Location work as tourism: William Wyler, Gregory Peck, and Audrey Hepburn at work on *Roman Holiday*. (Publicity still, *Roman Holiday*, Paramount Pictures, 1953, courtesy of Photofest.)

Joseph Cotten and Joan Fontaine pose in front of Old World splendors for *September Affair*. (Publicity still, *September Affair*, Paramount Pictures, 1950, courtesy of Photofest.)

Vacation sex exposed: *The Indiscretion of an American Wife*. (*The Indiscretion of an American Wife*, Columbia Pictures, 1954.)

Viewing Venice through a camera in *Summertime*. (Publicity still, *Summertime*, London Film Productions, 1955, courtesy of Photofest.)

The virginal American in the gothic Old World: June Allyson and Rossano Brazzi in *Interlude*. (Publicity still, *Interlude*, Universal International Pictures, 1957, courtesy of Photofest.)

Living like princesses on a secretary's salary: *Three Coins in the Fountain*.
(*Three Coins in the Fountain*, Twentieth Century-Fox, 1954.)

The French Riviera: A nice place to visit, but I would hate to make a film there.
(Publicity still, *To Catch a Thief*, Paramount Pictures, 1955, courtesy of Photofest.)

The postwar love triangle
in *A Foreign Affair*.
(*A Foreign Affair*, Paramount
Pictures, 1948.)

The triumph of fashion over feminism: Audrey Hepburn in *Funny Face*. (Publicity still, *Funny Face*, Paramount Pictures, 1957, courtesy of Photofest.)

Repackaging Germany and the war bride: Cary Grant and Ann Sheridan in *I Was a Male War Bride*. (Publicity Still, *I Was a Male War Bride*, Twentieth Century-Fox, 1949, courtesy of Photofest.)

left: Strolling down Victory Boulevard in defeated Berlin: *The Big Lift*. (*The Big Lift*, Twentieth Century-Fox, 1950.)

Germany as woman in *Fraulein*. (Publicity still, *Fraulein*, Twentieth Century-Fox, 1958, courtesy of Photofest.)

From subversive sexuality to puppet shows: Elvis in *GI Blues*. (*GI Blues*, Paramount Pictures, 1960.)

Coca-Cola, Communists, and Cagney at the Brandenburg Gate in *One, Two, Three*. (*One, Two, Three*, The Mirisch Corporation, 1961.)

The troubling American presence in *Town Without Pity*. (*Town Without Pity*, The Mirisch Corporation, 1961.)

A Different Kind of Romance on the Spanish Steps: *The Roman Spring of Mrs. Stone*. (*The Roman Spring of Mrs. Stone*, Warner Brothers Pictures, 1961)

Arriving at Hollywood's home-away-from-home in *Two Weeks in Another Town*. (*Two Weeks in Another Town*, Metro-Goldwyn-Mayer, 1962.)

Hepburn parodies herself in *Paris, When it Sizzles*. (*Paris, When it Sizzles*, Richard Quine Productions, 1964.)

5

Marrying the Enemy

The Occupation Romance

In the immediate aftermath of World War II, America found itself in a situation that far exceeded the ideological reach of the Weltanschauung around which it had previously organized itself. Although ventures into colonialism at the turn of the century had made the country somewhat familiar with global politics and its consequences, little prepared the country for the stage on which it would find itself after 1941. Any hopes of utilizing the distance from Europe in order to hide from Old World troubles vanished. The postwar occupations of Germany and Japan highlighted this new relationship to the world perhaps more than any other set of events. America and Americans were now operationally dedicated to other parts of the world for the long term. The occupation was not a war with an end in sight, but a new kind of relationship that, at least from the viewpoint of 1945, appeared to be permanent. Hollywood films served as one of many venues in which Americans tried to interpret their new role vis á vis their former enemies.

The American military served as the most consistent contact between the Old World and the New in the fifty years following World War II. So it is not surprising that the Hollywood films that were both made and set in Europe in the postwar years, those runaway films that form the focus of this book, include stories of American GIs. Perhaps a bit more surprising is how much these films resemble the films we have already examined. First, the films are romances. In fact, the films that depict encounters between uniformed Americans and Europeans represent some of the initial instances of the use of romance as metaphor for the new set of relations between the

Old World and the New. Secondly, the films use travel abroad as a part of the characters' justification for entering into the relationship. Thus, while the military duties of the characters add something to the general plotline, many of the distinctive features of the travelogue romance as we have come to recognize it remain intact, down to filmic tours of Old World landscapes and architectural beauties. Thus, the "occupation romance" forms a subcategory of the travelogue romance. The military and the representation of it in its European setting reveal much about the attitudes Hollywood reproduced regarding American–European relations in general.

The ways in which Germans and Americans related to each other after 1945 provided film writers with a rich ground for romance. Over the course of a decade the American role shifted from enemy to conqueror to occupier to educator to savior and finally to ally. The Germans morphed from enemy to vanquished to beggar to schoolchild to victim and then to ally. Likewise, the GI entering Germany initially found himself in a battle, but as time went by, on a much more pleasant tour of duty, namely as a soldier in a generally welcomed protection force. The travelogue romance under the conditions of occupation animates the various arguments regarding what it meant for America to be an occupying world power, forced into an intimate relationship with those who were very recently brutal enemies. Thus, a subset of the travelogue romances, which we will refer to as 'occupation romances,' emerges in which the asymmetrical political and economic relationship between the lovers in question, their differing experiences of war, and the external bureaucratic forces of the U.S. military combine to create the narrative tension and comic situations necessary to drive the films.

The discussion begins and ends with films directed by Billy Wilder in Berlin. *A Foreign Affair* (1948) depicts the newly conquered Berlin as a den of iniquity in which American morality must prevail over the remnants of National Socialist ideology. When Wilder returns to Berlin in 1961 for *One, Two, Three,* the aggressions of World War II have been replaced by Cold War tensions. Berlin, now a much more charming den of iniquity, is the last bastion of Western freedom against the tyranny of Soviet rule. The occupation troops have been replaced by the soldiers of capitalism, in the form of a Coca-Cola executive. In between the two Wilder Berlin films we find a set of films, including *I Was a Male War Bride* (Howard Hawks, 1949), *The Big Lift* (George Seaton, 1950), *Fräulein* (Henry Koster, 1958), and *GI Blues* (Norman Taurog, 1960), in which the discourse of distrust and occupation gradually gives way to a narrative of empathy and integration. The films narrate the ideological transformation in American popular sentiment of Germany as a symptom of moral decay to an example of successful rehabilitation.

Gender Politics at War's End

One very early issue that would take on metonymic characteristics for the entire range of feelings regarding American attitudes toward their vanquished enemy would be the policies regarding fraternization. The ever-shifting rules and attitudes regarding the regulation of sexual activity between the GIs and the local population became a barometer of the state of the relations between the United States and Germany. While initially uttered as a slur, a decade after the war the term 'war bride' had lost most of its pejorative implications and descriptive power.

Even before the war's end, many Germans fled toward and not from the Americans. They presumed they would be governed by a more liberal set of values than those they faced with the Soviet invaders. There was no vibrant insurgency against American occupation after May 8, 1945. Moreover, unlike its previous colonial experiences and even unlike the occupation of Japan, in Germany and Italy, the United States found itself in the position of a friendly occupier of a country with which it shared a common, hegemonic cultural heritage and racial identity.[1] Because of the ensuing Cold War split of Germany, the questions of occupation and of protection became more acute north of the Alps than they did in Italy. The military, economic, and political asymmetry between Americans and Germans led to a complicated set of relationships that had to be negotiated. Americans had to explain to themselves what their new role as occupiers meant. Who were the peoples who were being 'occupied,' and how were Americans, specifically the members of the occupational forces, meant to relate to their new European 'neighbors'?

At the same time that Americans were adjusting to their new global role, they also had to adjust to changing conditions at home. The 'Rosie the Riveter' generation of American women had gained self-confidence and work skills through their own part in the war effort. Their wartime experiences would, in coming decades, feed into the rise of second-wave feminism and women's greater presence in the public sphere. However, at the moment of the war's end, victory meant a return to a prewar normalcy. At least initially, the women who staffed the factory floors, mines, and mills during the war offered little public protest regarding the loss of their newfound autonomy and economic independence.[2]

If the women on the home front exhibited no sense of entitlement about their jobs at the end of the war, hegemonic culture did express strong opinions about their claim on returning men. If the women were to return home to the victorious soldiers, public discourse presumed that the victorious soldiers would return home to them. Thus, the marriageable men and women, having endured the privations of the depression and the war, could begin to construct new and prosperous lives together. Achievement of this "happily ever after," this reward for victory, was complicated by a number of factors, not the least of which were the changing expectations of women and the psychological scars of warfare left on the returning vets.[3] But, at least at home, the social fantasy of the returning hero as bridegroom was the broadly accepted normative ideal.

For the soldier who continued to serve in Europe, however, the role of victor was less clear. The politics of the postwar era demanded that the occupying soldiers change themselves from barbaric warriors to benevolent conquerors. Yet the model of the victor as husband and father that formed the norm at home was denied to the occupation soldier. Moreover, the home front demanded strict antifraternization policies, so that these men would eventually return home to the American women awaiting them.

The phenomenon of the war bride, defined as the foreign spouse of U.S. military personnel stationed abroad, found its way into the American popular press as soon as the war ended. In fact, panic about the morale and sexual activity of troops abroad began even before the war in the Pacific had concluded. "Stories about G.I.s and German women appear frequently in the American press, and wives in the States sent a flood of letters to their husbands overseas."[4] These concerns led to the formation of Bring Back Daddy clubs, which caused considerable political furor in the summer of 1945.[5] Regardless of how one framed the issue, it was easy to detect tremendous fear on the part of many, especially young women, that easing restrictions on fraternization would disrupt domestic sexual politics. Polls taken in the summer of 1945 suggest that Americans on the home front were notably concerned about the question of GI conduct in Germany. Sixty-seven percent of the women (70% of those 30 and under) and 59 percent of all respondents expressed interest in keeping GIs away from the recently vanquished Germans.[6] Yet, despite this strong opposition, General Eisenhower and the U.S. occupation authorities had difficulty enforcing the Congressional ban on contact between soldiers and the civilian population, especially women. As Petra Goedde notes, "by the summer of 1945, not even its strongest supporters deemed the continuation of the ban practical or even possible."[7]

Did giving up the fraternization ban mean that Americans were again losing the peace after winning the war, just as they had after World War I? Some Americans thought so. By not being able to control the social conduct of troops, the military government could not impose the rigid occupation it had outlined in the occupation directive. Yet others, among them high ranking military officials, came to doubt the wisdom of such a harsh occupation directive in light of the conditions

in postwar Germany. These officials played a crucial role in overturn-
ing the fraternization ban and allowing GIs to interact freely with
German civilians. For them, fraternization was an integral aspect of
the social and political reeducation of Germany.[8]

Goedde's summary of the debate about fraternization shows what a hot but-
ton issue it was at the end of the war.

The reversal of fraternization policies in October 1945 was less a matter
of a change in home front attitudes than it was a response to military needs.
In the States, fear that the soldiers were simply on sexual holiday persisted.
When the soldier returned home with a foreign bride, it was not seen as a
sign of this holiday having been concluded; rather it was a symptom of the
libertine attitude now brought home. Not only was the GI sleeping with the
enemy, insofar as he brought her home, he was flaunting his sexual decadence. Furthermore, he was not living up to his end of the presumed bargain
that, upon the cessation of hostilities, everyone would resume the story the
way they had left it.

The violation of an unspoken sexual contract was not the only concern
that surrounded the GIs' relationships with German women. There were, in
fact, real public health issues at stake as well. The collapsed German economy combined with the economic power of the Allied forces sent a large
number of women into the sexual work force. This, in turn, led to an epidemic
of sexually transmitted diseases. "In July 1946, the VD rate exceeded one in
four among American troops."[9] In short, revised sexual expectations were not
the only things that women on the home front feared their soldiers would
bring back from Germany. These anxieties provide the tension that underlies
the first of the occupation romances we will examine, Billy Wilder's *A Foreign
Affair,* and that are moderated by the other films in the cycle.

Working Woman v. War Bride
in *A Foreign Affair*

As we noted in Chapter One, the American film industry arguably had a longer
and more closely tied relationship with Germany than with any other country.
Long before the rise of National Socialism forced many German filmmakers
to flee to America, the studios had fostered close ties with the successful
German film industry of the 1920s. Hollywood products had long enjoyed
success in German markets and, at least until the advent of the talkies, German films had played well in America. Moreover, Hollywood studios invested
in German film production in the 1920s and early 1930s. The immigration

in the 1920s and 1930s, first economically and then politically motivated, of so many German speaking actors, directors, and producers, as well as a vast array of film technicians, only intensified the long-standing relationship. Therefore, it is not surprising that, at the end of the war, studio executives would take an interest in what would become of the German market.

Billy Wilder, who was born in Vienna and worked in Berlin, fled Germany when the Nazis came to power. He immigrated to southern California in 1933. In the summer of 1945, Wilder took up an invitation by the Office of Military Government of the United States (OMGUS) to travel to the devastated German territories to assess the state of the German film industry. The supposed purpose of the trip was to suggest ways in which Hollywood could assist the occupational authorities. The report that Wilder drew up at the end of the trip offered a virtual Hollywood takeover as the best possible solution.[10]

As a part of the comments published regarding the ideological potential of film in Germany, Wilder suggested that entertaining films regarding German–American relations would be the best tool for reeducating Germans. Citing *Mrs. Miniver* (William Wyler, 1942) as an example, Wilder pitches a love story between an American GI and a German "Fräulein" as the ideal vehicle for propaganda through entertainment. He, of course, offers his services to write and direct such a film. Thus, although he does not stick to his initial plot outline, *A Foreign Affair* appears to have been conceived of from the start as an occupation film in two senses of the word. First of all, it is a film set in the conditions of American military occupation of Berlin. Secondly it is a film designed to provide a model of how Hollywood itself might occupy and monopolize the German film industry.

Wilder initially intended to create a model for how Hollywood could replace German films for Germans with American films for Germans. By the time the production was in place, however, Germans had already begun making their own films again. Moreover, there is no indication that Wilder's 'Morgenthau Plan' for German filmmaking resonated with anyone other than Wilder himself.[11] But the chaotic and exotic setting of a destroyed Germany was proving to be an interesting location for filmic storytelling. Two German films, *The Murderers Are Among Us* (Wolfgang Staudte, 1946) and *Somewhere in Berlin* (Gerhard Lamprecht, 1946), as well as Roberto Rossellini's *Germania, Anno Zero* (1948), all received good reviews in the United States.[12] Moreover, by the end of the war, the studios had strong working relationships with the U.S. armed forces, which had been built both through collaboration on the combat and propaganda films made during the war and the military service, whether symbolic or real, of many members of the film industry. Thus, with Western control of much of German territory, Paramount and other American studios began looking for ways to make use of the narrative and scenic possibilities of occupied Germany.

The opening sequence of *A Foreign Affair* serves two primary purposes. Through its use of famous aerial file footage of war-ravaged Berlin it situates this romantic comedy in the heart of what the popular press referred to at the time as the world's most dangerous city. The footage, some of the most thorough depictions of the devastation wrought by the Allied air campaign and the Battle of Berlin, reveals the former capital of the Third Reich to have been reduced to canyons of rubble. The sequence also presents a congressional delegation sent to Berlin to investigate the morale and work of the American occupying forces. This delegation, led operationally if not officially by Phoebe Frost, seems to take as its mission to curtail the sexual decadence of the occupation forces. The sequence also sets up caricatures of the congressional factions of the time. The Texan lauds the work of the American military in the war. The Bronx Jewish leftist reminds his interlocutors that the Soviets were also responsible for the victory. The Democratic chair of the committee is sickly and ineffectual, whereas Frost, a Republican from Iowa, is the picture of straight-laced efficiency and decorum.

The rest of the story follows Congresswoman Frost as she discovers the rampant fraternization of the U.S. occupation forces with German women. She casts her eye on Captain John Pringle, a fellow Iowan, as an example of the upright soldier worthy of praise (and eventually affection). Actually, Pringle is having an affair with a sultry German nightclub singer. The inevitable love triangle ensues, one that pits the career woman Frost (played by Jean Arthur) against the seductive Nazi, Erika von Schlütow (Marlene Dietrich), in competition for the affections of Captain Pringle (John Lund).

Phoebe Frost presents a relatively two-dimensional character. Overplayed in the tradition of the screwball comedy of the 1930s, Frost caricatures the working women of the war era. Although she is shown as clearly more competent than her male colleagues, she is also depicted as absurdly uptight and prudish. The plot rests on the joke that this no-longer-young career woman will become sexualized. The joke of her sexuality is set up when Captain Pringle inquires after Frost's history of intimacy. She tells of having fallen for a smooth-talking Southerner, whose political, and therefore in her case professional, affiliations prevented their romance. In essence, the humor of the scene, and of the film in general, only functions if her career is construed as an obstacle to be overcome. As a congresswoman, she stands for upholding the moral integrity of the troops; as a woman, she comes to understand the pull of sexuality so far away from home.

Herein lies the construction of the fraternization issue in this film. Pringle is allied with the enemy. Frost sets out to expose the treachery of intimacy with foreign women. She quite literally asserts herself as the representative of the girls back home when she delivers to Captain Pringle a cake from his hometown sweetheart. Pringle, in turn, sells this symbol of affection for a mattress for his German lover. When Frost discovers the cake in a seedy nightclub, it confirms her suspicions that the women at home are being forsaken for the morally questionable "Fräuleins." This attitude persists when she herself becomes the one who is fighting for Pringle's affection.

Her sexual competitor, von Schlütow, is portrayed as having clear political ties to the Nazis. Yet, the film uses her to complicate the depiction of the German women of whom Frost is suspicious. Despite the film's effort to give von Schlütow an objectionable past, she retains a kind of legitimacy. Among other things, even as she reveals Pringle's deception to Frost, she sympathizes with Frost's plight. If the film portrays von Schlütow as in material need, Frost appears, at that moment, to be even more disadvantaged. She may be able to attract voters, but she does not seem able to attract a man. Thus, the sexual depravity of the soldiers confronts the sexual deprivation of the congresswoman.

While apparently junior to her male colleagues in age, Frost is both every bit their political equal and equally as desexualized as they are. The film constantly equates middle age with lack of sexuality. When Colonel Plummer, who generally serves as the voice of reason in the film, is accused of fraternization, the joke centers on the impossibility of this scenario, as he has just become a grandfather.[13]

The film suggests in the end that Pringle and Frost will marry, but getting them to that point requires an ideological adjustment. Frost defrosts herself by resorting to the black market to purchase a dress. The dress replaces her professional attire, namely her grey congressional suit. At least visually, Frost is only able to make herself attractive to Pringle, and thereby win out over her German competitor, by giving up the trappings of her career. Thus, the message of the film is that the American woman can win back the soldier, but only by rededicating herself to beauty and subservience.

Regulating the War Bride

A *Foreign Affair* addresses the perceived problem of war brides, sexual opportunism in postwar Germany, and the redomestication of career women. Foreign amorous liaisons appear as transgressions of American ideals. *I Was a Male War Bride* places war brides in an entirely different light. By parodying the bureaucratic machinations to which those who married U.S. military service personnel were submitted, the film offers a more sympathetic portrayal of the conditions under which such relationships might develop.

This sympathy is made possible by the film's primary conceit, namely that of gender reversal, and helped along by making the beloved foreigner a member of the Allied Forces. Moreover, the film assures the viewer that such relationships are under the paternalistic eye of government bureaucracy.

I Was a Male War Bride was a Twentieth Century-Fox production made approximately a year after *A Foreign Affair* and directed by Howard Hawks. The screenplay, based on a memoir entitled *I Was an Alien Spouse of Female Military Personnel Enroute to the United States Under Public Law 271 of the Congress* by Henri Rochard and credited to Charles Lederer, Leonard Spigelgass, and Hagar Wilde, was an autobiographical account of Rochard's own experiences with U.S. Military bureaucracy. This screwball comedy filmed on location in western Germany tells the story of a Women's Air Corps officer, Catherine Gates, and her tumultuous professional relationship with the French captain, Henri Rochard. Assigned to their third mission together, the two finally fall in love and decide to marry. The rest of the film centers on the couple's efforts to get Army permission to marry, to find a place to consummate their marriage, and to ensure that Henri can accompany Catherine back to the United States. While there are strictly outlined procedures for brides accompanying their new husbands back to the United States (the Public Law 271 of the book's title), a foreign groom confuses the military bureaucracy. The couple is finally united on the ship bound for the United States after Henri resorts to cross-dressing in order to be allowed on board.

The film takes place, for the most part, in the war-torn American sector of western Germany, where significant portions of it were filmed. Unlike *A Foreign Affair*, which portrays Germans as crooked and unreliable, *I Was a Male War Bride* shows them as capably reassuming the administration of their laws. The only exception is found in the opening sequence in which spoken German itself is deployed as a source of humor, as a taxi driver and a traffic cop argue about how to get to Heidelberg. This is the kind of humor made possible by the increased contact that Americans had with Germans due to the occupation. The black market, a central theme in Wilder's film, functions here as nothing more than a slapstick device exploited as part of a prank Gates plays on Rochard. In short, Germany is not the problem *I Was a Male War Bride* is trying to solve. On the contrary, in portraying a functional Germany, the film sets up the notion that the choice of a European to marry an American could be based on something other than opportunism.

In its attempt to offer a Germany that exhibits more than merely the scars of defeat, director Howard Hawks deploys location footage of berubbled Germany relatively sparingly. Equally as often, he sets the actors in front of intact Old World facades that suggest the two characters' missions together have been anything but a hardship. More so than *A Foreign Affair*, *I Was a Male*

War Bride offers Germany as a travelogue locale. Gates and Rochard's trip down the Rhine reveals both towering vineyards and a bombed out bridge. Later, they ride their motorcycle through farm fields for hours, suspecting that there is no passable road nearby, only to discover that they have been driving parallel to one the whole time. In short, the film counterbalances almost every instance of lingering destruction with one of infrastructural normalcy. Their trip through the bucolic German countryside sells the scenery as everything but a battleground.

Set far from Berlin, where the Cold War was raging, *I Was a Male War Bride* is significant for its normalization of the notion that Americans were a part of the administrative fabric of Germany. The expedition forces are portrayed as a relatively tight-knit and functional community working out of the quaint university town of Heidelberg. Catherine is shown to have many suitors, such that her choice of Henri is a deliberate one. Her main American admirer exhibits frustration at her choice of the Frenchman, but even then refrains from the kind of xenophobic slurs that one might have expected in 1949.

The sequence opens up with a long shot of Rochard sitting alone at a table. The cut reveals it to be a POV of three of Catherine's friends (a man, Ramsey, and two women) sitting at another table discussing her choice.

> RAMSEY: I can't understand an American marrying a foreigner she hardly knows. It's ridiculous and disgraceful.
> LAWRENCE: I declare, I just can't see why she wants to.
> BILLINGS: You all better get glasses.
> RAMSEY: Why are you women such pushovers for this (p)arlez vous hand-kissing stuff?

The conversation reveals both a bit of the prejudice attached to war marriages and a defense of Catherine's choice.

The spectator roots for Rochard, as he works his way through the bureaucratic process, which requires him to fill out paperwork on his gynecological history. His emasculation only creates more sympathy for the women who share his experience and allies him with them more strongly. His intentions appear serious, that is, we do not assume that he intends to abuse the privilege of immigrating to America. Moreover, their relationship is built on continued shared experience, not a one-night fling. Thus, Rochard is trustworthy. The film animates this trust as much through the deployment of the star system, Rochard being played by Cary Grant, as through the diegesis. Sympathy for a French male war bride rides squarely on Grant's status. It is easy to imagine that a French star in that role would have offered a different interpretation.

Curiously enough, the bureaucracy makes no differentiation between the French and the Germans; they are equally alien. The German brides are portrayed as sympathetic, quietly and respectfully working their way through a process that will allow them to go to America. The fact that Cary Grant, a powerful sex symbol in 1949 Hollywood, would ally himself with these women suggests that the figure of the war bride, at least one that seems to have resonated commercially, was becoming transformed. *I Was a Male War Bride* came in as one of the three top-grossing films of 1949.

What was at stake in the late 1940s such that Twentieth Century-Fox would have taken on this project? First of all, the subject of the war bride, regardless of how it might have been treated, fit the formula of a timely topic that would guarantee commercial success. Fox's production executive, Darryl Zanuck, had a history of productive cooperation with the armed forces, one that would continue throughout the 1950s and early 1960s. The U.S. expedi tion forces, whose cooperation was necessary for this production, needed to maintain troop morale. The latter could have been seriously undermined by any domestic attempt to curtail the amorous ambitions of American GIs. In fact, it is significant that Rochard continually quotes Public Law 271 that legalizes and legitimates marriage between American service personnel and foreign nationals. This law undid previous antifraternization legislation and came at the urging of Dwight D. Eisenhower and other military leaders who found the fraternization prohibition unworkable. Unlike Wilder's film, which sides heavily with an earlier domestic discourse of distrust regarding war brides, this occupation romance merely continues the cooperation between Hollywood and the military that began during World War II.

Germania, Anno Quattro

The idea that Fox would use military interest as its guide for negotiating the terrain of the travelogue romance under conditions of occupation also explains why it would not have remained one-sided in its approach to the question of war brides. If Americans had an ideological need to stabilize the story they would tell about West Germans in the late forties, the question of Berlin and where it would fall into the Cold War equation was still very open.[14]

In June 1948, the Soviet forces in Berlin began a blockade intended to force the Western allies to concede control of the former German capital. All land routes through the Soviet-occupied eastern zones of the country were blocked, and only air traffic could reach the city. On June 27, 1948, General Lucius D. Clay, who had succeeded Eisenhower as Commander of OMGUS (Office of the Military Government of the United States), ordered an airlift of food and supplies to sustain the city and keep those parts controlled by the Western allies from falling into Soviet hands. A few days later, President Harry S. Truman approved the order. Thus began a new relationship between Germans and Americans, one that placed Americans quite literally in the role of protectors and providers for their former enemies.

This reversal of the relationship to Germany had been three years in the making. Nevertheless, Americans still needed to explain to themselves their new role as savior of a people who had recently caused so much death and destruction. Illustrated magazines in the United States were filled with stories of the daring and skill of the American flyers. George Seaton's *The Big Lift* (1950), most of which was filmed after the blockade was lifted in May 1949, moves the discussion of the relationship beyond merely the terms of occupation. It is a didactic film that organizes the German–American relationship between the poles of isolation and integration, a narrative structure for which romance is well suited.

The Big Lift opens with a procedural description that situates the film as much within the Italian cinematic landscape of the moment as it does within its central European political context.

> This picture was made in occupied Germany. All scenes were photographed in the exact locale associated with the story, including episodes in the American, French, British, and Russian Sectors of Berlin. With the exception of Montgomery Clift and Paul Douglas, all military personnel appearing in this film are actual members of the U.S. Armed Forces on duty in Germany.

It reads as much as a rhetorical documentary film as a feature film romance. *The Big Lift* deploys the political and emotional appeal of neorealism in the service of selling Operation Vittles to the American public. Although the Berlin airlift was over by the time the film was made, U.S. military officials understood that American engagement in Berlin was going to be a long-term commitment.

The film begins with its main characters happily stationed in Hawaii watching a Movietone News segment on the Soviet blockade of Berlin and the American decision to commence an airlift. With the war over, the soldiers' current duties seem to revolve mainly around romancing the women of the island. This idyllic situation will soon be contrasted with their new orders to report to Frankfurt. Thus, the film begins by suggesting the degree to which the airlift was a sacrifice on the part of those who performed it. The soldiers arrive in Germany unprepared for the cold climate in which they find themselves. The temperature shift itself has metaphorical implications. The airmen are being sent into the chill of the Cold War. Coats appear as important props throughout the film, suggesting something like ideological as well as thermal protection.

Of the occupation romances discussed here, none structures itself more like a lesson than does *The Big Lift*. The story concentrates on two soldiers stationed at the airlift, one a handsome young playboy, Danny McCollough (played by Montgomery Clift), who appears young enough not to have taken part in the war itself and who sees his assignments as sexual opportunities. The other, Hank Kowalski, a somewhat older ground control expert and veteran of the war, resents the thought that he must help a people whom he finds morally despicable. We will soon discover that Kowalski's anger toward the Germans stands in for a broader public attitude toward Germany at which the film will aim its rhetoric. Having set up this friendship, the film will follow the two through their romantic experiences in Berlin.

Before the film sets up the romances that will make the case for why the airlift is necessary, it first sells the technical wonder of the mission. Planes take off every three minutes, fly two hours from Frankfurt to Berlin, unload in twenty minutes and then return to Frankfurt. Unlike the glorious life they led in Hawaii, these airmen are now hard at work. A reporter convinces Danny to allow him to do a feature story for Danny's hometown newspaper about the airlift. Danny agrees so as to win some time in Berlin to track down a young German woman he has just met. When the reporter is asked why he thinks he will succeed in freeing up Danny for a few days of touring Berlin, the reporter answers: "You know, the Air Force doesn't mind a little publicity now and again." During the tour given to the reporter, the technological advances of the Air Force are put on display. The display functions like a military procession, parading the military's newest gadgets for friend and foe alike. The sequence sells the airlift as an opportunity both to help the Germans and to display to the Soviets American air superiority.

Once the first half of the film has made the case for the military mission, the second half dedicates itself to justifying America's political mission in postwar Germany. It does this by setting up the two GIs with two contrasting German women. Danny uses the extra day he has gained in Berlin to find Frederika Burkhardt, a German woman whom he met at a celebration in honor of the airlift a few days earlier. Hank develops a complicated relationship with Gerdi, whom he treats with the same disrespect that he affords the rest of the Germans.

Danny's twenty-four-hour leave in Berlin allows the film to follow him through the war-torn city. He meets up with Frederika at her work place. The film sets her up in the stereotypical shot of the postwar German woman, with a scarf on her head and working as a *Trümmerfrau*, a "rubble woman" employed to clear the debris of the destroyed city. Despite her middle-class background and professional skills, Frederika, who is, by German law, required to work, explains that this difficult and dirty work provides more ration coupons than other jobs. When Danny's uniform becomes soiled, he is forced into German civilian clothing and thereby given an understanding of the life of a Berliner without proper identification. He must hide from the U.S. military police, he is trapped by the Soviet police, he buys cigarettes underground, and he is generally treated with suspicion.

The film offers some of the most authentic depictions of bombed-out Berlin available. Danny and Frederika stroll through the Tiergarten, a former forest in the middle of the city that has been stripped of all of its trees, which were harvested and used for fuel in the first winter after the war. The segment also contains numerous sequences in which whole conversations held in German are presented without subtitles. This allows the audience to identify with Danny's already enhanced confusion. Thus, the film not only employs nonprofessional actors in the military scenes, it also offers a filmic documentation of the aftermath of the war in Berlin that is equal to any film on the subject.[15] The entire sequence is designed to portray the physical destruction of the city and make a case for why it requires help.

It is during Danny's tour of berubbled Berlin that the film offers a concrete explanation of Hank's resentment of the Germans. While sitting at a nightclub, Hank recognizes a former POW camp guard who had tortured him during the war. He pursues the man through the streets of Berlin. When Hank finally catches up with him, he explains how it was that the man forced him to learn German by making him learn tongue twisters and then beating him when he mispronounced them. This is Hank's explanation for why he now refuses to speak German. He then proceeds to offer his former captor English lessons by the same method, beating him within an inch of his life. Later, he breaks down in front of Gerdi, because the revenge he had hoped for actually makes him feel worse rather than better. This scene serves as the film's lesson regarding the proper approach to a former enemy. Revenge merely reduces one to the level of the former perpetrator, thereby destroying one's moral position.

Hank is the film's agent of reeducation, the idealist American policy towards postwar Germans. Gerdi, a working-class daughter of former Nazis, strives to understand what democracy means. Through explanation, provocation, and insult, Hank endeavors to answer her. In so doing he offers some radical suggestions for 1949. At a time when Hollywood was recovering from the first round of HUAC investigations and red-baiting, Hank provides a clear defense of rights of free speech and the right to disagree with one's government. He admits American anti-Semitism and lauds efforts to address it. Of all of the American social ills the film could have mentioned at that point, it picks up the one most closely associated with the HUAC investigations. At another point in the film, a German character who had traveled widely in America notes that thing he liked about Americans was their willingness to openly criticize their government. In the end, Gerdi becomes an ideal democratic subject, one unwilling to put up with tyranny, even from Hank. She becomes the film's ideological poster child. Curiously enough, the film does not end with the couple's intention to go to the United States. Rather, it sticks to a much more conciliatory message. Hank and Gerdi express a desire to stay in Germany to continue the reeducation campaign.

The film makes a plea for democratic values and insists that not only Germans but also Americans live up to them. At the same time, it lampoons the Soviets. They are portrayed as obsessively distrustful and corrupt. The Soviet military police are keystone cops, incapable of both comprehending and then enforcing the laws. Their spy ring reveals itself to be a gravy train off of which clever West Berliners survive. Frederika's neighbor is employed by the Soviets to count the number of planes deployed in the airlift. The Americans know of his work and view it as harmless. He keeps the numbers he reports low so as to help the Soviets prove their suspicion that the Americans, in their reports, are inflating the number of flights made to Berlin. In short, while their actions make the airlift necessary, the film depicts the Soviets as more ridiculous than dangerous.

Frederika, in turn, embodies all of the difficulties of the new relationship between Germans and Americans. She has close ties to the Nazi past, which she both refuses to reveal and to relinquish. She abuses Danny's love and sympathy in order to convince him to marry her and take her to the United States, where her SS German husband is living. Danny discovers her plot at the last minute and pulls out. He is left disillusioned both by love and by the humanitarian military mission of which he had been a part.

This is where the film leaves us. Danny does not berate Frederika for her deception, which goes unpunished. But the film's conclusion insists that she is a symptom that Americans must continue to work hard to address. Rebuilding Germany into an ally will require finding the right Germans to start the effort. The right German, as embodied in Gerdi, is someone willing to make a break with her past and embrace American ideological principles. *The Big Lift* offers a cautionary tale regarding war brides. Danny learns that sympathy is a sentiment provoked by present suffering that is itself caused by a troubled past. It is portrayed as an inappropriate emotion upon which to build a relationship. Such cannot be the basis of an American–German partnership. The successful affiliation, namely Hank and Gerdi's, builds its foundation on shared values. They are 'Marshall Plan Missionaries,' intent upon democratizing Germany. Despite having had its main character deceived by a German woman, the film insists that America must stay in Germany to assure that Germans arrive at a position where they make their decisions based on moral rather than material principles.

Understanding the *Fräulein*

By the mid-1950s, American troops stationed in Germany had become an established fact of U.S. foreign policy. West Germany had rearmed and joined the North Atlantic Treaty Organization (NATO) and thus counted as an ally, even more so than France, which initially shunned NATO and only later accepted provisional membership. The United States was thus committed by treaty to the defense of the Federal Republic of Germany and much of the rest of Western Europe.

Interestingly, during the same period in which the United States was normalizing its ties to the new West German state, the trope of the war bride seems to disappear from American discourse. Ultimately, this disappearance relates as much to changing domestic circumstances as it does to attitudes toward Germany. A decade past the war, the questions of the loyalty of the veterans to the "Rosie the Riveter" generation were gradually replaced, at least in popular film, by the mating rituals of a younger set. Moreover, with the war long over and Germans again enjoying economic prosperity, the accusation of sleeping with the enemy no longer packed a punch. The Twentieth Century-Fox production of *Fräulein* (dir. Henry Koster) in 1958 is therefore all the more interesting. If the figure of the war bride was unlikely to resonate to the same degree in the late 1950s as it had a decade before, what would have moved the studio to develop the James McGovern novel into a film? While the production efficiencies of runaway filmmaking may have made the decision easier, the answer, it would seem, lies in the genderized notion of Germany that had developed alongside many of the films about the occupation.

Fräulein weaves a tale about the fate of a woman in postwar Germany. It begins during the war in Cologne, where a U.S. Army captain POW, Foster McClain, has avoided his captors and taken brief refuge in the home of Professor Ulrich Angermann and his daughter, Erika. They assist him, allowing him to return to the front and continue the war. At war's end, Erika finds herself in Berlin looking for her fiancé, whom she believes to be lying wounded in a hospital near there. In the ensuing months, she has to avoid rape by one Soviet soldier and marriage to another. She is almost tricked into prostitution by some acquaintances. She toils as a rubble woman clearing away the debris of the war by hand, and finally, she works in a humiliating act involving a dunk tank in a nightclub for Americans. There Major McClain recognizes her and begins to court her.

In the course of their courtship the true power imbalance of their relationship emerges. The American military authorities, of which McClain is one,
exercise economic and administrative power over German civilians. The film
shows that the Americans have power over Erika's history as well. Depending
on what files they keep and use, Erika can be seen either as a victim running
to escape the advances of a Russian officer or as a prostitute willing to sell
her body for creature comforts. In the end, when a sympathetic American
serviceman cleans her record, we are both relieved for her and fully aware of
how little she can control how her story plays out.

While the film plays with many of the tropes recognizable in the travelogue romance, including the use of a tourist locale to set the stage for the
romantic turning point, the setting and romance animate a different set of
concerns. *Fräulein* asks the spectator to identify with a foreign national rather
than with an American. While the film starts out with Foster's escape from
his German captors, that is merely a device to introduce Erika, whose fate
the rest of the film will follow. When the two unite at the end of the film, we
see the union as a solution to her problems. The film offers little clue as to
what he might get out of the relationship. In fact, that question seems almost
irrelevant. McClain and the rest of the characters in the film function as little
more than signposts for the myriad of problems Erika faces in reestablishing
her life after the war.

So, why would Twentieth Century-Fox decide to make an expressly pro-
German film in 1958? While the studio had always shown itself ready to
provide ideological support to the military for whatever issues that were in
need of public persuasion, it is hard to see what they might have been in 1958.
By then, West Germany had already entered NATO, thereby changing the
Federal Republic to official ally instead of an occupied former enemy. Soviet
creation of the Warsaw Pact in the wake of German entry into NATO insured
that American troops were unlikely to leave German soil for a long time. At
best, the film provides a sympathetic view of a former adversary: a view that
underscored West Germany's need for American solidarity. It seems more
likely, however, that the reasons for pursuing this production were practical in
nature. The production would have been an efficient use of resources already
deployed to Europe. The production did not need to set up a large first unit
in Germany since it makes, at best, only partial use of location work. In fact,
there are no scenes in which one could be certain that the characters were
actually shot on location. All of the Berlin work appears to be a combination
of process shots and studio reconstruction of rubble scenes. Thus, the studio
could easily deploy a crew working on the many combat films produced in
the era to shoot the footage necessary for the rear projection work. The trip
along the Rhine marks the only spot in the film in which the main characters

actually appear to be on location, but even that could be attributed to good process work.[16] No German actors, at least German actors working in Germany in the 1950s, appear in the film. In short, the studio combined a war story with a romance using an amalgamation of stock footage, second unit production, and studio work to produce a film it hoped would appeal to both male and female audiences.

The films under discussion above had, by 1957 when this film went into production, already established the trope of Germany as woman. *A Foreign Affair* set it up with Erika von Schlütow marking Germany as both corrupt and of suspicious ideological loyalties, a trait that continued in *The Big Lift*.[17] The much more sympathetic depiction of Erika Angermann in *Fräulein* extends the equation, revealing the improved standing Germany enjoyed in American public opinion by the mid-1950s. Moreover, the film presents no leading male German characters, making the viewer identify the woman's fate as that of the country as a whole.

The identification of Germany as woman begins with the very title of the film. This now somewhat dated term for girl in German goes untranslated. Thus the film's title is necessarily understood as "German girl." Yet, in the popular American discourse of the time, "Fräulein" also contained a suggestion of sexual promiscuity, the catcall employed by the linguistically inept GI It is a word that Erika comes to understand as an insult or at least an identification of something with which she does not want to be associated. It is a term that will, over the course of the film, also come to be rehabilitated.

If Erika is offered as the stand-in for Germany as a whole, the supporting characters fill out the picture as well. Erika's father, who reluctantly provides refuge for the fleeing Captain McClain, appeals, if somewhat feebly, to the long German philosophical tradition. While her personal history is grounded in the Enlightenment, she has also fallen in love with a darker side of German history, having been engaged to Hugo von Metsler, an officer of the Wehrmacht. Though not depicted as a Nazi, he is certainly co-opted by them. The Graubachs, whom Erika first encounters in Berlin when she arrives at the house of a cousin, suggest a kind of German from whom Erika differentiates herself. They are refugees from the eastern German territories who have just arrived in Berlin. The film depicts them as political opportunists, black marketers, and pimps. More than once they sell out Erika in order to protect or advance themselves.

Her encounter with the Russians presents even more evidence of the film's attempt to retell German history through the figure of Erika Angermann. The Russian colonel who rescues and then courts her constantly equates her behavior with German behavior and his own behavior as representatively Russian. When she resists him, he reads it as Germany resisting the Russians.

His marriage proposal is delivered like a unilateral peace treaty that he presumes she will accept, if only because of the asymmetry of their relationship. She literally escapes this treaty by fleeing to the American sector.

Erika's troubles do not end once she leaves the Russian occupation zone. She finds employment initially as a rubble woman, a job from which she is 'rescued' by the newly prosperous Graubachs, who attempt to trap her into their prostitution ring. Rather than succumbing to their entrapments, Erika flees into the hands of the U.S. military police.

The encounter with the M.P.s introduces an aspect of American domestic conflict into the film that is rare among the travelogue romances. It marks the first appearance of an African–American character in such films. Moreover, the film thematizes bigotry. When Herr Graubach refuses to take orders from the black M.P., Corporal Hanks, Erika apologizes as a German for Graubach's comments. The obvious sexual tension between Erika and Hanks goes undeveloped. Yet, in the end, it is Hanks who clears her record by removing a charge of prostitution, thereby making it possible for her to marry McClain.[18] Control of the files means control of history, a theme that also appears in *A Foreign Affair.*

Erika's relationship with Foster McClain then takes the allegorical reading of the film to its logical conclusion. The film depicts Erika as a problem and sympathetic Americans such as Hanks and McClain as the solution.[19] McClain himself has one American counterpart whose resistance he must overcome, namely that of the only American woman in the film. Lieutenant Dubbin, who serves as McClain's secretary, mouths the anti-war-bride position attributed to American women on the home front. She is unthreatened by the women of Berlin as long as they remain objects of sexual spectacle to be laughed at or pitied. The threat comes when McClain expresses his much more earnest intentions regarding Erika. Dubbin scoffs at the notion that an offer of marriage is required: "Don't you think that is a bit extreme," she suggests. "With these women a half dozen pair of nylons will do." McClain counters her comments with his own conflation of Erika with Germany. "Don't you think our war against the Germans should end now that it's over?" While Dubbin might resent Erika for luring the affections of McClain, McClain mouths a statement of Allied policy that she is hard-pressed to counter.

McClain does not court Erika as much as he attempts to reeducate her. In order to gain her love, he must convince her to confront her own past. The film sets up a cruise along the Rhine, a route steeped in romantic tradition both for Erika personally and Germany generally. He asks her to remember her own previous trips down the river with her father, or friends, or fiancé. It is a pseudo-Freudian experiment in which McClain makes her recall her past in order to purge her emotions. McClain tries to bring her to free herself from the binds to the past, both to the idealism of her father's philosophical tradition and to the blindness of her ex-fiancé's political choices. Erika cries briefly and then accepts McClain's romantic advances. It would seem that she accepts that the past is gone and the future lies with McClain.

The film constructs this allegorical analysis both structurally and narratively. That is to say, both the audience and fellow characters in the film conflate Erika's identity with that of Germany. Before she can be integrated into an alliance with the American, she must first free herself of an unwanted one with a Russian. She must be careful not to prostitute herself and to avoid exploitation by postwar racketeers. And, she must liberate herself from both her idealistic and militaristic German past, while retaining a sense of honor, an honor that is, in part, saved by Hanks's alteration of her file. The American soldier is then no longer marrying the enemy, but a fully rehabilitated, if still junior, partner.

GI Blues: Domesticating Elvis Abroad

In the boom years of the 1950s, the idea of the war bride ceases to threaten the American sexual economy as it did in the immediate aftermath of the war. The fact that GIs serving in Europe often returned home with brides became as normalized as relations with Europe did. This attitudinal shift is evident in *GI Blues* (Norman Taurog, 1960), an Elvis Presley vehicle that mines Presley's recently completed military service in Germany as source material. It tells the story of a company of GIs who make a bet as to who can seduce a German nightclub singer. The film can hardly be branded a runaway production, as only second unit shots of Germany were used. Nevertheless, as the military occupation film most dependent upon the tropes of the travelogue romance, it extends the picture of the sexual discourse between GIs and Germans.

Juliette Prowse plays Lili, a sanitized version of Erika von Schlütow. She is a nightclub singer, but one actively avoiding contact with randy American soldiers. While her act suggests sexual promiscuity and the nightclub owner himself seems to want to peddle her to the wealthy businessmen who frequent the club, Lili remains aloof. Set in a much more prosperous Germany, her charms cannot be purchased with stockings and Spam. Her charms are to be won by a combination of old-fashioned courting and screwball antics. But, it is not obvious that the American GI, even if it is Elvis Presley, will win her affections. In the end, he does so as the cleaned-up, postservice Elvis, who no longer represents the threat that he once did to domestic sexual order in America. As Bosley Crowther puts it in his review of the film, "Whatever else the Army has done for Elvis Presley, it has taken that indecent swivel out of his hips and turned him into a good, clean, trustworthy, upstanding American."[20] Thus, the film succeeds in showing that not only is Elvis now good clean fun for the entire family, but Germany is too. Even Elvis has to be on his best behavior to get a bride there.

The fact that the actors were not shot on location in Germany limits their interactions with the natives to a few staged moments, including Elvis singing *"Muss I' Denn"* at the puppet show. Nor does it take as its subject matter something intrinsic to recent German history, such as the fate of Erika Angermann in *Fräulein*. The film could have just as easily been set outside of a base anywhere in the United States. *GI Blues* concentrates less on cultural understandings and misunderstandings and more on the domestication of Elvis. The threat of foreign sexuality in the form of the war bride has been replaced with the homegrown threat of youthful sexuality as represented by Presley. Nevertheless, one of the constant traits of the travelogue romance remains the containment of sexuality. The foreign locale, while seemingly perfect for sexual experimentation, almost inevitably leads the characters to desire to return home to sexual rituals they better understand.

CocaColonization and the Travelogue Romance

The presence of the U.S. military in Western Europe ceased to be an occupation in the 1950s with the founding of the North Atlantic Treaty Organization and West Germany's entry into it. At that point, if not already before, the troops' mission was to protect and defend Germany from possible Soviet incursions rather than to regulate its conversion to democracy. Germany, at least the one governed from Bonn, had gone from an adversary to an ally. Also in the course of the same decade, West Germany's economy expanded rapidly, providing the United States with a significant trading partner. U.S. companies took advantage of America's new place in the world as a lever to open markets worldwide.

Germany remained a Cold War hot spot. The expanding West German economy proved increasingly irresistible for East Germans, especially well-educated ones, such that thousands annually crossed from East to West. This massive brain drain threatened the collapse of the economy in East Germany. On August 13, 1961, the government of the German Democratic Republic took measures to completely seal its border, including the construction of the Berlin Wall to divide Germany's capital city.

Billy Wilder took a crew to Berlin in the summer of 1961 to produce a comedy about East–West tensions. In the course of filming, the production crew encountered numerous difficulties in their attempt to shoot the film in both parts of the city. Wilder and crew were finishing up their production in Berlin on August 13, when the East German government erected the wall. By the time *One, Two, Three* premiered in December 1961, the Wall had been completed, and the division of Germany was not a laughing matter. In fact, one reviewer quotes a moviegoer as saying, "They'll be gagging up lung cancer next." Yet the review goes on to praise the comedic value of the film.[21]

The basic plot outline of *One, Two, Three* centers on the Berlin head of Coca-Cola. C. R. MacNamara, played by James Cagney, is a philandering diminutive dictator (to whom his wife, played by Arlene Francis, refers as "Mein Führer"), who is trying to work his way up the corporate ladder. One day he receives a phone call from the Coca-Cola CEO, Arthur Hazeltine, asking MacNamara to host his seventeen-year-old daughter, who is on a tour of Europe. Scarlett Hazeltine turns out to be a nymphomaniac who promptly sneaks off to East Berlin, falls in love with and marries a young Communist, Otto Piffl. When the CEO telephones to announce his imminent arrival in Berlin, it is incumbent upon MacNamara to either break up the marriage or turn the communist into a fitting son-in-law for an American captain of industry.

The building of the Berlin Wall created a set of narrative problems that the film needed to solve in postproduction. Thus, the film begins with a brief voice-over prologue in which MacNamara notes that the Berlin Wall is merely a sign of just how untrustworthy the East Germans are and that the story to follow supposedly serves as further illustration of the same. The subsequent narrative does not bear out MacNamara's interpretation. Yet the opening sequence introduces the contrasting visions of Berlin: East Berliners as political ideologues who spend more time parading than producing and West Berliners whose primary occupations are rebuilding and consuming. These are the stereotypes that will populate the film. The task of the film is not to contrive some sort of East–West integration narrative. Rather it is to convert the propagandistic ideologue into a Coca-Cola loving consumer.

One, Two, Three animates a variety of positions that the travelogue romance, including the occupation romances, had been developing in the course of the previous decade. While the film's main character does not go abroad in order to find romance, he does use the ruse of "language lessons" to carry on affairs with the secretaries in each of the countries in which he is stationed. His wife understands the affairs as a symptom of an international lifestyle of which she has long since grown weary. She presumes that if they return to America the 'foreign affairs' will cease. The real travelogue romance happens between Scarlett Hazeltine and the East German, Otto Piffl (played by West German heartthrob, Horst Buchholz). *One, Two, Three* calls upon both the long Ernst Lubitsch tradition of international romance, to which Billy Wilder was a direct heir, and the screwball comedy. The problem that the film narrative needs to solve is how to tell a triumphalist tale of American capitalism in the shadow of Cold War escalation.[22]

The film's humor derives from the notion that MacNamara must maintain the myth of the boss's daughter's virginal innocence in the face, not only of European sexual decadence, but also of Scarlett's own blatant promiscuity. The trope of Europe as stage for sexual experimentation and self-discovery becomes part of the lampoon. Europe offers her merely the opportunity to escape her father's gaze. She was kept under watchful eye in Paris and Rome such that, as far as her own romantic adventures are concerned, they were no different there than in her Atlanta home. Only the confusions of Cold War tensions provide enough chaos for her to find a properly inappropriate liaison. Thus, the European difference that fuels other travelogue romances is now animated by the Iron Curtain.

The other films in this chapter construct the U.S. military occupation or the stationing of American troops abroad as a background for a travelogue romance. In *One, Two, Three*, the continued American military presence in Berlin is combined with American economic dominance to set a romance in which the American's right to determine the outcome is assumed. The sites of Berlin, most prominently the Brandenburg Gate, are not presented as timeless, romantic monuments. Rather, they are depicted as trouble spots. East Berlin is a combination of the Brandenburg Gate and berubbled ruins. West Berlin is effectively a construction site covered with ads for American consumer goods. The film parodies the notion of the Old World as a site for romance.[23] When asked why she has come to Berlin in search of sexual adventure, Scarlett naïvely explains that "everybody says that Berlin is the hottest spot in the world right now." Thus, the film will make a travelogue romance out of a place that might be better avoided.

A Foreign Affair portrays Germany as an unapologetic cesspool of Nazis. By the time Wilder turns his attentions to it again in *One, Two, Three*, the Nazi past is turned into schtick and a point of shame that MacNamara can turn to his advantage. Instead of a young woman with a compromised past, as we have seen in *A Foreign Affair*, *The Big Lift*, or *Fräulein*, the German woman here, Ingeborg (played by Liselotte Pulver), is a sexually assertive secretary with neither a dark, Nazi secret nor any old-fashioned notions of virtue, only an insatiable desire for old bosses and new clothes.

Consumerism, however, holds no sway for Otto Piffl. He fights all advances made to him on material grounds. He wears old clothes and sandals (and, much to Scarlett's delight, no underwear). The film depicts him as a walking cliché, an effusive ideological machine, spouting Communist propaganda in every sentence. MacNamara's first plan is to frame him, have him arrested by the East German police, and then secretly have the marriage annulled before Scarlett's parents arrive. That plan fails when they learn that Scarlett is pregnant. The only way MacNamara can think to save his job is to transform the dirty, obnoxious communist into a capitalist aristocrat. Aristocracy, in the film, amounts to nothing more than a set of trinkets and crests, which can be bought from a count who works as a men's room attendant.

MacNamara's attempts to disguise the young communist as a young capitalist succeed, but lead to MacNamara's own defeat. Mr. Hazeltine is so enamored with the new Piffl that he offers him the job in London for which MacNamara has been vying. While, in the opening voice-over, MacNamara had claimed that the story would reveal how deceptive the East Germans are, in the end, deception has been shown to be just another tool in the capitalist's toolbox. Piffl does not so much deceive MacNamara as outmaneuver him in his own game.

Piffl's capitalist conversion is explained neither by the appeal of consumerism, nor by MacNamara's attempts to convince him that the communist regime is corrupt. Piffl is tamed by the fact that his bride is pregnant. Domestic interests come to dominate political ones. MacNamara, too, is drawn back into the domestic sphere by the end of the film. He has spent fifteen years, effectively the entire postwar era, abroad. His wife insists that life abroad is harming their family, and MacNamara's well-laid plans have continually been ruined by political turmoil. Working abroad has proven to be a sucker's game for the ambitious capitalist. In the end, the message of *One, Two, Three* is rather isolationist. Whether the communist or the capitalist, everyone ends up at home with the wife and kids.

Conclusion

How do the occupation romances fit into the larger category of the travelogue romance? At first sight, they seem to operate under a different premise. The Old World scenery used as backdrop seems more appropriate for dark tourism than sexual adventurism. For the most part, soldiers roam among the ruins of a war-torn Germany, a place in which they are charged with controlling the locals. Yet, the various forms of American intervention abroad, whether military or commercial, provided a setting for plots that parallel and occasionally overlap the travelogue romances. In fact, because many of them predate the other travelogue romances discussed up to now, the occupation romance performs necessary groundwork for the genre. Occupied Germany functions as a locale in which love will be found, because, despite the destruction of war, the settings remain romantic. Whatever difficulties external conditions might pose, sentimentality will easily overcome them. In the occupation romances, as opposed to travelogue romances generally, the American–European relationships are allowed to survive and be brought home. The necessarily political content of films in which the characters are in uniform brings with it a more openly expressed interest in using the love story as an integration device. Whether it is the former enemy turned war bride, the local boy gone sexually astray abroad, or the East German communist, the occupation romances employ the love story to redomesticate and incorporate the outlier into the dominant fiction of the 1950s American nuclear family. As in the travelogue romances, being abroad is equated with a certain sexual libertinism. The only way to contain that libidinal adventure is to repatriate the characters. The contemporary viewer was still asked to ascribe to the idea that nothing like that would happen at home.

6

The End of the
European Romance

ravelogue romances did not end at the beginning of the 1960s, but
it was clear by the beginning of the decade that they no longer held
the same position with filmmakers and audiences that they did a few
years earlier. In this concluding chapter, I would like to first survey what we
have learned about the travelogue romance as a genre. Then we will look at
a series of films that question some of the basic conceits of the travelogue
romance. Finally, we will conclude by questioning both what became of the
genre and of the larger industrial practice of runaway filmmaking.

Rick Altman has long advocated a certain structural understanding of
generic tropes that centers around a distinction between what he calls semantic and syntactic elements.[1] The semantic elements consist of particular building blocks of meaning (like words in a language) that are then arranged in a
characteristic structure (akin to a grammar). The semantic components of
the travelogue romance would include, for instance, a setting in Europe, copi-
ous shots of Old World monuments, palaces, comically small cars, location
shooting, nondiegetic traveling shots, depictions of various local rituals, and
a presumption of Europe as seat of American cultural heritage. In Altman's
system the syntactic components are those that combine the genre's various
semantic tropes into systems of meaning, that is, in this case, the standard
romantic relationship, the combination of cultural differences that make that
relationship at first attractive and then often fragile, and the traveler's choice
to stay or return home. As we have seen in earlier chapters, the genre also
develops stock characters, such as the virginal American woman looking for

sexual awakening in Europe, the American man in midlife doldrums, the poor but compelling European with nothing to offer but romance, and the down-in-the-world aristocrat drawn to American naïveté. We have seen how these and a number of other semantic and syntactic elements developed to form the travelogue romance as a genre.

In general, it is clear that not only do these films share a set of readable tropes, they are products that emerge out of a specific set of production practices, with a patterned set of actors and directors. Audrey Hepburn appears in two of the films discussed at length so far and stars in two other films of the era in which the sexually transformative qualities of the European trip play a large role, namely *Sabrina* (Billy Wilder, 1954) and *Love in the Afternoon* (Billy Wilder, 1957). Rossano Brazzi shows up in *Three Coins in the Fountain*, *Summertime*, and *Interlude*, while starring in other films in the genre including *The Barefoot Contessa* (Joseph L. Mankiewicz, 1954), *Rome Adventure* (Delmer Daves, 1962), and *Light in the Piazza* (Guy Green, 1962). As European-born actors, both Brazzi and Hepburn add something to the authenticity drive to which the travelogue romances seem to be responding, even when Hepburn plays an American.

An impulse similar to the one that made the European-born actors attractive seems to have also influenced the choice of directors for the travelogue romances. The great majority of the directors of the films in question were born in Europe, including William Wyler, Alfred Hitchcock, Jean Negulesco, David Lean, Vittorio De Sica, Douglas Sirk, William Dieterle, Billy Wilder, and Henry Koster. Some, such as Lean and De Sica, were simply European directors who had developed working relationships with Hollywood. The rest were expatriates who were returning to the continent that they had, at least professionally, long since abandoned. The travelogue romance provided these directors with the opportunity to tell tales about the complex relationship between America and Europe.

At the production level, we have also seen the centrality of the Cinecittà studios outside of Rome (and to a lesser degree, the Studios de Boulogne outside of Paris and the Geiselgasteig facilities near Munich) as a production outpost that made possible the location work that serves as such a critical semantic device in the genre. Thus, if we include production similarities in genre constructions, these films take on even greater similarity. ·

While we can be rather certain about the fact that many of these films share common conditions of production, it is equally as important to note whether or not they were understood as similar when they premiered. In order to see if anyone else perceived these films as belonging to a category, one place to look would be in the press reviews the films received. Of course, we are arguably free to diagnose a genre even if historical reviewers did not do so. But a failure to notice what seem to us to be distinct patterns of filmmaking would require an explanation. The case of travelogue romances offers a somewhat middle case. While never consistently referring to these films as a genre, reviewers often picked up upon and commented on their distinctive semantic traits.

Bosley Crowther, for instance, reviewed films for the *New York Times* from the early forties until 1968. Known for unapologetically middlebrow tastes, Crowther serves as a suitable representative of the kind of aesthetic judgment prevailing in the expanding postwar American middle class. Crowther gave his take on many of the films discussed in this study, beginning with *A Foreign Affair*. His reviews pick up on many of the semantic features, most notably the extensive use of the sightseeing tour. In his review of *I Was a Male War Bride*, Crowther notes of the tour "to be sure, the scenery is pretty, being the genuine article."[2] His pan of *September Affair* argues that "not even the lovely background settings of Naples, Pompeii, Capri and beautiful city of Florence . . . succeed in conveying apt illusion to this low-grade yarn."[3] He refers to *Three Coins in the Fountain* as "a nice way to take the movie audience on a sightseeing tour of Rome."[4] He pushes the case for the Old World backdrop even further in his review of *Summertime*: "The beautiful city of Venice, with its ancient buildings, its mingling of vivid sounds and colors and its bewitchingly romantic air comes off as the principal performer in David Lean's and Ilya Lopert's 'Summertime.'"[5] His review of the film suggests that its travelogue qualities redeem the film's otherwise improbable romance. This is a judgment he makes even more strongly in reference to *Fräulein*. "Come to think of it, shots of bomb-torn Berlin and Cologne and the picturesque Rhine wine country contribute more color to 'Fraulein' than its plot."[6] The travelogue settings of these romances offer a stable category upon which Crowther passes judgment.

When confronted with a travelogue romance, Crowther was not the only reviewer who often had more to say about the travelogue than the romance. The films are clearly read as romances with a distinctive kind of scenery. More often than not, reviewers note an incongruity between that beautiful backdrop and the romance that unfolds. The *Variety Weekly* review of *Interlude* asserts that the "best feature of the Ross Hunter production is the striking photographic tour it provides."[7] Branch Corey in the *Hollywood Citizen News* suggests that "Perhaps the movie doesn't offer a brand new story, but it does offer an old love story in a Technicolor setting that somehow becomes appealing with its foreign charm."[8] On the other hand, when a film such as *Roman Holiday* succeeds, reviewers note that the success comes because of a good combination of plot and scenery. "The director and his scenarists . . . have sensibly used the sights and sounds of Rome to dovetail with the facts of their story."[9] A reviewer of *Summertime* for the New York culture and entertainment magazine *Cue* struggles with how to refer to the genre, referring to it as "the most dramatic travelogue and/or the most sublimely scenic drama of its time."[10] While the reviewer may not have a name for it, he certainly knows that it belongs to a category. The *New Yorker* review comes closer to generic classification when it refers to the film as "an ingenious combination of travelogue and romantic comedy."[11] This is as close as it gets.

If the critics of the time could not name it, can we be so presumptuous as to do so? Is there another readily accepted genre into which these films can more easily be catalogued? To be sure, they belong to the family of romance, a category so large as to not be descriptive by itself. The category of the "woman's film" described so adroitly by Jeanine Basinger accounts for many aspects of the romance including perhaps the target audience, but fails to address the particular location features or production factors. If a genre category's title is meant to evoke, "travelogue romance" gives an accurate sense of what these films are trying to do. It brings together both the visual and narrative distinctions of a set of films.

What then do we gain by asserting that the travelogue romance constitutes a genre? By calling attention to the fact that these films belong to a genre, we have been able to see them as working on a similar project. Altman argues that genres are "regulatory schemes facilitating the integration of diverse factions into a single unified social fabric."[12] Indeed, we can read the travelogue romance genre as attempting a unifying interpretation of both the emotional economy of the new cosmopolitan American and the changing relationship between the Old and the New World. Just as Westerns and gangster films helped narrate new relationships to the law, urbanization, and community, so too did travelogue romances serve an important function as Americans attempted to understand for themselves how they were to respond to the larger world in which they suddenly found themselves enmeshed. And just as Americans traveled the world sometimes as tourists, sometimes as soldiers, and sometimes as capitalists, so too do these stories reflect the larger range of hats worn by the Yankee abroad.

Thomas Schatz's genre theory suggests that genres enjoy a natural life cycle. He argues that, as genres mature, the characters develop more complex relationships with the situation and mise en scène in which they interact. "A newborn genre's status as social ritual generally resists any ironic, ambiguous, or overly complex treatment of its narrative message."[13] As genres "age," according to Schatz, they begin to experiment more with narrative tropes, evincing patterns of increasing self-awareness. While this organic treatment of narrative genre reads as a bit reductive, it does seem likely that once genres work out a particular set of recognizable patterns, the producer–consumer pact might demand increasing sophistication. This sophistication includes knowledge of what previous contributors to the genre have accomplished and what has not been seen before.

In the case of the travelogue romance, the shifting attitudes of the early 1960s, as well as the continuing collapse of the influence of the Production Code Administration, affect the evolution of the genre. Always sexually charged, travelogue romances simply paralleled larger industrial trends about the kinds of sexual relationships that would be explicitly portrayed on the screen. More important for the evolution of the genre, however, is the shift in the nature of the intercontinental relationship presented in the films. The happy sexual adventure abroad gradually transforms into a dark tale about the troubled relationship between America and Europe. In studying the films of the early 1960s, we will note that the genre, which always contained a potentially darker interpretation of the transatlantic relationship, now uses it as a form of introspection. The travelogue romance becomes the object of narrative criticism either through darker versions of the generic formula, metafilms, or parodies.

In this chapter we will look at some of these tales of the darker side of romantic adventures abroad in *Town Without Pity* (Gottfried Reinhardt, 1961), *The Roman Spring of Mrs. Stone* (José Quintero, 1961), and *Two Weeks in Another Town* (Vincente Minnelli, 1962). This evidence of the maturation of the travelogue romance will provide further evidence that the practice of runaway production in Europe in the 1950s eventually formed a small but important genre. Finally, I will consider another bit of evidence for the claim that by the 1960s the travelogue romance formed a mature genre: the parody. *Paris, When it Sizzles* (Richard Quine, 1964) rests on the assumption that the structures to be lampooned are well known. Quine's film suggests that the structure of the travelogue romance were so well worn as to be worn out.

Town Without Pity: Reconfiguring the Occupation as Rape

Our inclusion of occupation romances as a part of a discussion of travelogue romances derives from the way in which those films developed a progressive story of improving relations between the United States and Germany. The love interests move from the unrepentant Nazi consort in *A Foreign Affair* to the domesticating tamer of the oversexualized Elvis Presley in *GI Blues* and the reformed communist in *One, Two, Three*. Cinematically, Germans as objects of desire prove to be much more reliable and worthy of marriage than their Italian or French counterparts. As a result, a tour of duty in postwar

Germany, as represented in the films, begins to take on much more the feel of a holiday than a hazard. Like the lovers in the other travelogue romances, the revelers in uniform stage their relationships against the backdrops of Old World historical splendor.

The worldview of Europe as romantic playground propagated by the occupation romances changes considerably when the narrative perspective shifts to the Germans. One of the transformations of the travelogue romance as a whole in the early 1960s is a move toward more thoroughly investigating whether or not the sexual desire with which the genre has associated Europe is reciprocated by the Old World. In this vein, Gottfried Reinhardt's *Town Without Pity* rejects "romance" for a much more troubling metaphor.

Reinhardt's film is an adaptation of a 1960 German novel, *Stadt ohne Mitleid* by Manfred Gregor. The dedication of Gregor's novel reads "To a better understanding between two peoples."[14] The epigram suggests that something in the German–American relationship is troubled. Moreover, the fact that the first three films discussed in this chapter, as well as a number of others discussed in the book, are adaptations, offers evidence that the cinema was not the only outlet in which Americans and Europeans were giving serious thought to their contemporary relationship.

Son of the famous stage director, Max Reinhardt, Gottfried Reinhardt emigrated with his father from Berlin to California in 1934. Starting as a writer and producer in the 1930s, Reinhardt directed a number of films in the 1950s including the runaway production, war film *Betrayed* in 1954. In the mid-to-late 1950s he returned to Germany, spending five years solely on German productions. *Town Without Pity*, essentially an international coproduction, marks Reinhardt's return to working mostly within the American system, albeit still in Germany. Although Reinhardt's work history tracks that of many expatriate Germans who returned to Europe to direct American-financed productions, the perspective taken up by the film diverts mightily from those offered by the other Hollywood-controlled endeavors abroad. Here Europe begins to talk back to the Hollywood fantasy of Europe.

Town Without Pity uses the story of a rape of a teenaged German girl by four American GIs to motivate a larger story about the tensions caused by the U.S. presence in Germany. As the film sets up no mystery regarding the actual crime, the real tension of the ensuing court martial derives from the legal strategy pursued by defense attorney Steve Garrett (played by Kirk Douglas). Here we have something that amounts to a genre conflict. The group of randy GIs no longer serves as the cast of a travelogue romance, but of a courtroom drama, one in which the notion of Germany as sexual playground is put on trial. In the action that unfolds yet another generic split occurs. The German public, looking for a public trial about the American presence in Germany, witness instead a courtroom drama, where the technicalities of American jurisprudence prevail over retributive desires.

We have been treating the romances as metonymical devices for the German–American relationship. This film's use of rape as the rhetorical device offers a more complicated sense of the American connection to occupied Germany. The film alters permanently the set-up that provided background for *A Foreign Affair*, *GI Blues*, or even a much more serious film such as *Fräulein*. The quaint Bavarian town is troubled both by closed-minded Germans and imperialistic Americans. Here, the U.S.–German encounter is either rape or prostitution—a radical departure from the conciliatory occupation romances. The film puts to trial the sense of sexual entitlement that motivates most of the stories of Americans abroad.

One of the interesting changes the film makes in its adaptation of the Gregor novel is the addition of Inge Koerner (played by Barbara Rütting), a reporter for a German tabloid whose voice also serves as the film's voice-over narrator. By placing a representative of the German public sphere, even if in the problematic form of a yellow press reporter, in the narrator position, *Town Without Pity* broadens its perspective. Koerner's monologues not only provide the voice-over, but also a loose translation of the significant amount of German spoken in the film. Serving as both an extradiegetic omniscient storyteller and a character who provides Garrett with offscreen information, the Koerner figure locates the narrative perspective on the German side of a very polarized situation. It relieves the film of the untenable possibility of sympathizing with the rapists.

The film's opening sequence establishes the four American soldiers as unsympathetic and menacing. The ensuing trial will not be about the guilt or innocence of the GIs, but about how the German public reacts to American officialdom. Moreover, although Garrett will later be forced into making insinuations about the character of the victim, Karin Steinhof, the film's portrayal of the attack leaves no reason for the spectator to believe that it was anything but a rape. The trial then turns on the question of how Americans respond to German public pressure and how Germans respond to the fact that they are not completely sovereign in their own country.

The rape causes a crisis between the local German population as represented by the town's mayor and the victim's father, a local bank president. Responding to pressures from the mayor, the commanding general of the base demands not only that justice be done, but that it be done in public, so as to offer the Germans a civics lesson. A fair and open court martial is to be held in which the four GIs, if convicted, will face the death penalty. Both the trial and the eventual penalty are meant to show the Germans that the U.S. Army takes as its mission their welfare and protection. But the film sets up a scenario whereby the rape victim's sexuality must be put on stage in order for the death penalty, upon which the victim's father insists, to be considered. Thus, seeking the death penalty in this case ends up appealing to the local population's pruriency rather than their sense of justice.

If the general and mayor represent the geopolitical interests at stake in the case, defense attorney Garrett and reporter Koerner give voice to a different set of interests, interests that contradict each other. Garrett is an idealist who opposes the death penalty. He does not attempt to claim that the soldiers are innocent, instead he seeks justice rather than vengeance for their actions. He pins his hopes on an article of the occupation agreement between the United States and West Germany that stipulates that, in a rape case, the victim must testify in order for the death penalty to be applied. Koerner sees herself representing Karin's interests. She does not show any sympathy for the American notion of the right to a rigorous defense. Instead she voices the concern that Garrett's defense of the rapists relies on an evocation of the petty jealousies and frustrations of the local population. Garrett allows the trial to become about a wealthy girl's immodesty and sexual activity, rather than about the violence that was perpetrated upon her. While Garrett uses Karin to spare the soldiers' lives, the townspeople convict Karin of having provided another opportunity for the Americans to dominate them. By having allowed herself to be raped by them, she has yet again proved that they are powerless in the face of the occupiers. Her suicide at the end of the film only punctuates the degree to which all sides have failed to protect her.

The reviews of the film, which ranged from pan to praise, could not even in this case resist noting the authenticity of the locale. A. H. Weiler in the *New York Times* claims that "the story evolves as authentically as the actual German locales at which it was filmed."[15] While the film fared well with Weiler, Stanley Kauffmann of *The New Republic* was less enamored. He notes that the film establishes four very important themes, namely the corrupting effect of occupation, the lasciviousness of public morality, the psychosexual relationship between father and daughter, and the complexities of the American legal system. "The film starts all these hares, then lets them scamper free, never having decided which of them it is following."[16] Indeed Kauffmann's critique is indicative of much of the reception, all of which felt that the film was ambitious if unsuccessful in its attempt to make more than a mere joke out of the conditions of American occupation in Germany.

One of the issues that comes under severe criticism by, among others, the *Los Angeles Times* reviewer John L. Scott was the film's ending. Garrett's strategy for saving the defendants' lives is to confront Karin so aggressively on the witness stand that she, in the end, refuses to complete her testimony. If she does not testify in full, the men cannot be put to death. Karin Steinhof and her beau, Frank Borgmann, are both so humiliated by the trial and the subsequent scorn that Frank illegally withdraws money from his mother's bank account and attempts to flee town with Karin. When the police arrest him, Karin commits suicide by jumping in the river. It is in this choice that Scott accuses Reinhardt of dodging issues that he initially offers as important.[17] The film, according to Scott's critique, does not put the town's prurient attitudes to the same trial that it puts the GI's actions and Karin's desires.

Given this set-up, the question remains how this film relates to the dozen or so films about the American–European encounter that have been presented here. Obviously, it offers an antidote to the rosy picture painted by *GI Blues* the previous year. Far from being a blind defense of romantic German virtue, the film deploys the picturesque *Heimat* as a petty and vicious mise en scène for a confrontation between rule of law and vengeance. In many ways, the filmmakers could have as easily used the backdrop of a Western for this tale. The use of small-town Germany suggests that the film wants to say something about transatlantic relations as well. While certainly not a travelogue romance, *Town Without Pity* only makes sense with the story line established by the films in Chapter Five. After *Town Without Pity*, whatever romantic appeal the idea of randy American soldiers roaming the picturesque Bavarian countryside in search of giggling fräuleins contained no longer looks innocent. And, behind the Old World facades lurk arcane and brutal attitudes.

Sexuality, Stardom, and the Spanish Steps: *The Roman Spring of Mrs. Stone*

Town Without Pity reveals the troubling nature of some of the basic premises upon which the travelogue romance was built. The first premise is that the notion of Americans living, working, and, indeed, occupying the Old World was necessarily a benevolent and democratizing force. Reinhardt's film suggests that the American–German relationship was complicated, uncomfortable, and perhaps unsuitable fodder for romance. The second notion upon which the genre was built is that the American move abroad was only an American story. Another film from 1961, *The Roman Spring of Mrs. Stone*, takes up this theme in its own critique of the American sexual adventure abroad.

In 1961 José Quintero, a noted stage director, took up production of *The Roman Spring of Mrs. Stone*, an adaptation of Tennessee Williams' eponymous novella from 1950. The film did not adhere to the same modes of production found in most of the other films discussed in this book. Because of its subject matter, the producers were unable to attain a license to take the first unit to Rome. Instead, they set up headquarters in London and sent a second unit to Rome.

The film is about an actress, Karen Stone, played by Vivien Leigh, who is approaching fifty years of age and whose critics and friends are beginning to suggest loudly that she might be a bit long in the tooth for the roles that she is playing. In order to escape inevitable critical failure, Stone breaks off her engagement in a play about to open on Broadway in order to join her ailing husband on a trip to Rome intended to rejuvenate them both. On the flight to Europe her husband dies of a heart attack. Thus, Stone arrives in the Eternal City a widow. Her mourning period is eventually interrupted by an impover-ished Eastern European aristocrat who works as a procuress of gigolos for the Roman tourist elite.

Most of the travelogue romances carefully exclude a full account of the life of the principal American back in the States. Whether in *Summertime*, *The Indiscretion of an American Wife*, or *To Catch a Thief*, the genre tends to avoid full disclosure of the events surrounding the character's departure to Europe. Neither *The Roman Spring of Mrs. Stone* nor the next film in our discussion, *Two Weeks in Another Town*, shy away from such discussions. Both films center on the attempts of aging actors to rejuvenate their lives and perhaps their careers by going abroad. The former utilizes its precredit sequence to offer a much more brutal, indeed sexist, assessment of the fate of an actress who is no longer qualified to play the ingénue. The film begins with Stone's out-of-town opening in the role of Rosalind in Shakespeare's *As You Like It*. The film's first dialogue, conducted among theater patrons, mocks Stone for having aged. Knowing it herself, Stone must force herself to finish the performance, only to be told afterward by her friend, Meg, that she is too old to play sexualized roles. Everything from the dialogue to Stone's makeup to the role she plays asks us to view Karen Stone as a grotesque.

Once Stone arrives in Rome, the film cuts to a title sequence that, as do many in the genre, offers a travelogue montage of the sites of the Eternal City. We are offered long shots of Stone in front of the fountains and monuments of the city, with the sequence culminating in her ascending the Spanish Steps. The film must use a body double in these shots, as the production company was not granted a license to set up its first unit there. Thus, all of the shots are long shots with Stone's face veiled in order to conceal the fact that Vivien Leigh was not on site. It is an attempt at offering the same authenticity that spectators of the genre had come to expect. The title sequence is set to mel-ancholy music, suggesting a different type of adventure than the genre had offered heretofore.

As soon as the credits fade, the film cuts to a long shot of Stone surveying the cityscape accompanied by an authoritative voice-over narrator: "Because so much of Rome seemed to exist in the past, Mrs. Stone decided that it was both an appropriate and comfortable place to lead what she was sure would be an almost posthumous existence." And then, as if to introduce a different kind of tourism than had been presented in the genre up to now, the film cuts to a shot of people, primarily men, loitering around the Spanish Steps as the voice-over narrates: "For almost two centuries, the immense cascade of stone stairs descending from Trinità dei Monti to the Piazza di Spagna has been a favorite place of assignation." The film cuts to various shots of young men approaching older men or women, indicating either an expected encounter or a proposition, as well as a shot of a young man napping face down on the stone steps. This famous landmark of the Eternal City is introduced as little more than a whorehouse. The voice continues: "A multitude of assorted humanity comes every day to crouch in the sun, to seek fulfillment of some desire, or to dream. And here, in one of the ancient Palazzi flanking the higher reaches of this fountain of stairs Karen Stone chose to make her home." With this introduction, given in a narrative form that the film abandons shortly thereafter, *The Roman Spring of Mrs. Stone* both presents itself as working closely within the geographic expectations of the travelogue romance, while at the same time announcing its considerably less sentimental take on the conventions at hand.

This brief omniscient narration is remarkable in terms of the generic positioning in the reading it gives of this particular Roman monument. For this is the same backdrop against which the runaway princess Ann discovers her freedom, where the indiscreet American wife, Mary Forbes, first meets her Italian lover, and where the young secretaries of *Three Coins in the Fountain* discuss the possibility of finding true love in Rome. In short, the travelogue romances have treated the Spanish Steps as the iconic site of their sentimental projections. *The Roman Spring of Mrs. Stone* interprets the Piazza di Spagna, amidst the prostitutes and the homeless, as a backdrop for almost anything but a healthy relationship. If all of these films serve as, among other things, filmic travel guides, then we are being led here on a remarkably different tour than those the other films provided.

After introducing the seediness of the milieu, the film takes great pains both to offer an interpretation of Mrs. Stone and to introduce a character whom it will treat more as an apparition than a reality, a homeless young man who will stalk Stone around Rome. The voice-over narrator continues:

> Simultaneously, a solitary young man with no regular or legitimate occupation had appeared on the Spanish Steps to spend all his time keeping watch on Mrs. Stone's apartment, as if waiting to give or receive some sort of secret signal. What puzzled Mrs. Stone was

why this strange youth should make any impression on her consciousness. Self-knowledge was something that Karen Stone had
always been able to avoid. The obsessive, ruthless pursuit of her
career and the childlike adoration of an indulgent husband had kept
this proud and arrogant woman from exploring the dark corners of
her own nature.

The sequence then cuts briefly to the arrival of a well-dressed young man and
an older woman, whom we will come to know as Paolo and the Contessa. The
voice-over continues:

As her body began adjusting to its new condition and her self to the
upheavals which had so greatly unnerved her, Mrs. Stone was also
becoming alarmingly conscious of a sense of drifting if not of drown-
ing in a universe of turbulently rushing fluids and vapors, but now the
drift was beginning to take direction.

Thus, the film reveals both the psychological makeup of its eponymous character and the fact that it will not treat her sympathetically. That very change
of narrative attitude radically differentiates this film from the genre in which
it sets itself. The film will not pretend that this is an innocent American moving about in an otherwise corrupt world. Indeed, the presentation of the spec-
tral drifter, who is linked in the narration with "the dark corners of [Stone's]
own nature," suggests that the entire scene of the Spanish Steps that Stone
surveys from her apartment is an erotic–thanatic fantasy being performed for
her pleasure.

Karen Stone's purpose for being in Rome does, in fact, resemble the various justifications offered by the many films discussed up to this point. From
September Affair through *One, Two, Three*, the characters of the travelogue
romances have justified their sojourn abroad by a search for a set of sexual
experiences unavailable to them stateside. The addition of the death drive to
The Roman Spring of Mrs. Stone separates this film from the rest of the group.
Moreover it reflects back onto the other films, suggesting that the titillating
sexual adventure upon which the narratives are founded is inextricably bound
to controlling one's own demise. If previously Rome was the backdrop of a
harmless sexual encounter, it has now become little more than a decadent sex
den into which Karen Stone retreats to die.

Not only does the film spoil the fantasy of Rome as a metonymic locale
for innocent sexual tourism in Europe, which Hollywood had so carefully constructed in the previous decade, it also draws attention to the growing frustration with American dominance that was also evident in *Town Without Pity*.

Rome is no longer populated by the servile landlords or comic civil servants as depicted in *Roman Holiday*, but by an army of sex workers who know how to exploit their American colonizers.

This shift to resentment in *The Roman Spring of Mrs. Stone* is gradual. The Contessa initially expresses sympathy for Stone when she hopes to secure her as a client for one of the men in her stable, Paolo (played by Warren Beatty), but then turns on her as soon as Stone proves difficult to exploit. When Paolo suggests that the relationship he is developing with Stone is more complicated and perhaps less sexual than the Contessa presumes, he insists that Stone is a "great lady." This comment gives the Contessa an opening to proffer one of the oldest European clichés about Americans: "Listen, Paolo, there is no such thing as a great American lady. Great ladies do not occur in a nation less than two hundred years old." Americans, according to this attitude, are merely consumers of taste provided for them by Europeans.

Eventually, Paolo and Mrs. Stone do establish a primarily commercial relationship, while both of them try on sentimentality on occasion to see if it fits. In a scene shortly after they have consummated their relationship, the film makes it clear that both characters see the other more as a type than an individual. When Stone complains that it is about to rain, Paolo breaks into an unexpected rant: "I don't suppose it would concern you that there is something in this country to consider other than the amusement of rich foreigners. You don't care if the grain in the country is all dry or that the water supply is so low that there is not even enough for electricity." When Stone expresses surprise that Paolo is suddenly something other than a beautiful plaything he continues his resentments: "You rich American women think that you are the new conquerors of Rome. Well you let me warn you something. This city has all 3000 years [sic] and every one of its conquerors has gone right back to the dust." Stone continues not to take his speech seriously as the conversation turns to his feelings for her. "Beside my family the only person that I ever loved was my second cousin . . . She was raped by your soldiers in Naples and has spent the rest of her life in a convent. So you can laugh all you want to at me. But I don't love anybody." This is the only bit of Paolo's history with which the film provides us, and given his tendency to use lies and melodrama to manipulate his clients to give him money, it is unclear whether we are meant to take it seriously. The story used for this manipulation is nonetheless interesting. Stories of trauma, from Stone's perspective, are no more than gimmicks the locals will use to extract more money out of the Americans. Both Paolo's resentful remarks and Stone's infantilizing response lay bare the nature not only of their relationship, but also of the American–European affair as it has been constructed in the travelogue romance. For Stone, Paolo is no more real than the stalker who shadows her through the streets of Rome. Both represent Stone's desire to determine the conditions of her own demise. They are merely the faces of sex and death.

The idea that the film barely treats any of the Europeans whom Stone encounters as real is not new to the travelogue romance. We have reached that conclusion about a number of films discussed here. But if the American characters in *Interlude, Summertime,* or *The Indiscretion of an American Wife* arrive in Europe in hopes of an authentic encounter, Karen Stone harbors no such illusions. *The Roman Spring of Mrs. Stone* not only undermines the romantic tropes established in its predecessors, it also does away with the other fantasies of what might be gained through a European sojourn, namely the cultural sophistication that Europe is meant to provide. This dark tale of sexual adventurism maintains very strictly the notion of the Old World as nothing more than the decadent hideaway from American life.

If escapism in Europe were all that is at stake in *The Roman Spring of Mrs. Stone,* the film would not take us any further than we were a decade earlier with *September Affair.* In fact, the film's critique of the travelogue romance tropes goes even further. For not only is Karen Stone quite open about her unreal perceptions of Rome, she is equally dismissive of the suggestion that her life would somehow improve through a return to the United States. Stone's trip to Rome will not be a troubled but edifying experience that will fortify her in her return to a productive American life. Although the film's title misleadingly suggests Stone will experience a reawakening in the Eternal City, it is forceful in equating Rome with death, something that appeals to her far more than her careerist life in America. Thus, sexual adventurism abroad is emptied out of both its pleasure and its lesson, moving quite in sync with Sigmund Freud beyond the pleasure principle.[18]

The film utilizes one of the spats that Paolo instigates in order to try to manipulate Karen to reveal her expectations of her European sojourn. Paolo, attempting to threaten, queries:

> Has it ever occurred to you, Karen, that women of your kind are very often found assassinated in bed?
>
> KAREN: What?
>
> PAOLO: It's true. Only last week on the French Riviera a middle-aged woman was found in bed with her throat cut from ear to ear. There was no broken lock, no forced entrance, just stains of hair oil on the other pillow. Obviously, the lady had asked the assassin to come in.
>
> KAREN: Does this mean you are going to kill me?

PAOLO: That's very funny. Make a joke. Show your sense of humor.
And in three or four years I pick up a paper and read about your
death.

KAREN: Three or four years is all I need. After that a cut throat will
be a convenience.

With this exchange the film announces the inevitability of its conclusion.
When her relationship with Paolo and with it her brief sexualized respite from
her looming demise come to an end, Stone quite calmly throws her keys to
Paolo's dark double, namely the drifter who has been stalking her throughout
the story. The film ends with the drifter entering her apartment and approaching Stone. It leaves open the interpretation of what is to happen next. Given
the film's pairing of *eros* and *thanatos*, it would seem that Stone gives up
her resistance to the latter and, as Paolo predicted, welcomes it through the
door. In fact, Paolo's prediction adds to the film's suggestion that both he and
his double were little more than phantasmagoric apparitions to accompany
Karen Stone into death. Thus, *The Roman Spring of Mrs. Stone* offers an
extreme version of the idea, found throughout the travelogue romances, that
Europeans are something less than real and the trip to Europe is nothing but
a fantasy.

Runaways or Cast-Offs?

Up to now, we have viewed the runaway film movement and the genre of
the travelogue romance that formed out of it as a relatively positive development, one that served Hollywood's various postwar needs quite well. While
the labor unions and various feeder industries in southern California always
decried the moving of productions abroad, producers benefited from lower
negative costs, artists escaped Red Scare scrutiny, and studios found exotic
backdrops that differentiated their products from television fare. Yet, as
the production trend grew and various international coproduction financing schemes developed, runaway productions ceased to be the exclusive
domain of cost-conscious American filmmakers. European producers began
to view the new mode of production as a way to gain access to the American
market through the use of Hollywood personnel living and working abroad.
However historically equitable this new economic situation may have been,
for a still-struggling Hollywood industry, it served as yet another example
of what was wrong with the industry's flight from southern California. *Two
Weeks in Another Town* (Vincente Minnelli, 1962) presents a dark view of
the "runaway" culture of the late 1950s and early 1960s that reinforces the
notion that such productions did not enjoy a stellar reputation within the

industry. Adapted from a novel by Irwin Shaw, who was himself blacklisted and spent the 1950s and 1960s in Europe working as a screenwriter, the film, which is set in Rome and at the Cinecittà studios, treats runaway productions as the most recent symptom of an aesthetically and morally moribund industry.

Jack Andrus (Kirk Douglas) is a former Oscar-winning actor who has fallen on hard times. The end of a rocky marriage has sent him into a professional and personal tailspin. This is one of the few films under discussion here that begins with the traveler's life in the States before the call to go abroad is received. We meet Andrus languishing in a high-end psychological care facility in Connecticut, where he apparently spends inordinate amounts of time playing shuffleboard. This is presumably included in the film to provide a sort of threat, that is, this is not the place to which he will want to return at the end of the film. Nevertheless, it also has the function, so typical of the travel ogue romance, of making his trip to Rome a flight from home as well.

He receives notice that Maurice Kruger (Edward G. Robinson), the director who made him famous, wants him to come to Rome to act in his new film. Upon arrival in Rome, Andrus confronts the range of problems facing runaway productions. Kruger, who like many of the actual runaway production directors is a German–Jewish European immigrant, faces a ruthless producer whose only concern is that the film come in on time and on budget. The actors are apparently both untalented and unmotivated to improve. Kruger, a formerly decorated director, has lost his apparently once-famous rapport with his cast. A gossip columnist refers to him as "the prototype of the obsolete Hollywood type." He is reduced to casting actresses with whom he can do little more than enjoy an occasional tryst. His runaway production is out of control and without a commanding sense of the film that should come out of it. Andrus is put to work in the dubbing studio but discovers there his untapped skills in directing. When Kruger suffers a heart attack, Andrus takes over direction of the picture, promising to finish the film "the Kruger way." Andrus turns around the production, getting promising performances out of untalented actors and finishing the shooting ahead of schedule.

Yet, old ghosts threaten Andrus' comeback. Once in Rome, Andrus also discovers that his ex-wife Carlotta, played by Cyd Charisse, is in town with her current husband, a Greek shipping tycoon. Andrus' troubles began with their initial breakup, and her reappearance threatens the stability that he is trying to regain.

The film also presents a typical travelogue romance. While still working on the production, Andrus encounters Veronica, an Italian woman who is the abused lover of the troublesome lead actor, Davie Drew. In clichéd midlife crisis fashion, Andrus discovers youthfulness and renewal of purpose through his association with Veronica. Her only potential benefit from the relationship is the suggestion that she might eventually return to America with him. Andrus remains, however, haunted by his ex-wife until he realizes that the latter was not the real cause of his misery, as he had always believed. When Andrus and Drew finally come to terms with one another, their deal is sealed by Andrus 'giving' Veronica to Drew. The two reconciled young lovers escort the rejuvenated Andrus to his plane as he heads back to Hollywood to make films the way they are meant to be made. Ultimately Andrus redeems himself by discovering that he can still make films and that the seedy conditions of Roman runaway productions, with washed-up actors and foreign investors, are the wrong place to prove it.

In order to set up its premise, the film requires the travelogue backdrop. It certainly does not take location shooting to the experimental extreme we find in *Roman Holiday* or *Summertime*, but the film goes beyond merely projecting Andrus onto the background of Rome. Rather, like many of the films discussed here, it uses location work to integrate him into that scenery. It is an acknowledgment of the imaginary geography of the Old World that Hollywood had spent the previous decade constructing the necessary tour of that terrain that a character must undertake. Thus Andrus walks the Spanish Steps, observes a group of clerics walking by, drives his car across a famous Roman piazza, climbs into an undersized Roman taxi, and, most important, at least for our metafilmic understanding, he pulls up in front of the Cinecittà studios. These typical authenticators for the film's travelogue credentials reveal Rome to be an appealing yet unsuitable location for the proper work of filmmaking.

In addition to using the full range of travelogue work to establish place, the basic plot line of *Two Weeks in Another Town* does not deviate tremendously from *September Affair*. Both are stories about American men who go to Europe to escape bad marriages, only to have those marriages find them there. Both men pin their hopes of masculine rejuvenation on younger European (or Europeanized) women, only to use that rejuvenation to restart their careers. In both cases, resumption of their work requires a return to America. Thus, it is not as a travelogue romance that the film adds anything new to our discussion. Instead, it is on the story line about a runaway production in Rome that we will focus our attention.

While a metafilm about the decadence of American-interest productions abroad makes for relatively dull movie entertainment, it does some useful work for our discussion here. The film that they are shooting is a low-budget costume drama designed for immediate international distribution. It resembles more the later international coproduction work of Carlo Ponti or Dino De Laurentis than the Hollywood runaways. *Two Weeks in*

Another Town does, however, pose questions about the mode of production that Hollywood had pursued in Europe for more than a decade. Runaway productions come off as the last refuge for a generation of directors with little left to offer and actors who lack either the discipline or the talent to work in southern California.

Two Weeks in Another Town reveals an awareness of the history of runaway production. It uses as a plot point one of the weaknesses of working in Rome that William Wyler mentions in his letters to Paramount Studios regarding *Roman Holiday*, namely the use of dubbed rather than live sound. Because of the Italian sound facilities, in Kruger and Andrus's film, all dialogue is recorded in the sound studio and dubbed into the film. After being denied the role in the film that he is promised, Andrus takes over the direction of the dubbing. George Hamilton plays the young heartthrob, Davie Drew, whose bad attitude has ruined his promising Hollywood career and reduced him to playing in what is obviously a second-rate runaway production. The scene in which Andrus directs Drew through the performance of the voice track furthers the film's suggestion that Rome is filled with washed-up (and overweight) former Hollywood stars who earn their livelihood dubbing voice tracks in mediocre technical facilities. *Two Weeks in Another Town* animates on the screen the production notes of a variety of runaway productions.

The film suggests a reading of the ex-wife, Carlotta, as metaphor for the fleeting allures of stardom, whether gained in southern California or abroad. She represents the misguided priorities of Andrus's career. When she turns up in Rome at the same time that he is there, those same destructive temptations follow him. As with many of the travelogue romances, the film's denouement comes when Andrus realizes that he wants something more real out of life. He rejects the unreal baubles of stardom. Of direct importance for our discussion here, these baubles are equated with being an American star abroad. Moreover Cinecittà, which, with the *Roman Holiday* production, initially served as a location of renewal for Hollywood filmmaking, reads in this film as a symptom of a dysfunctional industry. As Drew puts it when he has a change of heart and wants to work his way back into the industry: "One more runaway and I would be finished." He is referring simultaneously to his tendency to tempestuously leave the set and to the second-rate runaway roles to which his career has been reduced.

Two Weeks in Another Town ultimately falls victim to the same phenomena that it sets out to critique. That is to say, Minnelli and crew seem no more in control of their film than Kruger and crew are. Like *Town Without Pity*, it sets up a critique of America in its new global context, but falls short of drawing a useful synthesis about it. For our purposes, the important point is that the film demonstrates the degree to which the travelogue romance in its many guises had become established enough by the beginning of the 1960s that it could assume knowledge of generic semantics in order to commence upon a critical assessment of them. *Two Weeks in Another Town* does not quite tell us what it is that is wrong with the films made abroad. It portrays runaway productions as staffed by money-grubbing, low-end producers and crew members with bad technical facilities at their disposal and a cast of players that no longer represents Hollywood quality—many of the complaints that labor leader Roy Brewer had offered a decade earlier regarding foreign productions. While *Two Weeks in Another Town* accomplishes very little of what it sets out to do, it does reveal to us how a certain Hollywood attitude had begun to again shift. If one of the initial appeals of the runaway production was to go abroad to show something new on the screen, in the early 1960s, the Old World was no longer new.

Whether or not the assessment that the Hollywood experiment in European production had run its creative course is fair, it is interesting that a similar depiction of Hollywood abroad emerges in the French *nouvelle vague* tradition a year later, namely in Jean-Luc Godard's *Le Mèpris* (1963). While the general conceit of Godard's film differs considerably from *Two Weeks in Another Town*, both address the hopeless conditions of American runaway productions at Cinecittà. Godard's film depicts a Hollywood team led by a loud and uncultured producer, Prokosch (played by Jack Palance), and the famous director Fritz Lang (played by Lang himself) in the midst of work on a screen adaptation of Homer's *Odyssey*. The film presents a range of themes, not the least of which is Hollywood's attempt to co-opt ancient Old World culture in the service of commercial cinema. More importantly for our tale of American productions abroad, *Le Mèpris* is, at the very least, a sign that European filmmakers were every bit as aware of the hopes Hollywood studios had invested in runaway productions, whether they were making romances, as presented in Minnelli's film, or epics, as in Godard's film. Arguably, even much of Fellini's *La Dolce Vita* (1960) owes the culture it is depicting to the ubiquitous Hollywood star in the Eternal City in 1960.[19]

The three films discussed in this chapter up to now suggest that, by the early 1960s, both the Hollywood experiment in foreign production and the imaginary geography of the Old World are less appealing and perhaps more troubling than they had been a decade earlier. While this would, in no way, spell the end of runaway production work, the romantic attachment to Europe was a story that was winding down. The Spanish Steps began to look much more like a seedy tourist trap and less like a backdrop to romantic self-discovery.

The travelogue romance was also a genre that best served its narrative purpose during U.S. ascendancy to world power. By the beginning of the

1960s, the factors that had established the transatlantic relationship at the end of World War II were once again in flux. With the help of the Marshall Plan, Western Europe had reestablished a consumer economy and a financially sound middle class. The partnership with the United States was based more on military dependency in the Cold War clash with the Soviet Union than on economic aid. As the relationship changed, so did the stories required to explain it. The story becomes less about romance and more about intrigue in the spy films that were soon to take over the screens. Also, by the 1960s, the historical films about World War II begin to investigate more thoroughly how America got into this relationship with Europe in the first place. The travelogue romance, it would seem, had little left in it but a parody.

Parody and Paris

Thomas Schatz ends his chapter of *Hollywood Genres* with a reading of John Ford's *The Man Who Shot Liberty Valence* (1962), noting that Ford uses the film as a commentary on the genre that the director was central in constructing. He argues that Ford's attitude toward the Western, visible throughout the film, undergoes an ideological shift. "Time has turned Ford's—and the genre's—initial optimism into a mixture of cynicism and regret."[20] For Schatz, this serves as an important example of a genre exhibiting a lifespan. Genres are like organisms that change as they age but retain key defining features throughout their lifespan. He employs a similar "lifespan" rhetoric in his treatment of the gangster film, pointing to the deaths of the classical gangster heros in *Key Largo* (John Huston, 1948) and *White Heat* (Raoul Walsh 1949) as evidence of the maturation of the gangster genre. The animalistic urban gangster had made himself irrelevant as well as difficult to sustain under the Production Code.[21] Such a life cycle model, as Rick Altman observes, allows for an explanation of genre continuity that is neat and teleological. "Always contained, generic types are forever separated by the isolating action of a historical logic according to which genres can only unfold, but never mate or select."[22] Altman's view of film genres, in contrast, insists that they exist on a continuum in which they are always in the process of morphing from or into something else, like species that can evolve in radical ways over time rather than single, comparatively stable organisms.

While I generally agree with Altman's more evolutionary approach to genre history, I believe we would be ill served if we dispensed with the lifespan model completely. Each is capable of illuminating phenomena overlooked by the other. For example, one aspect of genre history that Altman tends to ignore but that Schatz's model can help interpret is Hollywood's long history of generic parody. Parody as a practice affirms the lifespan approach to genre in one very important way, namely in the presumption it makes of a stable category over which it is discoursing.

In his crisply argued monograph on the subject, Simon Dentith begins with a definition of parody as including "any cultural practice which provides a relatively polemical allusive imitation of another cultural production or practice."[23] While Dentith generally confines his study of parody to literary expression, his working definition provides a productive guide to how the lampooning style functions in film as well. What I find particularly appealing is the way in which the term "cultural practice" is employed here. Rather than a fixed set of texts situated firmly in a particular narrative tradition, we have viewed the travelogue romance up to this point as a cultural practice in which studios and audiences engaged in order to take advantage of and explain a shifting set of conditions regarding both the new relationship between the United States and Western Europe and Hollywood's negotiation of a variety of postwar conditions.

Since the late 1960s, if not earlier, the genre parody has been a mainstay of film comedy. Mel Brooks made a career out of it with films such as *Silent Movie*, *High Anxiety*, *Young Frankenstein*, and *Blazing Saddles*. Arguably, the metafilm about genre films goes all the way back to the Marx Brothers and extends to this very moment. The current *Scary Movie* franchise that lampoons the teen slasher pics as well as the Will Ferrell send-ups of sports movies depend heavily upon an audience knowing how to read the genres being spoofed.

In the case of the travelogue romance as cultural practice, any parody of it would necessarily have to acknowledge its existence as a narrative mode of address. In order to lampoon the practice, it would have to allude to some initial traits that would be recognizable to the spectator as such. Richard Quine's *Paris, When it Sizzles* (1964) is a metafilmic send-up of both the travelogue romance and the Hollywood practice of runaway filmmaking in Europe. As such, it is evidence that, by the 1960s, the travelogue romance constituted a stable generic construct that a broader audience could identify.

Paris, When it Sizzles sends up runaway films with the story of a screenwriter living in Paris, Richard Benson, who has been contracted to write a script for a Hollywood production set in the French capital. With just two days left to finish the screenplay of "The Girl Who Stole the Eiffel Tower," Benson (played by William Holden) hires a typist, Gabrielle Simpson (played by Audrey Hepburn), to type a manuscript that he has, of yet, failed to write. This sets in motion both a romance between Benson and Simpson and a metanarrative about the kinds of films that Hollywood had been making abroad for the previous decade.

Reconstructing the plot of *Paris, When it Sizzles* does not fully account for the wild number of narrative strands woven together in the film. Benson and Simpson trade ideas for possible story lines, which the audience sees played out in dream-sequence-like episodes, wherein Benson and Simpson play the main characters and provide voice-over narration. The given plot provides a loose structure for a number of spoofs that are all put into play. The film either mentions or alludes to most of the films, especially the travelogue romances, in which Audrey Hepburn had played. The French New Wave comes in for lampooning when Simpson reveals that she had worked for a *nouvelle vague* director in whose films nothing ever happens. Tony Curtis plays an uncredited bit part in which he is constantly reminded that he is playing a bit part.

The conceit of *Paris, When it Sizzles* derives from the presumption that the spectator has seen a number of the films under consideration here. The establishing shot of *Paris, When it Sizzles*, taken from a helicopter as it courses the coastline of the French Riviera, recalls a similar opening shot in *To Catch a Thief*, only this time the culprit is a Hollywood producer lounging around an upscale resort adorned by scantily clad young women. As if pulled straight from the production files of previous runaway films, the producer, Alexander Meyerheim (played by Noël Coward) assures Paramount executives at home that he is working much harder than his colleagues in southern California. When the film then dissolves to the scene of the scriptwriting in Paris, it establishes the City of Lights with the only possible backdrop, namely the Eiffel Tower, of which the apartment of every travelogue romance set there apparently has a view. When the film cues the pending arrival of Gabrielle Simpson as a secretarial assistant to Benson, it cuts to a shot of her in a train station that mimics similar set-ups in *Three Coins in the Fountain* and *Interlude*. Other Hepburn films such as *Funny Face* and *Charade* employ similar shots. The film also overlays a soundtrack of Fred Astaire singing "That Face" during her arrival at the Metro station. In short, the film announces from the start that it is a metafilm about the travelogue romance, runaway productions, and the Audrey Hepburn star vehicles. The film references, either directly or indirectly, *Funny Face, My Fair Lady, Charade,* and *Breakfast at Tiffany's* and alludes to *Sabrina* and *Love in the Afternoon* as well.[24]

In addition to these allusions to her other films, Audrey Hepburn plays a stock Audrey Hepburn character. Gabrielle Simpson is a wide-eyed, young American woman working in Paris as a secretary. She came to Paris following vaguely romantic and artistic ambitions. Specifically, she wanted to write. She, like Benson, came to Paris looking for a story. Benson's is also a stock character by now. A cynical, philandering, middle-aged American filmmaker looking to live well while doing as little work as possible.

The idea of Paris as backdrop for a story that brings together otherwise unlikely lovers provides only one of a number of generic parodies that the film offers as Benson and Simpson try out ideas for the script. In fact, genre film as such offers a target as well. When Simpson asks Benson what kind of film he is writing, he replies: "It's an action suspense romantic melodrama with lots of comedy, of course. And deep down underneath, a substrata of social comment." As the two construct the plot of the screenplay, they set it in gothic horror, the spy thriller, the Western, the air combat film, and the detective film, each of which attempts to highlight a European setting, before returning it to the romantic comedy. The mockery of both New Wave minimalism and Hollywood genres can, in itself, be seen as a parodying of the notion of auteurism. If *Paris, When it Sizzles* sustains any critique of travelogue romance, it is that the latter often mix together too many generic elements without simply sticking to the simple love story set against a European backdrop. At the end of the film, Benson and Simpson throw their pastiche of generic story lines into a fountain at the foot of the Eiffel Tower and kiss, both suggesting that the travelogue romance is not worth doing anymore and participating in it at the same time. The genre has run its course, but it was fun while it lasted.

Conclusion

As with most genres, the travelogue romance did not disappear. In some cases, it morphed into the action thriller, such as in the Audrey Hepburn and Cary Grant star vehicle *Charade* (Stanley Donen, 1963). *Charade* seems to have applied the combination of Hitchcockian drama and travelogue romance slightly more effectively than *To Catch a Thief*. Hepburn worked the genre even further while reuniting with William Wyler in *How To Steal a Million* (1966). The late 1960s saw a much more sexualized contribution to the travelogue in *If It's Tuesday, This Must Be Belgium* (Mel Stuart, 1969) in which the European adventure is condensed down to an eighteen-day tour.

While the Cold War context motivated the utilization of the European backdrop for a different narrative line in later years, aspects of the travelogue romance remain. Even the occupation romance returned in the Goldie Hawn vehicle, *Private Benjamin* (Howard Zieff, 1980). Curiously enough, with the end of the Cold War, the 1990s saw a resurgence of the genre. In 1995 alone three films, *Forget Paris* (Billy Crystal), *French Kiss* (Lawrence Kasdan) and *Before Sunrise* (Richard Linklater), allude strongly to the generic traditions of the 1950s travelogue romance. By the 1990s, the United States and the new European Union had a new relationship to negotiate, one no longer based on American protection and patronage. But, the fact that a long-standing commitment on the part of all sides continued to be in place gave the narrative a much different take than it had a half-century before. The story of a chance meeting between a young American and a handsome European might have given way to a story of a marriage celebrating its golden anniversary. The latter, however, has rarely been the fodder of commercial cinema, and so the stories of these later travelogue romances continue to portray new love.

Although the studios began to find other stories to tell in the early 1960s, it did not mean that they returned permanently to southern California. In fact, Twentieth Century-Fox, which had survived a near-death experience in the early 1960s, released *The Sound of Music* (Robert Wise) in 1965, its most successful film ever. The film benefited from the studio's experience with European location production, especially the more extensive World War II combat films that were a staple of the studio for decades. Hollywood studios continue their global production, using foreign set-ups both as real foreign settings and as lower-cost substitutes for American settings. First and second unit production abroad is now a phenomenon that attracts very little comment.

One of the biggest hits of 1950 was Billy Wilder's *Sunset Blvd.*, a film about a washed-up movie star who is unaware of her own demise. It is not hard to extrapolate from this story an attitude about the Hollywood industry and its fears that its best days were behind it.[25] The studios were losing their audience and with it their place as the stars of the American media landscape. They feared that just as talkies had made Norma Desmond irrelevant, so too would television and the suburbs force them into retreat in their decrepit mansions. In their journey to the Old World they found new ways to fill the screen and new stories to tell, all at a production price that was easy to pay. Whether or not the old star of Hollywood was worth saving is an issue for another day. But runaway productions and the travelogue romances they spawned did much to help classical Hollywood bridge the gap to New Hollywood.

Notes

INTRODUCTION

1. See, for example, William Wyler's *Dodsworth* from 1936 or, for a more recent example, Richard Linklater's *Before Sunset* from 2004.

2. Luce, "The American Century," 160.

3. Of course, for many previous generations of Americans, the contact with another country came from having been born there. In this book, we are essentially concerned with American rediscovery of Europe, whether or not the country in question is a part of the characters' direct ancestry.

4. Neale, *Genre and Hollywood*, 26.

5. Schatz, *Hollywood Genres*, 6.

6. Schatz, *Hollywood Genres*, 15.

7. Altman, *Film/Genre*, 17.

8. Basinger, *The World War II Combat Film: Anatomy of a Genre*, 14–15.

9. Bordwell, *Making Meaning: Inference and Rhetoric in the Interpretation of Cinema*, 147.

10. Aristotle, *Nicomachean Ethics*, 2.

11. Rosch, "Natural Categories," 328–350. Rosch has advocated a paradigm theory in order to explain how human minds categorize ordinary objects into categories such as "cup" or "bird." Put much too simply, the idea is that one is able to think "bird" upon seeing a canary for the first time because it bears so many similarities to the paradigms of birds we store in our heads (say, sparrows or pigeons). Less paradigmatic birds, such as a penguin, will give us pause upon first encounter because it is so different from the paradigm.

CHAPTER 1

1. "Yank Prod. Abroad at Peak," *Variety*, September 24, 1952.

2. *Variety*, September 24, 1952.

3. "Movies' Decline Held Permanent: Survey by Film Unions Finds '46 Status 'Gone Forever,'" Pryor, *New York Times*, April 7, 1958. Peter Lev also cites this article in *Transforming the Screen, 1950–1959*, 150.

4. "Film Making Abroad Shows Signs of Reversed Trend," *Los Angeles Mirror*, October 11, 1961.

5. Later "runaway productions" would come to connote any film not shot in southern California.

6. Abel, "History Can Work for You, You Know How to Use It," 108.

7. Guback, "Hollywood's International Market," 468–469.

8. For a greater summary of early European–American film industrial relations, see Kristin Thompson, *Exporting Entertainment: America in the World Film Market*.

9. See Thomas J. Saunders' *Hollywood in Berlin: American Cinema and Weimar Germany*.

10. See Eric Rentschler's *The Ministry of Illusion: Nazi Cinema and Its Afterlife*.

11. Belton, *Widescreen Cinema*, 73.

12. For an investigation of what the breakup meant to the value of the studios themselves, see DeVany and McMillan, "Was the Antitrust Action that Broke Up the Movie Studios Good for the Movies?: Evidence from the Stock Market."

13. Williams, "Learning to Scream," 14–17.

14. Belton, *Widescreen Cinema*, 76.

15. See Thomas Schatz, *Boom and Bust: American Cinema of the 1940s*, 293.

16. Schatz, *Boom and Bust*, 293.

17. The "Hollywood Ten" included screenwriters Alvah Bessie, Lester Cole, Ring Lardner, Jr., John Howard Lawson, Albert Maltz, Sam Ornitz, Robert Adrian, and Dalton Trumbo, as well as directors Herbert Biberman and Edward Dmytryk. Bertolt Brecht was also scheduled to testify, but fled to East Germany before the hearings.

18. Guback, "Hollywood's International Market," 471.

19. Schatz, *Boom and Bust*, 297.

20. Schatz, *Boom and Bust*, 300.

21. For a discussion of the economics of the cinema in immediate postwar Germany see my *Rubble Films: German Cinema in the Shadow of the Third Reich*.

22. For a further discussion of frozen currencies and their effects on the studios see Guback, "Hollywood's International Market," 474.

23. Guback, "Hollywood's International Market," 477–478.

24. "U.S. Locations Hurt Italian Production Rossellini Says," *Hollywood Reporter*, January 1, 1949.

25. Lev, *Transforming the Screen*, 150.

26. Wilkerson, "Tradeviews," January 15, 1953.

27. *Hollywood Reporter* "Roy Brewer Explains IA's 'Runaway' Pix Complaint," February 2, 1952.

28. *Hollywood Reporter* "Roy Brewer Explains IA's 'Runaway' Pix Complaint," February 2, 1952.

29. Schatz, *Boom and Bust*, 297.

30. *Hollywood Reporter* "Roy Brewer Explains IA's 'Runaway' Pix Complaint," February 2, 1952.

31. *Hollywood Reporter* "Roy Brewer Explains IA's 'Runaway' Pix Complaint," February 2, 1952.

32. *Variety Daily*, February 11, 1953.

33. "Overseas Film Probe Asked by SAG," *Hollywood Citizen-News,* June 18, 1953.

34. "First Pair of U.S. Films Shot Abroad Give New Horizon," *Los Angeles Times,* July 12, 1953.

35. "Wanger Brands Labor's Drive against 'Runaway' Prod'n 'Injurious' to AFL," *Variety Daily,* September 27, 1954.

36. "Eric Johnston Defends Majors' Prod'n Abroad," *Variety Daily,* January 11, 1954.

37. *Variety Daily*, January 11, 1954.

38. Guback, "Hollywood's International Market," 479.

39. Guback, "Hollywood's International Market," 479.

40. "Coast Kids Self; European Film Production is Still Third Cheaper; Preminger Raps U.S. Standbys," *Variety Weekly,* January 30, 1963.

41. *Variety Weekly*, January 30, 1963.

42. *Variety Weekly*, January 30, 1963.

43. "Crafts Hear Zanuck Assurances of 20th Resumption in Hollywood; Costs No Longer Favor Overseas," *Variety Weekly,* January 30, 1963.

CHAPTER 2

1. Herman. *A Talent for Trouble: The Life of Hollywood's Most Acclaimed Director, William Wyler*, 342.

2. Ray, *A Certain Tendency of the Hollywood Cinema*, 138.

3. Ray, *A Certain Tendency of the Hollywood Cinema*, 142.

4. Ray, *A Certain Tendency of the Hollywood Cinema*, 139.

5. Henry Henigson to William Wyler, April 12, 1952. *Roman Holiday* [Production-Location]. Paramount Production Records Collection. Margaret Herrick Library. Academy of Motion Picture Arts and Sciences.

6. Jacob H. Karp to Henry Henigson, June 21, 1952. *Roman Holiday* [Production-Location]. Paramount Production Records Collection.

7. Lewis, "'We Do Not Ask You to Condone This': How the Blacklist Saved Hollywood."

8. Ceplair and Englund, *Inquisition in Hollywood*, 455.

9. Ceplair and Englund, *Inquisition in Hollywood*, 455.

10. Navasky, *Naming Names*, 148.

11. Navasky, *Naming Names*, 148.

12. Navasky, *Naming Names*, 154.

13. Henigson to Wyler, April 12, 1952.

14. In turn, Trumbo's work was an obvious reworking of Robert Riskin's treatment of *It Happened One Night*, which itself was based on Samuel Hopkins Adams' story "The Night Bus." *It Happened One Night* was also remade in 1956 under the title *You Can't Run Away from It* (Dick Powell).

15. *Additional Dialogue: Letters of Dalton Trumbo, 1942–1962*, ed. Helen Manfull.

16. While it is clear that whether credit was given to Ian McClellan Hunter or Dalton Trumbo, Wyler was willing to credit a blacklisted writer, his later behavior

in crediting *Friendly Persuasion* seems to undermine his reputation as an advocate of blacklisted artists. See Joseph Dmohowski "The *Friendly Persuasion* (1956) Screenplay Controversy: Michael Wilson, Jessamyn West, and the Hollywood Blacklist."

17. Herman, *Talent for Trouble*, 341.

18. Herman, *Talent for Trouble*, 342.

19. Trumbo, *Additional Dialogue*, 230.

20. See Internet Movie Database "Roman Holiday." Available at http://www.imdb.com

21. According to Hunter in 1981, Trumbo gave him the treatment, which Hunter submitted to Paramount and for which he was paid $40,000. Hunter was then asked to write the screenplay. Reported in Peter H. Brown's "Blacklist: The Black Tale of Turmoil in Filmland."

22. Henigson to Wyler, April 12, 1952.

23. Henigson to Wyler, April 12, 1952.

24. Frank Caffey to Henry Henigson, May 19, 1952. *Roman Holiday* [Production-Location]. Paramount Production Records Collection.

25. Frank Caffey to Henry Henigson, May 21, 1952. *Roman Holiday* [Production-Location]. Paramount Production Records Collection.

26. Caffey to Henigson, May 21, 1952.

27. Caffey to Henigson, May 21, 1952.

28. Jacob Karp to Henry Henigson, July 22, 1952. *Roman Holiday* [Production-Location]. Paramount Production Records Collection.

29. Karp to Henigson, July 22, 1952.

30. Henigson to Wyler, April 12, 1952.

31. Noted screenwriter Ben Hecht had completed a rewrite in November 1951, over six months before the production left for Rome: it was in no way ready for shooting by the summer of 1952. Given Hecht's prominence as a screenwriter, it is noteworthy that Henigson does not refer to the script as the "Hecht script." It suggests perhaps that the Hecht rewriting was not used. He did not receive screen credit for his work, and in fact the final film does not reflect the Hecht script.

32. Jacob Karp to Henry Henigson, July 21, 1952. *Roman Holiday* [Production-Location]. Paramount Production Records Collection.

33. William Wyler to Don Hartman, July 26, 1952. *Roman Holiday* [Production-Location]. Paramount Production Records Collection.

34. Comencini's portrayal of the *carabinieri*, the Italian local police, earned him censorship from governmental officials. See Millicent Marcus's *Italian Film in the Light of Neorealism*.

35. Wyler to Hartman, July 26, 1952.

36. Comencini's *Bread, Love and Dreams* premiered in 1953 and was successful enough to warrant a sequel, *Bread, Love and Jealousy*, in 1954 as well as a series of similar films throughout Europe in the subsequent decade.

37. Wyler to Hartman, July 26, 1952.

38. Wyler to Hartman, July 26, 1952.

39. Wyler to Hartman, July 26, 1952.

40. Wyler to Hartman, July 26, 1952.

41. Herman, *Talent for Trouble*, 351.

42. Wyler to Hartman, July 26, 1952.

43. Wyler to Hartman, July 26, 1952.

44. Wyler to Hartman, July 26, 1952.

45. Wyler to Hartman, July 26, 1952.

46. Wyler to Hartman, July 26, 1952.

47. William Wyler to Don Hartman, cable, November 17, 1952. *Roman Holiday* [Production-Location] Paramount Production Records Collection.

48. Bordwell, *Figures Traced in Light*, 40.

49. Ray, *A Certain Tendency of the Hollywood Cinema*, 111.

50. I owe this insight to my colleague, Terry Hoagwood.

51. "ROMAN HOLIDAY" PREVIEW FOR MEMBERS OF RADIO AND TELEVISION INDUSTRIES taken from the clipping files for *Roman Holiday* in the Margaret Herrick Library, Academy of Motion Picture Arts and Sciences.

52. *Holiday*, September 1953.

53. *Los Angeles Times,* October 1, 1953.

54. All of the quotes from the preview cards are taken from the Paramount Production Records Collection. *Roman Holiday* [preview cards]. Margaret Herrick Library. Academy of Motion Picture Arts and Sciences.

55. *Holiday*, September 1953.

56. *Los Angeles Daily News*, October 1, 1953.

CHAPTER 3

1. This is, of course, the current strategy of runaway filmmaking in which Vancouver doubles for San Francisco or Toronto for New York.

2. Max Horkheimer and Theodor W. Adorno, *Dialectic of Enlightenment: Philosophical Fragments*, 119.

3. Schatz, *Boom and Bust*, 323.

4. Joseph Breen to Hal Wallis, September 2, 1948. Motion Picture Association of America, Production Code Administration records. Margaret Herrick Library Special Collections. Academy of Motion Picture Arts and Sciences. Referred to hereafter as the "MPAA, PCA records."

5. Joseph Breen to Hal Wallis, September 10, 1948. MPAA, PCA records.

6. Breen to Wallis, September 10, 1948.

7. Robert Theoren to Joseph Breen, October 6, 1948. MPAA, PCA records.

8. Theoren to Breen, October 6, 1948.

9. Joseph Breen to Hall Wallis, October 14, 1948. MPAA, PCA records.

10. Jacobs, *The Wages of Sin: Censorship and the Fallen Woman Film, 1928–1942.*

11. Jacobs, *The Wages of Sin*, 108.

12. Joseph Breen to Margaret Young, December 13, 1949. MPAA, PCA records.

13. Breen to Young, December 13, 1949.

14. J. A. Vizzard to Joseph Breen, interoffice memo, December 20, 1949. MPAA, PCA records.

15. Vizzard to Breen, December 20, 1949.

16. Joseph Breen to David O. Selznick, November 11, 1952. MPAA, PCA records.

17. Joseph Breen to David O. Selznick, November 20, 1952. MPAA, PCA records.

18. See Lev, *Transforming the Screen*, 92.

19. Joseph Breen to Irving Paul Lazar, January 5, 1953. MPAA, PCA records.

20. Breen to Lazar, January 5, 1953.

21. Geoffrey Shurlock to Robert F. Blumofe, May 20, 1955. MPAA, PCA records.

22. Robert F. Blumofe to Geoffrey Shurlock, June 20, 1955. MPAA, PCA records.

23. Ralph Hetzel to Geoffrey Shurlock, June 17, 1955. MPAA, PCA records.

24. Shurlock asks for a removal of an embrace, the dropping of a shoe, and subsequent fireworks, all of which he reads as overly suggestive of an illicit sexual encounter. Moreover, he asks them to omit a later scene in which the character played by Katharine Hepburn mentions the fact that her lover prefers to do something other than sleep during the night. These and other cuts that Shurlock requests remain a part of the 35mm, VHS, and DVD prints in circulation today.

25. Robert F. Blumofe to Geoffrey Shurlock, June 17, 1955. MPAA, PCA records.

26. Geoffrey Shurlock William Gordon, May 2, 1956. MPAA, PCA records.

27. Geoffrey Shurlock to William Gordon, May 23, 1956. MPAA, PCA records.

28. Shurlock to Gordon, May 23, 1956.

29. This is even more apparent in the films discussed in Chapter Four.

30. *Summertime*, in fact, offers three different marriages. The McIllhennys' serves as the old-fashioned, American version, the Yeagers' as the troubled contemporary version, and Renato's as the feudalist European sort.

31. See Bourdieu, *Distinction: A Social Critique of the Judgement of Taste.*

32. Lee Rogow, "One Touch of Venice," *Saturday Review*, June 18, 1955.

33. *Hollywood Reporter*, May 7, 1957.

34. Halliday, *Sirk on Sirk*, 127.

35. As producer Ross Hunter was putting together the *Interlude* production, another reworking of Cain's *Serenade* premiered. Directed by Anthony Mann, *Serenade* (1956) was to serve as a vehicle for Mario Lanza's attempted comeback. It sticks relatively close to the novel's plot of a failed opera singer who finds redemption and renewed success with the help of a prostitute.

CHAPTER 4

1. Belton, *Widescreen Cinema*, 114. Most of the following account of the advent of widescreen cinema is derived from Belton's excellent history of the medium.

2. Belton, *Widescreen Cinema*, 119.

3. Belton, *Widescreen Cinema*, 89.

4. Belton, *Widescreen Cinema*, 96.

5. Belton, *Widescreen Cinema*, 1.

6. *Newsweek*, May 31, 1954.

7. John Rosenfeld, *Dallas Daily News*, May 29, 1954.

8. Belton, *Widescreen Cinema*, 77.

9. Behlmer, *Memo From Darryl F. Zanuck: The Golden Years at Twentieth Century Fox*, 232.

10. Behlmer, *Memo From Zanuck*, 235.

11. Behlmer, *Memo From Zanuck*, 236.

12. Behlmer, *Memo From Zanuck*, 197.

13. Secondari, *Coins in the Fountain.*

14. Behlmer, *Memo From Zanuck*, 238.

15. Behlmer, *Memo From Zanuck*, 248.

16. Twentieth Century-Fox did not grant me the rights to reprint the letter. So, readers will have to go to Los Angeles to check this out for themselves.

17. The title, *Three Coins in the Fountain*, won out against another competitor as well, "We Believe in Love," which was favored by Fox's East Coast financial and marketing offices. Producer Sol Siegel wanted "Three Coins in the Fountain." As W. R. Wilkerson reports,

> On an eve when it began to look as if the sales department selection would win out over the studio's, Sol Siegel, in a frantic effort to get a title switch, called in Sammy Kahn and Jule Styne who were in the studio working on another picture and asked them to write him a song with the title 'Three Coins in the Fountain,' explaining to the composers the story content of the picture. In 24 hours the music team sang and played the song for Siegel, who then rushed it to Zanuck and with his okay rushed the recording to NY and won the battle for the title of 'Three Coins in the Fountain' over 'We Believe in Love.' Not only was the new title a hit, but the song is rated at 20th as increasing the gross better than $2,000,000 on the picture which is now safely headed for a $10,000,000 take. (Wilkerson, "TradeViews" *Hollywood Reporter*, March 8, 1954)

18. Behlmer, *Memo From Zanuck*, 229–230.

19. Behlmer, *Memo From Zanuck*, 215.

20. Behlmer, *Memo From Zanuck*, 234.

21. Pomerance, "Neither Here nor There: *eXistenZ* as 'Elevator Film.'"

22. Pomerance, "Neither Here nor There," 4.

23. The practice of paying local employees of embassies, agencies, etc., according to local pay scales is, indeed, common and generally enforced. It is intended to prevent such agencies from having a disruptive function in local economies.

24. Review of *Three Coins in the Fountain*. *Time*, May 31, 1954.

25. Pomerance, "Neither Here nor There," 12.

26. Truffaut et al., *Hitchcock*, 223.

27. For a productive examination of Hitchcock and the Death Drive see Laura Mulvey's chapter "Death Drives" in *Hitchcock Past and Future*.

28. "Foreign Travel by Americans Has More Than Tripled," *U.S. News and World Report*, May 24, 1957.

29. "Earn Credits For Your Trip Abroad," *Scholastic* 65, December 1, 1954, 107.

30. It is interesting to note that, in the dozens of Hollywood films that fit into the general category of the European romance with which I am working, Europe remains an entirely "white" continent.

31. "Grace Kelly Tells How to Travel Light" *Woman's Home Companion*, April, 1955. 46–47

32. Endy, *Cold War Holidays: American Tourism in France*, 32.

33. *Cold War Holidays* provides a thorough discussion of postwar tourism in France from 1945 through the 1970s. See especially Chapter Three, which offers the most useful discussion of the class tensions inherent in early debates regarding tourism development.

34. For a thorough explanation of the relationship between editing and widescreen format see David Bordwell, Janet Staiger, and Kristin Thompson, *The Classical Hollywood Cinema*, 363.

35. "Screen in Review: *To Catch a Thief,*" September 2, 1955.

36. I would argue that Hitchcock's obsession with the faces on Mt. Rushmore in *North by Northwest* is a reference to his earlier inability to depict a close-up face with the anamorphic process.

37. C. O. Erickson to Frank Caffey, June 13, 1954. *To Catch a Thief* [Production-Location]. Paramount Production Records Collection. Margaret Herrick Library. Academy of Motion Picture Arts and Sciences.

38. Lears, "A Matter of Taste: Corporate Cultural Hegemony in a Mass-Consumption Society," 46.

39. Levin, "Introduction" to *The Ambassadors.*

40. Nash, "Who Wants to Travel All Over Europe," 28.

41. Krantz, "Those 'Frightful' American Tourists," 61.

42. Durgnat, *The Strange Case of Alfred Hitchcock*, 253.

43. Durgnat, *Strange Case of Hitchcock*, 254.

44. Durgnat, *Strange Case of Hitchcock*, 254.

45. Durgnat, *Strange Case of Hitchcock*, 254.

46. See Jameson, "The Vanishing Mediator: Or, Max Weber as Storyteller," in *The Ideology of Theory: Essays 1971–1986*, 3–34.

47. Slavoj Žižek's most thorough discussion of the vanishing mediator, a term he lifts from Frederic Jameson, is found in *For They Know Not What They Do: Enjoyment as a Political Factor*, 179–188.

48. My mother-in-law is one such spectator who remembers going to these films to look at the clothes more than to watch the story.

CHAPTER 5

1. This identity, as it often has in America, ignored the interests and backgrounds of millions of Americans, including those of Japanese heritage, whose cultural and racial heritage was not bound to Europe.

2. My mother, a personnel office employee of General Dynamics during the war, often told the story of how, upon hearing the news of the Japanese surrender on VJ day, the shop floor workers, almost all women, simply walked out of the plant and on to the streets. They apparently returned a few days later to collect their pay, without making any claims on further employment, either immediately or in the near future.

3. Kaja Silverman uses gender upheaval in wake of the war as the organizing principle for her study of postwar constructions of masculinity in film in *Male Subjectivity at the Margins*. In her chapter on the World War II coming home story, Silverman describes a set of films in which "the hero no longer feels 'at home' in the house or town where he grew up . . . he has been dislodged from the narratives and subject positions which make up the dominant fiction" (53). The primary films that constitute her study are *The Best Years of Our Lives* (William Wyler, 1946), *It's a Wonderful Life* (Frank Capra, 1946), and *The Guilt of Janet Ames* (Henry Levin, 1947). Each of the films she discusses depicts men struggling to insert themselves into the dominant fiction of the triumphant World War II veteran. In so doing, the films reveal how flimsy and unsatisfying this ideological structure may have been.

4. Shukart and Scibetta *War Brides of World War II*, 131.

5. Shukart and Scibetta, *War Brides*, 131.

6. "The Quarter's Poll," *Public Opinion Quarterly*, 385.

7. Goedde, *GIs and Germans*, 75.

8. Goedde, *GIs and Germans*, 79.

9. Shukart and Scibetta, *War Brides*, 135.

10. For a more thorough discussion of Hollywood's relations with OMGUS see my Chapter One, "Dismantling the Dream Factory: The Film Industry in Berubbled Germany," in *Rubble Films: German Cinema in the Shadow of the Third Reich*, 9–24.

11. Henry Morgenthau was the Roosevelt administration official who proposed briefly the notion that, upon capitulation, Germany should be completely deindustrialized and reverted solely to an agricultural economy.

12. The American premiere of *Germania, Anno Zero* was in September 1949.

13. In actuality, the actor Millard Mitchell who plays Plummer was younger than both Dietrich and Arthur, the latter being the oldest of the film's stars. In a casting choice rare in Hollywood, she was thirteen years older than her paramour in the film, John Lund.

14. On May 23, 1949 the basic law of the Federal Republic of Germany was ratified thus calling the newly formed state into being. Berlin's status vis-à-vis the Federal Republic remained in question until German reunification over forty years later.

15. Not only did early German postwar filmmaking dedicate itself to telling moral tales set against the destroyed urban German background, Italian, French, and British filmmakers found the scenario similarly fascinating. See for instance Roberto Rossellini's *Germania, Anno Zero* (1948) or Carol Reed's *The Third Man* (1949). For further discussion of the documentary qualities of the film see Ralph Stern's "*The Big Lift* (1950): Image and Identity in Blockaded Berlin."

16. After watching dozens of runaway films, certain indicators of location and Hollywood studio work emerge. Studio set designers were almost never sensitive to small details of architectural difference. For instance, European doors and door handles are generally shaped differently than American ones, and windows usually function differently. Moreover, the layout of the apartments themselves can also often indicate whether a scene was shot on location or on a southern California back lot.

17. Interestingly enough, the German films of the early postwar era tend to identify Germany with its defeated male soldier returning from war. The films seek to rehabilitate the men as a way of rehabilitating the community. See my *Rubble Films*.

18. Another runaway film from 1958 that takes up the American racial discourse is Delmer Daves' *Kings Go Forth*. A combat film set late in the war in southern France, it presents a love triangle between two GIs from the same company and a young girl they meet while on leave at the French Riviera. The plot twists when they discover that not only is the girl an American, but that her late father was an African–American. Her family fled to France before the war to escape miscegenation laws in the United States. While the film does not fit into the generic parameters under discussion here, being more of a combat film than a romance, it does point to a feature of all the films, except *Fräulein*, under discussion here. The travelogue romance allows a momentary reprieve from the discussions of race relations that were causing such furor stateside. The unsettling notion presented in *Kings Go Forth*, namely that African-Americans fled to Europe for civil rights unavailable to them at home, is not part of the Europe or the America presented in most of the films under discussion. Political enlightenment, to the degree that it plays out at all in these films, remains a one-way street.

19. The film also repeatedly refers to her as "Erika," while maintaining "Major McClain" when referring to him. This slight difference exaggerates the power gap between them. Only in the end, when the word "Fräulein" is rehabilitated, is she referred to as "Fräulein Angermann."

20. *New York Times,* November 5, 1960.

21. *Esquire*, March 1962.

22. Lubitsch was not only the mentor for many of the German speaking directors who moved to Hollywood, he was also the pioneer of the international romance, which was arguably the forerunner of the travelogue romance. A prime example of this type of film was *Ninotchka* (1939).

23. Wilder also participated in the travelogue romance, directing *Love in the Afternoon* (1957), which was filmed in Paris. He also directed *Sabrina* (1954), which while shot in the United States depends heavily upon the tropes developed in the travelogue romance.

CHAPTER 6

1. Originally published as "A Semantic/Syntactic Approach to Film Genre." Altman revisits the question in his conclusion to *Film/Genre*.

2. *New York Times*, August 27, 1949.

3. *New York Times*, February 2, 1951.

4. *New York Times*, May 21, 1954.

5. *New York Times*, June 22, 1955.

6. *New York Times*, June 9, 1958.

7. *Variety Weekly*, May 8, 1957.

8. *Hollywood Citizen News*, September 19, 1957.

9. A. H. Weiler, *New York Times*, August 28, 1953.

10. *Cue*, June 25, 1955.

11. *The New Yorker*, June 25, 1955.

12. Altman, *Film/Genre*, 195.

13. Schatz, *Hollywood Genres*, 41.

14. Vienna: Verlag Kurt Desch, 1960. My translation.

15. *New York Times*, October 11, 1961.

16. *The New Republic*, November 13, 1961.

17. *Los Angeles Times*, November 20, 1961.

18. *Beyond the Pleasure Principle* is where Freud discusses the death drive most thoroughly. See *The Standard Edition of the Complete Psychological Works of Sigmund Freud* translated from the German under the general editorship of James Strachey, in collaboration with Anna Freud.

19. *Two Weeks in Another Town* comes off, in some respects, as a Hollywood version of Federico Fellini's 8½ of the following year, a film about a director's inability to make the film he is contracted to make.

20. Schatz, *Hollywood Genres*, 80.

21. Schatz, *Hollywood Genres*, 110.

22. Altman, *Film/Genre*, 22.

23. Dentith, *Parody*, 9.

24. The film *My Fair Lady* (George Cukor, 1964) was actually released months after *Paris, When it Sizzles*, but the controversial decision to cast Audrey Hepburn in the starring role rather than Julie Andrews, who had created the role on Broadway, had been news for some time.

25. See Peter Lev's comments about the film in *Transforming the Screen*, 60.

Filmography[*]

8½
Premiere: 1963
Running Time: 138 min.
Director: Federico Fellini
Production Company: Cineriz and
    Francinex

All that Heaven Allows
Premiere: 1955
Running Time: 89 min.
Director: Douglas Sirk
Production Company: Universal
    International Pictures

An American in Paris
Premiere: 1951
Running Time: 113 min.
Director: Vincente Minnelli
Production Company: Loew's and
    MGM

L'Amore
Premiere: 1948

Running Time: 78 min.
Director: Roberto Rossellini
Production Company: Finecine and
    Tevere Film

The Barefoot Contessa
Premiere: 1954
Running Time: 128 min.
Director: Joseph L. Mankiewicz
Production Company: Figaro

Battle Hymn
Premiere: 1957
Running Time: 108 min.
Director: Douglas Sirk
Production Company: Universal
    International Pictures

Battleground
Premiere: 1949
Running Time: 118 min.
Director: William A. Wellman
Production Company: MGM

---

[*] Compiled using the Internet Movie Database, http://www.imdb.com

Before Sunrise
Premiere: 1995
Running Time: 105 min.
Director: Richard Linklater
Production Company: Castle Rock
    Entertainment

Before Sunset
Premiere: 2004
Running Time: 77 min.
Director: Richard Linklater
Production Company: Castle Rock
    Entertainment

Ben-Hur
Premiere: 1959
Running Time: 212 min.
Director: William Wyler
Production Company: MGM

Berlin Express
Premiere: 1948
Running Time: 87 min.
Director: Jacques Tourneur
Production Company: RKO

The Best Years of Our Lives
Premiere: 1946
Running Time: 172 min.
Director: William Wyler
Production Company: Samuel Goldwyn
    Company

Betrayed
Premiere: 1954
Running Time: 108 min.
Director: Gottfried Reinhardt
Production Company: MGM

Bhowani Junction
Premiere: 1956
Running Time: 110 min.
Director: George Cukor
Production Company: MGM

The Bicycle Thief
Premiere: 1948

Running Time: 93 min.
Director: Vittorio De Sica
Production Company: Produzioni
    De Sica

The Big Lift
Premiere: 1950
Running Time: 120 min.
Director: George Seaton
Production Company: Twentieth
    Century-Fox

Bigger Than Life
Premiere: 1956
Running Time: 95 min.
Director: Nicholas Ray
Production Company: Twentieth
    Century-Fox

Blazing Saddles
Premiere: 1974
Running Time: 93 min.
Director: Mel Brooks
Production Company: Crossbow and
    Warner Brothers

Bonjour Tristesse
Premiere: 1958
Running Time: 94 min.
Director: Otto Preminger
Production Company: Wheel Productions

Bread, Love, and Dreams
Premiere: 1953
Running Time: 92 min.
Director: Luigi Comencini
Production Company: Titanus

Bread, Love, and Jealousy
Premiere: 1954
Running Time: 97 min.
Director: Luigi Comencini
Production Company: Titanus

Breakfast at Tiffany's
Premiere: 1961
Running Time: 115 min.

Director: Blake Edwards
Production Company: Jurow-Shepherd

The Cabinet of Dr. Caligari
Premiere: 1920
Running Time: 71 min.
Director: Robert Wiene
Production Company: Decla-Bioscop
    AG

Casablanca
Premiere: 1942
Running Time: 102 min.
Director: Michael Curtiz
Production Company: Warner Brothers

Catch-22
Premiere: 1970
Running Time: 122 min.
Director: Mike Nichols
Production Company: Filmways and
    Paramount

Charade
Premiere: 1963
Running Time: 113 min.
Director: Stanley Donen
Production Company: Universal

Cleopatra
Premiere: 1963
Running Time: 192
Director: Joseph L. Mankiewicz
Production Company: Twentieth
    Century-Fox

Come September
Premiere: 1961
Running Time: 112 min.
Director: Robert Mulligan
Production Company: Universal
    International Pictures, 7 Pictures,
    and Raoul Walsh Enterprises

Dial M for Murder
Premiere: 1954
Running Time: 105 min.

Director: Alfred Hitchcock
Production Company: Warner Brothers

The Dirty Dozen
Premiere: 1967
Running Time: 145 min.
Director: Robert Aldrich
Production Company: MKH and MGM

Dodsworth
Premiere: 1936
Running Time: 101 min.
Director: William Wyler
Production Company: Samuel Goldwyn
    Company

La Dolce Vita
Premiere: 1960
Running Time: 174 min.
Director: Federico Fellini
Production Company: Riama Film, Pathé
    Consortium Cinema, Gray Film

Elephant Walk
Premiere: 1954
Running Time: 103 min.
Director: William Dieterle
Production Company: Paramount

eXistenZ
Premiere: 1999
Running Time: 97 min.
Director: David Cronenberg
Production Company: Alliance Atlantis
    Communications

Father of the Bride
Premiere: 1950
Running Time: 92 min.
Director: Vincente Minnelli
Production Company: MGM

The Fifth Element
Premiere: 1997
Running Time: 126 min.
Director: Luc Bresson
Production Company: Gaumont

A Foreign Affair
Premiere: 1948
Running Time: 116 min.
Director: Billy Wilder
Production Company: Paramount

Forget Paris
Premiere: 1995
Running Time: 101 min.
Director: Billy Crystal
Production Company: Castle Rock
    Entertainment

Fräulein
Premiere: 1958
Running Time: 95 min.
Director: Henry Koster
Production Company: Twentieth
    Century-Fox

French Kiss
Premiere: 1995
Running Time: 111 min.
Director: Lawrence Kasdan
Production Company: Polygram Filmed
    Entertainment

Funny Face
Premiere: 1957
Running Time: 103 min.
Director: Stanley Donen
Production Company: Paramount

Gentlemen Prefer Blondes
Premiere: 1953
Running Time: 91
Director: Howard Hawks
Production Company: Twentieth
    Century-Fox

Gentleman's Agreement
Premiere: 1947
Running Time: 118 min.
Director: Elia Kazan
Production Company: Twentieth
    Century-Fox

Germania, Anno Zero
Premiere: 1948
Running Time: 78 min.
Director: Roberto Rossellini
Production Company: Produzione Salvo
    D'Angelo and Tevere Film

GI Blues
Premiere: 1960
Running Time: 104 min.
Director: Norman Taurog
Production Company: Paramount

Grapes of Wrath
Premiere: 1940
Running Time: 128 min.
Director: John Ford
Production Company: Twentieth
    Century-Fox

The Guilt of Janet Ames
Premiere: 1947
Running Time: 83 min.
Director: Henry Levin
Production Company: Columbia

High Anxiety
Premiere: 1977
Running Time: 94 min.
Director: Mel Brooks
Production Company: Twentieth
    Century-Fox

How to Marry a Millionaire
Premiere: 1953
Running Time: 95 min.
Director: Jean Negulesco
Production Company: Twentieth
    Century-Fox

How to Steal a Million
Premiere: 1966
Running Time: 123 min.
Director: William Wyler
Production Company: World Wide
    Productions

I Was a Male War Bride
Premiere: 1949
Running Time: 105 min.
Director: Howard Hawks
Production Company: Twentieth
    Century-Fox

If It's Tuesday, This Must Be Belgium
Premiere: 1969
Running Time: 105 min.
Director: Mel Stuart
Production Company: Wolper Pictures

Indiscretion of an American Wife
Also known as: *Stazione Termini*
Premiere: 1953 (US Premiere: 1954)
Running Time: 72 min.
Director: Vittorio De Sica
Production Company: Columbia
    Pictures, Produzioni De Sica

Interlude
Premiere: 1957
Running Time: 90 min.
Director: Douglas Sirk
Production Company: Universal
    International Pictures

Island in the Sun
Premiere: 1957
Running Time: 119 min.
Director: Robert Rossen
Production Company: DFZ Productions
    and Twentieth Century-Fox

It Happened One Night
Premiere: 1934
Running Time: 105 min.
Director: Frank Capra
Production Company: Columbia
    Pictures

It Started in Naples
Premiere: 1960
Running Time: 100 min.
Director: Melville Shavelson

Production Company: Capri
    Productions and Paramount

It's a Wonderful Life
Premiere: 1946
Running Time: 130 min.
Director: Frank Capra
Production Company: Liberty Films

Key Largo
Premiere: 1948
Running Time: 100 min.
Director: John Huston
Production Company: Warner Brothers

Kings Go Forth
Premiere: 1958
Running Time: 109 min.
Director: Delmer Daves
Production Company: Frank Ross-Eton
    Productions

The Last Laugh
Also known as: *Der Letzte Mann*
Premiere: 1924
Running Time: 77 min.
Director: F. W. Murnau
Production Company: Universum Film
    Aktiengesellschaft (UFA)

Last Tango in Paris
Premiere: 1972
Running Time: 136 min.
Director: Bernardo Bertolucci
Production Company: Produzioni
    Europee Associati and Les
    Productions Artistes Associés

Last Time I Saw Paris
Premiere: 1954
Running Time: 116 min.
Director: Richard Brooks
Production Company: MGM

Le Mèpris
Premiere: 1963

Running Time: 103 min.
Director: Jean-Luc Godard
Production Company: Compagnia
   Cinematografica Champion

Light in the Piazza
Premiere: 1962
Running Time: 102 min.
Director: Guy Green
Production Company: MGM

Little Boy Lost
Premiere: 1953
Running Time: 95 min.
Director: George Seaton
Production Company: Paramount

The Longest Day
Premiere: 1962
Running Time: 178 min.
Producer: Darryl F. Zanuck
Production Company: Twentieth
   Century-Fox

Lost Honeymoon
Premiere: 1947
Running Time: 70 min.
Director: Leigh Jason
Production Company: Bryan Foy
   Productions

Love in the Afternoon
Premiere: 1957
Running Time: 130 min.
Director: Billy Wilder
Production Company: Allied Artists

Love is a Many-Splendored Thing
Premiere: 1955
Running Time: 102 min.
Director: Henry King
Production Company: Twentieth
   Century-Fox

Macao
Premiere: 1952

Running Time: 81 min.
Director: Josef von Sternberg and
   Nicholas Ray
Production Company: RKO

The Man in the Gray Flannel Suit
Premiere: 1956
Running Time: 153 min.
Director: Nunnally Johnson
Production Company: Twentieth
   Century-Fox

The Man on the Eiffel Tower
Premiere: 1949
Running Time: 97 min.
Director: Burgess Meredith
Production Company: A&T Film and
   Gray Film

Man on a Tightrope
Premiere: 1953
Running Time: 105 min.
Director: Elia Kazan
Production Company: Twentieth
   Century-Fox

The Man Who Knew Too Much
Premiere: 1956
Running Time: 120 min.
Director: Alfred Hitchcock
Production Company: Filwite
   Productions, Paramount

The Man Who Shot Liberty Valence
Premiere: 1962
Running Time: 123 min.
Director: John Ford
Production Company: John Ford
   Productions, Paramount

The Misfits
Premiere: 1961
Running Time: 124 min.
Director: John Huston
Production Company: Seven Arts
   Productions

Mogambo
Premiere: 1953
Running Time: 115 min.
Director: John Ford
Production Company: MGM

Mrs. Miniver
Premiere: 1942
Running Time: 134 min.
Director: William Wyler
Production Company: Loew's, MGM

The Miracle
See *L'Amore*

The Murderers Are Among Us
Premiere: 1946
Running Time: 85 min.
Director: Wolfgang Staudte
Production Company: DEFA

My Fair Lady
Premiere: 1964
Running Time: 170 min.
Director: George Cukor
Production Company: Warner Brothers,
    First National Pictures

Night People
Premiere: 1954
Running Time: 94 min.
Director: Nunnally Johnson
Production Company: Twentieth
    Century-Fox

Ninotchka
Premiere: 1939
Running Time: 110 min.
Director: Ernst Lubitsch
Production Company: MGM

North by Northwest
Premiere: 1959
Running Time: 136 min.
Director: Alfred Hitchcock
Production Company: MGM

Nosferatu
Premiere: 1922
Running Time: 94 min.
Director: F. W. Murnau
Production Company: Jofa-Atelier
    Berlin-Johannisthal, Prana-Film

On the Waterfront
Premiere: 1954
Running Time: 108 min.
Director: Elia Kazan
Production Company: Horizon
    Pictures, Columbia

One, Two, Three
Premiere: 1961
Running Time: 115 min.
Director: Billy Wilder
Production Company: Mirisch
    Corporation, Pyramid Productions

Open City
Also known as: *Roma, città aperta*
Premiere: 1945
Running Time: 100 min.
Director: Roberto Rossellini
Production Company: Excelsa Film

Paisa
Also known as: *Paisan*
Premiere: 1946
Running Time: 125 min.
Director: Roberto Rossellini
Production Company:
    Organizzazione Film
    Internazionali, Foreign Film
    Productions

Paris Blues
Premiere: 1961
Running Time: 98 min.
Director: Martin Ritt
Production Company: Diane
    Productions, Jason Films,
    Monica Corporation, Monmount,
    Pennebaker Productions

Paris Holiday
Premiere: 1958
Running Time: 103 min.
Director: Gerd Oswald
Production Company: Tolda Productions

Paris, When it Sizzles
Premiere: 1964
Running Time: 110 min.
Director: Richard Quine
Production Company: Richard Quine
    Productions, George Axelrod
    Productions

Pinky
Premiere: 1949
Running Time: 102 min.
Director: Elia Kazan
Production Company: Twentieth
    Century-Fox

Private Benjamin
Premiere: 1980
Running Time: 109
Director: Howard Zieff
Production Company: Warner Brothers

Quo Vadis
Premiere: 1951
Running Time:
Director: Mervyn Le Roy
Production Company: MGM

Rear Window
Premiere: 1954
Running Time: 112
Director: Alfred Hitchcock
Production Company: Paramount

Rhapsody
Premiere: 1954
Running Time: 115 min
Director: Charles Vidor
Production Company: MGM

The River
Premiere: 1938

Running Time: 31 min.
Director: Pare Lorentz
Production Company: Farm Security
    Administration

The Robe
Premiere: 1953
Running Time: 135 min
Director: Henry Koster
Production Company: Twentieth
    Century-Fox

Roman Holiday
Premiere: 1953
Running Time: 118 min
Director: William Wyler
Production Company: Paramount

The Roman Spring of Mrs. Stone
Premiere: 1961
Running Time: 103 min
Director: José Quintero
Production Company: Warner
    Brothers

Rome Adventure
Premiere: 1962
Running Time: 119 min
Director: Delmer Daves
Production Company: Warner Brothers

The Roots of Heaven
Premiere: 1958
Running Time: 121 min.
Director: John Huston
Production Company: Twentieth
    Century-Fox

Sabrina
Premiere: 1954
Running Time: 113 min
Director: Billy Wilder
Production Company: Paramount

Saving Private Ryan
Premiere: 1998
Running Time: 170 min

Director: Steven Spielberg
Production Company: DreamWorks and
Amblin Entertainment

Sayonara
Premiere: 1957
Running Time: 147 min.
Director: Joshua Logan
Production Company: Pennebaker
Productions and William Goetz
Productions

Scary Movie
Premiere: 2000
Running Time: 88 min
Director: Keenen Ivory Wayans
Production Company: Dimension Films

The Search
Premiere: 1948
Running Time: 105 min
Director: Fred Zinneman
Production Company: MGM

September Affair
Premiere: 1950
Running Time: 104 min
Director: William Dieterle
Production Company: Paramount

Serenade
Premiere: 1956
Running Time: 121 min
Director: Anthony Mann
Production Company: Warner Brothers

Shoeshine
Also Known As: *Sciuscià*
Premiere: 1946
Running Time: 93 min.
Director: Vittorio De Sica
Production Company: Societa
Cooperativa Alfa Cinematografica

Silent Movie
Premiere: 1976
Running Time: 87 min.

Director: Mel Brooks
Production Company: Crossbow
Productions

The Snows of Kilimanjaro
Premiere: 1952
Running Time: 114 min.
Director: Henry King
Production Company: Twentieth
Century-Fox

Somewhere in Berlin
Also Known As: *Irgendwo in Berlin*
Premiere: 1946
Running Time: 80 min.
Director: Gerhard Lamprecht
Production Company: DEFA

The Sound of Music
Premiere: 1965
Running Time: 174 min.
Director: Robert Wise
Production Company: Twentieth
Century Fox

Spartacus
Premiere: 1960
Running Time: 184 min.
Director: Stanley Kubrick
Production Company: Bryna
Productions

Stage Fright
Premiere: 1950
Running Time: 110 min.
Director: Alfred Hitchcock
Production Company: Warner Brothers

Stazione Termini
See *Indiscretion of an American Wife*

Stromboli
Premiere: 1950
Running Time: 107 min.
Director: Roberto Rossellini
Production Company: Berit Films and
RKO

Suddenly, Last Summer
Premiere: 1959
Running Time: 114 min.
Director: Joseph L. Mankiewicz
Production Company: Horizon Pictures
    and Columbia Pictures

Summertime
Premiere: 1955
Running Time: 100 min.
Director: David Lean
Production Company: London
    Film Productions and Lopert
    Productions

Sunset Blvd.
Premiere: 1950
Running Time: 110 min.
Director: Billy Wilder
Production Company: Paramount

The Ten Commandments
Premiere: 1956
Running Time: 220 min.
Director: Cecil B. DeMille
Production Company: Motion Picture
    Associates and Paramount Pictures

The Third Man
Premiere: 1949
Running Time: 104 min.
Director: Carol Reed
Production Company: London Film
    Productions and British Lion Film
    Corporation

This is Cinerama
Premiere: 1952
Running Time: 116 min.
Producer: Fred Waller
Production Company: Cinerama
    Productions

Three Coins in the Fountain
Premiere: 1954
Running Time: 102 min.

Director: Jean Negulesco
Production Company: Twentieth
    Century-Fox

To Catch a Thief
Premiere: 1955
Running Time: 106 min.
Director: Alfred Hitchcock
Production Company: Paramount

Torn Curtain
Premiere: 1966
Running Time: 128 min.
Director: Alfred Hitchcock
Production Company: Universal
    Pictures

Total Recall
Premiere: 1990
Running Time: 113 min.
Director: Paul Verhoeven
Production Company: Carolco
    International and TriStar Pictures

Town Without Pity
Premiere: 1961
Running Time: 105 min.
Director: Gottfried Reinhardt
Production Company: Mirish
    Corporation, Osweg, and Gloria
    Film

Trapeze
Premiere: 1956
Running Time: 105 min.
Director: Carol Reed
Production Company: Hill-Hecht-
    Lancaster Productions and Susan
    Production

Twelve O'Clock High
Premiere: 1949
Running Time: 132 min.
Director: Henry King
Production Company: Twentieth
    Century-Fox

Two Weeks in Another Town
Premiere: 1962
Running Time: 107 min.
Director: Vincente Minelli
Production Company: John Houseman
    Productions and MGM

Under Capricorn
Premiere: 1949
Running Time: 117 min.
Director: Alfred Hitchcock
Production Company: Transatlantic
    Pictures

Vertigo
Premiere: 1958
Running Time: 128 min.
Director: Alfred Hitchcock
Production Company: Alfred J. Hitchcock
    Productions and Paramount

When Tomorrow Comes
Premiere: 1939
Running Time: 90 min.
Director: John M. Stahl
Production Company: Universal
    Pictures

White Heat
Premiere: 1949
Running Time: 114 min.

Director: Raoul Walsh
Production Company: Warner Brothers
    and First National Pictures

The Wizard of Oz
Premiere: 1939
Running Time: 101 min.
Director: Victor Fleming
Production Company: MGM and
    Loew's

You Can't Run Away from It
Premiere: 1956
Running Time: 95 min.
Director: Dick Powell
Production Company: Columbia
    Pictures

Young Frankenstein
Premiere: 1974
Running Time: 106 min.
Director: Mel Brooks
Production Company: Gruskoff/
    Venture, Crossbow, and Jouer Ltd.

The World of Suzy Wong
Premiere: 1960
Running Time: 126 min.
Director: Richard Quine
Production Company: World
    Enterprises

Bibliography

Abel, Richard. "History Can Work For You, You Know How To Use It." *Cinema Journal* 44 (2004): 107–112.

Altman, Rick. *Film/Genre*. London: British Film Institute Publishing, 1999.

Anderson, Thom. "Red Hollywood." In *Literature and the Visual Arts in Contemporary Society*, edited by Suzanne Ferguson and Barbara Groseclose, 141–196. Columbus: Ohio State University Press, 1985.

Aristotle. *Nichomachean Ethics*. Translated by Terence Irwin. 2nd ed. Indianapolis: Hackett, 1992.

Basinger, Jeanine. *A Woman's View: How Hollywood Spoke To Women, 1930–1960*. New York: Alfred A. Knopf, 1993.

———. *The World War II Combat Film: Anatomy of a Genre*. Middletown, Conn.: Wesleyan University Press, 2003.

Behlmer, Rudy. *Memo from Darryl F. Zanuck: The Golden Years at Twentieth Century Fox*. New York: Grove Press, 1993.

Belton, John. *Widescreen Cinema*. Cambridge, Mass.: Harvard University Press, 1992.

Betz, Mark. "The Name Above the (Sub)Title: Internationalism, Coproduction, and Polyglot European Art Cinema." *Camera Obscura* 46 16 (2001): 1–44.

Bordwell, David. *Figures Traced in Light: On Cinematic Staging*. Berkeley: University of California Press, 2005.

———. *Making Meaning: Inference and Rhetoric in the Interpretation of Cinema*. Cambridge, Mass.: Harvard University Press, 1989.

Bordwell, David, Janet Staiger, and Kristin Thompson. *The Classical Hollywood Cinema: Film Style & Mode of Production to 1960*. New York: Columbia University Press, 1985.

Bourdieu, Pierre. *Distinction: A Social Critique of the Judgement of Taste*. Cambridge, Mass.: Harvard University Press, 1984.

Boyer, Paul. *By the Bomb's Early Light: American Thought and Culture at the Dawn of the Atomic Age*. Chapel Hill: University of North Carolina Press, 1994.

Bronfen, Elisabeth. *Home in Hollywood: The Imaginary Geography of Cinema*. New York: Columbia University Press, 2004.

Brown, Peter H. "Blacklist: The Black Tale of Turmoil in Filmland." *Los Angeles Times*, February 1, 1981.

Buhle, Paul, and Dave Wagner. *Hide in Plain Sight: The Hollywood Blacklistees in Film and Television, 1950–2002*. New York: Palgrave Macmillan, 2003.

Byars, Jackie. *All that Hollywood Allows: Re-Reading Gender in the 1950s Melodrama*. Chapel Hill: University of North Carolina Press, 1991.

Cain, James M. *Serenade*. New York: A.A. Knopf, 1937

Capra, Frank. *The Name above the Title: An Autobiography*. New York: Macmillan Company, 1971.

Casper, Drew. *Postwar Hollywood: 1946–1962*. Oxford: Blackwell, 2007.

Ceplair, Larry, and Steven Englund. *The Inquisition in Hollywood: Politics in the Film Community, 1930–1960*. Urbana: University of Illinois Press, 2003.

Coleman, Hebert. *The Man Who Knew Hitchcock: A Hollywood Memoir*. Lanham, Md.: The Scarecrow Press, 2007.

Corber, Robert J. *In the Name of National Security: Hitchcock, Homophobia, and the Political Construction of Gender in Postwar America*. Durham, N.C.: Duke University Press, 1993.

Dentith, Simon. *Parody*. The New Critical Idiom. London: Routledge, 2000.

DeVany, Arthur, and Henry McMillan. "Was the Antitrust Action that Broke Up the Movie Studios Good for the Movies?: Evidence from the Stock Market." *American Law and Economics Review* 6 (2004): 135–153.

DeZoysa, Richard, and Otto Newman. "Globalization, Soft Power and the Challenge of Hollywood." *Contemporary Politics* 8 (2002): 185–202.

Dmohowski, Joseph. "The *Friendly Persuasion* (1956) Screenplay Controversy: Michael Wilson, Jessamyn West, and the Hollywood Blacklist." *Historical Journal of Film, Radio and Television* 22 (2002): 491–514.

Durgnat, Raymond. *The Strange Case of Alfred Hitchcock: Or, the Plain Man's Hitchcock*. Cambridge, Mass.: MIT Press, 1974.

Dyer, Richard. "Never Too Thin: Richard Dyer on the Awkward Perfection of Audrey Hepburn." *Sight and Sound* 3 (1993): 59.

Eldridge, David N. "'Dear Owen': The CIA, Luigi Luraschi, and Hollywood, 1953." *Historical Journal of Film, Radio, and Television* 20 (2000): 149–196.

Elmer, Greg, and Mike Gasher. *Contracting Out Hollywood: Runaway Productions and Foreign Location Shooting*. Critical media studies. Lanham, Md.: Rowman & Littlefield, 2005.

Elsaesser, Thomas. "Tales of Sound and Fury." *Monogram* 4 (1972): 2–15.

Endy, Christopher. *Cold War Holidays: American Tourism in France*. The new Cold War history. Chapel Hill: University of North Carolina Press, 2004.

Fishelov, David. *Metaphors of Genre: The Role of Analogies in Genre Theory*. University Park, Penn.: Pennsylvania State University Press, 1993.

"Foreign Travel by Americans Has More Than Tripled." *U.S. News and World Report* 42 (May 24, 1957): 42–43.

Freud, Sigmund, James Strachey, Anna Freud, and Carrie Lee Rothgeb. *The Standard Edition of the Complete Psychological Works of Sigmund Freud. Volume 18, Beyond the Pleasure Principle; Group Psychology; and, Other Works.* London: Hogarth Press and the Institute of Psycho-Analysis, 1953.

Georgakas, Dan. "The Hollywood Reds: 50 Years Later." *American Communist History* 2 (2003): 63–76.

Goedde, Petra. *GIs and Germans: Culture, Gender, and Foreign Relations, 1945–1949.* New Haven: Yale University Press, 2003.

Gomery, Douglas. *Shared Pleasures: A History of Movie Presentation in the United States.* Wisconsin Studies in Film. Madison: University of Wisconsin Press, 1992.

Grant, Barry Keith. *Film Genre Reader III.* Austin: University of Texas Press, 2003.

Gregor, Manfred. *Stadt ohne Mitleid.* Vienna: Verlag Kurt Desch, 1960.

Guback, Thomas. "Hollywood's International Market." In *The American Film Industry,* edited by Tino Balio, 463–486. Madison: University of Wisconsin Press, 1985.

———. *The International Film Industry: Western Europe and America since 1945.* Bloomington: Indiana University Press, 1969.

Gussow, Mel. *Don't Say Yes Until I Am Finished Talking: A Biography of Darryl F. Zanuck.* New York: Pocket Books, 1972.

Halberstam, David. *The Fifties.* New York: Fawcett Books, 1993.

Halliday, Jon. *Sirk on Sirk.* London: Faber and Faber, 1971.

Handyside, Fiona. "'Paris isn't for Changing Planes; It's for Changing Your Outlook': Audrey Hepburn as European Star in 1950s France." *French Cultural Studies* 14 (2003): 288–298.

———. "Beyond Hollywood, into Europe: The Tourist Gaze in *Gentlemen Prefer Blondes* (Hawks, 1953) and *Funny Face* (Donen, 1957)." *Studies in European Cinema* 1 (2004): 77–89.

Harvey, James. *Movie Love in the Fifties.* New York: Alfred A. Knopf, 2001.

Herman, Jan. *A Talent for Trouble: The Life of Hollywood's Most Acclaimed Director, William Wyler.* New York: G. P. Putnam and Sons, 1995.

Higson, Andrew, and Richard Maltby. *Film Europe and Film America: Cinema, Commerce and Cultural Exchange 1920–1939.* Exeter: University of Exeter Press, 1999.

Hillier, Jim. *Cahiers du Cinéma.* Cambridge: Harvard University Press, 1985.

Hollywood Citizen-News, "Overseas Film Probe Asked by SAG," June 18, 1953.

Hollywood Reporter, "U.S. Locations Hurt Italian Production Rossellini Says," January 1, 1949.

———. "Roy Brewer Explains IA's 'Runaway' Pix Complaint," February 2, 1952.

Horkheimer, Max and Theodor W. Adorno. *Dialectic of Enlightenment: Philosophical Fragments* ed. Gunzelin Schmid Noerr, trans. Edmund Jephcott. Stanford: Stanford University Press, 2002.

Jäckel, Anne. "Dual Nationality Film Productions in Europe after 1945." *Historical Journal of Film, Radio, and Television* 23 (2003): 231–243.

———. "European Co-Production Strategies: The Case of Britain and France." In *Film Policy: International, National, and Regional Perspectives,* edited by Albert Moran, 85–97. London: Routledge, 1996.

———. *European Film Industries.* London: British Film Institute, 2003.

Jacobs, Lea. *The Wages of Sin: Censorship and the Fallen Woman Film, 1928–1942.* Berkeley: University of California Press, 1997.

Jameson, Fredric. "The Vanishing Mediator: Or, Max Weber as Storyteller." In *The Ideology of Theory: Essays 1971–1986. Vol. 2. The Syntax of History,* 3–34. Minneapolis: University of Minnesota Press, 1988.

Jarvie, Ian. *Hollywood's Overseas Campaign: The North Atlantic Movie Trade, 1920–1950.* Cambridge: Cambridge University Press, 1992.

Judt, Tony. *Postwar: A History of Europe since 1945.* New York: Penguin Press, 2005.

Kashner, Sam, and Jennifer MacNair. *The Bad & the Beautiful: Hollywood in the Fifties.* New York: W. W. Norton, 2002.

Kinsey, Alfred C., and Institute for Sex Research. *Sexual Behavior in the Human Female.* Philadelphia: Saunders, 1953.

Krantz, Judith. "Those 'Frightful' American Tourists." *Good Housekeeping* 143 (July 1956): 61.

Kroes, Rob. *If You've Seen One, You've Seen the Mall: Europeans and American Mass Culture.* Urbana: University of Illinois Press, 1996.

Kuisel, Richard. *Seducing the French: The Dilemma of Americanization.* Berkeley: University of California Press, 1993.

Landy, Marcia. *Italian Film.* National film traditions. Cambridge: Cambridge University Press, 2000.

Laurents, Arthur. *The Time of the Cuckoo.* New York: Random House, 1953.

Lears, Jackson. "A Matter of Taste: Corporate Cultural Hegemony in a Mass-Consumption Society." In *Recasting America: Culture and Politics in the Age of the Cold War,* edited by Lary May, 38–57. Chicago: University of Chicago Press, 1989.

Lev, Peter. *The Euro–American Cinema.* Austin: University of Texas Press, 1993.

———. *Transforming the Screen, 1950–1959.* History of the American cinema. Berkeley: University of California Press, 2003.

Levin, Harry. "Introduction." In *The Ambassadors,* by Henry James. Penguin Classics Edition. New York: Penguin Books, 1986.

Lewis, Jon. "'We Do Not Ask You To Condone This': How The Blacklist Saved Hollywood." *Cinema Journal* 39 (2000): 3–30.

Lipschutz, Ronnie D. *Cold War Fantasies: Film, Fiction, and Foreign Policy.* Lanham: Rowman and Littlefield Publishers, 2001.

Los Angeles Mirror, "Film Making Abroad Shows Signs of Reversed Trend," October 11, 1961.

Luce, Henry R. "The American Century." *Diplomatic History* 23 (1999): 159–171.

Marcus, Millicent. *Italian Film in the Light of Neorealism.* Princeton: Princeton University Press, 1986.

May, Elaine Tyler. *Homeward Bound: American Families in the Cold War Era.* Rev. and updated ed. New York: Basic Books, 1999.

May, Lary. *Recasting America: Culture and Politics in the Age of Cold War.* Chicago: University of Chicago Press, 1989.

McGilligan, Patrick, and Paul Buhle. *Tender Comrades: A Backstory of the Hollywood Blacklist.* New York: St. Martin's Press, 1997.

Miller, Toby, Nitin Govil, John McMurrin, Richard Maxwell, and Ting Wang. *Global Hollywood 2.* London: British Film Institute Publishing, 2005.

Morey, Anne. *Hollywood Outsiders: The Adaptation of the Film Industry, 1913–1934*. Minneapolis: University of Minnesota Press, 2003.

Moseley, Rachel. *Growing Up With Audrey Hepburn: Text, Audience, Resonance*. Inside popular film. Manchester: Manchester University Press, 2002.

———. "Trousers and Tiaras: Audrey Hepburn, A Woman's Star." *Feminist Review* 71 (2002): 37–51.

Motion Picture Association of America. Production Code Administration records. Margaret Herrick Library Special Collections. Academy of Motion Picture Arts and Sciences. Beverly Hills, Calif.

Mulvey, Laura. "Death Drives." In *Hitchcock Past and Future*, edited by Richard Allen and Sam Ishii-Gonzalés, 231–242. London: Routledge, 2004.

Naremore, James. "Hitchcock and Humor." *Strategies* 14 (2001): 13–25.

Nash, Ogden. "Who Wants To Travel All Over Europe and See Nothing But A Lot Of American Tourists? I Do." *New Yorker* 31 (July 30, 1955): 28.

Navasky, Victor S. *Naming Names*. 3rd ed. New York: Hill and Wang, 2003.

Neale, Steve. *Genre and Hollywood*. London: Routledge, 2000.

Nowell-Smith, Geoffrey, and Steven Ricci. *Hollywood and Europe: Economics, Culture, National Identity; 1945–95*. UCLA Film and Television Archive studies in history, criticism, and theory. London: British Film Institute, 1998.

Paramount Production Records Collection. Margaret Herrick Library, Academy of Motion Picture Arts and Sciences. Beverly Hills, Calif.

Pells, Richard. *Not Like Us: How Europeans Have Loved, Hated, and Transformed American Culture since World War II*. New York: Basic Books, 1997.

Pomerance, Murray. *American Cinema of the 1950s: Themes and Variations*. New Brunswick: Rutgers University Press, 2005.

———. "Neither Here nor There: *eXistenZ* as 'Elevator Film.'" *Quarterly Review of Film and Video* 20 (2003): 1–14.

Pryor, Thomas M. "Movies' Decline Held Permanent: Survey by Film Unions Finds '46 Status 'Gone Forever.'" *New York Times*, April 7, 1958.

"Quarter's Polls, The." *Public Opinion Quarterly* 9 (1945): 365–393.

Ray, Robert B. *A Certain Tendency of the Hollywood Cinema, 1930–1980*. Princeton, N.J.: Princeton University Press, 1985.

Rentschler, Eric. *The Ministry of Illusion. Nazi Cinema and Its Afterlife*. Cambridge, Mass.: Harvard University Press, 1996.

Rogow, Lee. "One Touch of Venice." *Saturday Review*, June 18, 1955.

Rosch, Eleanor. "Natural Categories." *Cognitive Psychology* 4 (1973): 328–350.

Saunders, Thomas J. *Hollywood in Berlin: American Cinema and Weimar Germany*. Berkeley: University of California Press, 1994.

Schallert, Edwin. "First Pair of U.S. Films Shot Abroad Give New Horizon." *Los Angeles Times*, July 12, 1953.

Schatz, Thomas. *Boom and Bust: American Cinema of the 1940s*. History of the American Cinema. Berkeley: University of California Press, 1999.

———. *The Genius of the System: Hollywood Filmmaking in the Studio Era*. New York: Henry Holt and Company, 1988.

———. *Hollywood Genres: Formulas, Filmmaking, and the Studios*. New York: Random House, 1981.

Schwartz, Vannessa R. *It's So French: Hollywood, Paris, and the Making of Cosmopolitan Film Culture*. Chicago: University of Chicago Press, 2007.

Secondari, John *Coins in the Fountain*. Philadelphia: Lippincott, 1952

Segrave, Kerry. *American Films Abroad: Hollywood's Domination of the World's Movie Screens*. Jefferson, N.C.: McFarland and Co., 1997.

Shandley, Robert R. *Rubble Films: German Cinema in the Shadow of the Third Reich*. Philadelphia, Penn.: Temple University Press, 2001.

Shukert, Elfrieda Berthiaume, and Barbara Smith Scibetta. *War Brides of World War II*. New York: Penguin Books, 1988.

Silverman, Kaja. *Male Subjectivity at the Margins*. New York: Routledge, 1992.

Smith, Dina M. "Global Cinderella: *Sabrina* (1954), Hollywood, and Postwar Internationalism." *Cinema Journal* 41 (2002): 27–51.

Stern, Ralph. "*The Big Lift* (1950): Image and Identity in Blockaded Berlin." *Cinema Journal* 46 (2007): 66–90.

Studlar, Gaylyn. "Chi-Chi Cinderella: Audrey Hepburn as Couture Countermodel." In *Hollywood Goes Shopping*, edited by David Dresser and Garth Jowett, 159–178. Minneapolis: University of Minnesota Press, 2000.

Thompson, Kristin. 1985. *Exporting Entertainment: America in the World Film Market, 1907–34*. London: British Film Institute Publishing.

Truffaut, François, Alfred Hitchcock, and Helen G. Scott. *Hitchcock*. Rev. ed. New York: Simon and Schuster, 1984.

Trumbo, Dalton. *Additional Dialogue: Letters of Dalton Trumbo, 1942–1962*. Edited by Helen Manfull. New York: M. Evans; distributed in association with Lippincott, 1970.

Variety, "Yank Prod. Abroad at Peak," September 24, 1952.

Variety Daily, "Labor Whips 'Runaway' Vidpix," February 11, 1953.

———, "Eric Johnston Defends Majors' Prod'n Abroad," January 11, 1954.

———, "Wanger Brands Labor's Drive against 'Runaway' Prod'n 'Injurious' to AFL," September 27, 1954.

Variety Weekly, "Coast Kids Self; European Film Production is Still Third Cheaper; Preminger Raps U.S. Standybys," January 30, 1963.

———. "Crafts Hear Zanuck Assurances of 20th Resumption in Hollywood; Costs No Longer Favor Overseas," January 30, 1963.

Von Moltke, Johannes. *No Place like Home: Locations of Heimat in German Cinema*. Berkeley: University of California Press, 2005.

Whitfield, Stephen J. *The Culture of the Cold War*. 2nd ed. Baltimore: Johns Hopkins University Press, 1996.

Wilkerson, W. R. "TradeViews." *Hollywood Reporter*, March 8, 1954.

———. "TradeViews." *Hollywood Reporter*, January 15, 1953.

Williams, Linda. "Learning to Scream." *Sight and Sound* 4 (1994): 14–17.

Willoughby, John. "The Sexual Behavior of American GIs During the Early Years of the Occupation of Germany." *The Journal of Military History* 62 (1998): 155–174.

Wilson, Elizabeth. "Audrey Hepburn: Fashion, Film and the 50s." In *Women and Film: A Sight and Sound Reader*, 36–40. Philadelphia, Penn.: Temple University Press, 1993.

Woman's Home Companion "Grace Kelly Tells How to Travel Light" April, 1955. 46–47

Wood, Robin. *Hitchcock's Films Revisited.* New York: Columbia University Press, 2002.

Žižek, Slavoj. *For They Know Not What They Do: Enjoyment as a Political Factor.* London: Verso, 1991.

Index

Robert R. Shandley is Associate Professor of Film Studies and German at Texas A&M University. He is the author of *Rubble Films: German Cinema in the Shadow of the Third Reich* (Temple) and editor of *Unwilling Germans? The Goldhagen Debate.*